GRAVE ON THE PRAIRIE

Seven Religious of the Sacred Heart and Saint
Mary's Mission to the Potawatomi

GRAVE ON THE PRAIRIE

Seven Religious of the Sacred Heart and Saint Mary's Mission to the Potawatomi

MAUREEN J. CHICOINE, RSCJ

TABLE OF CONTENTS

LIST OF ILLUSTRATIONS

Figure 27   Skyscraper on the Prairie, front view
Abbreviations:
 KSHS   Kansas State Historical Society
 TCHA   Tippecanoe County Historical Association
Note: Photos not otherwise attributed are by the author.

ACKNOWLEDGEMENTS

Special thanks to all who helped with this project especially: Carolyn Osiek, RSCJ, provincial archivist; her staff: Mary Lou Gavan, RSCJ, Frances Gimber, RSCJ, and Michael Pera; David P. Miros, director of the Jesuit archives, and staff member Mary Struckel. Thanks, too, for the hospitality offered by the RSCJ community, West Pine Boulevard, in Saint Louis during research.
Special thanks for sharing family oral tradition and research to Virginia Pearl, CSJ, and family, direct descendants of a Potawatomi[1] survivor of the March of Death: Theresa Slevin, who was a pupil at Sugar Creek Mission. Sincere appreciation to the Citizen Band Potawatomi Cultural Center and Dr. Kelli Jean Mosteller, director, whose doctoral dissertation helped clarify the complex history of the Potawatomi. Thanks to the Weld family, Citizen Band Potawatomi, who graciously allowed me to share this project with them.

---

[1] Except for quotations from sources that use other spellings, this spelling will be used in this writing, since it is the official one used by the tribe.

INTRODUCTION

In Mount Calvary Cemetery of Saint Marys, Kansas, there is a single grave holding the bodies of seven Religious of the Sacred Heart (RSCJ):[2] Lucille Mathevon, Mary Anne O'Connor, Louise Amiot, Mary Layton, Julia Deegan, Catherine Regan, and Rosa Boyle. While the histories of Lucille Mathevon and Mary Layton may be familiar, less is known about the other five. All lived with one another in the RSCJ community that ministered to the Potawatomi people from 1841 to 1879, except Rosa Boyle, who arrived after the others had died. For those who associate the mission to the Potawatomi only with Philippine Duchesne, it may be a surprise that it existed for thirty-seven years after she had returned to Missouri. This history will explore the lives of these women and the thirty-eight years of the mission of the Society of the Sacred Heart to the Potawatomi Indians of Sugar Creek, Kansas (1841-48), and Saint Marys,[3] Kansas (1848-1879).

Close-up of gravestone with names of RSCJ

---

[2] The initials "RSCJ" stand for the French "*Religieuses du Sacré-Cœur de Jésus*" or Religious of the Sacred Heart of Jesus and will be used throughout this work to indicate the members of the Society of the Sacred Heart.

[3] While the mission was Saint Mary's, the modern town is called Saint Marys.

During the course of this research, originally intended for a short article, it became necessary to understand each woman in the context of the period in which she lived at the mission to the Potawatomi. That need expanded this writing into a history of the Society of the Sacred Heart's work with the Potawatomi at Sugar Creek and in Saint Marys, Kansas. The mission that originated with Philippine Duchesne's call to work with native people continued for almost four decades after her brief stay with them in 1841-1842. This study will try to understand how the missionaries viewed the natives, how their work with the natives shaped the way they lived and worked, and, as far as possible, what the natives might have thought of the black-robed women who came to live and work among them. Since the Potawatomi left no written record of their feelings, their impressions will be gauged through observation of their behavior toward the missionaries and the mission school.

There is no doubt that the Religious of the Sacred Heart shared many of the misconceptions and prejudices of their time about native peoples. The French were influenced by romantic notions of the "noble savage" living in a state of primitive virtue untainted by civilization's defects.[4] On the other hand, the Americans had a history of conflict with native people on the frontier. This conflict was aggravated by the push to extend the United States across the continent as their national "manifest destiny."[5] Both the missionaries and the United States government officials assumed that the best outcome was the "civilization" of the native peoples and their

---

[4] Phil Belfrey, "Savage and Savagism," *Encyclopedia of the North American Indian*, ed. Frederick Hoxie (New York: Houghton Mifflin, 1995). "The concept of the savage predates the European colonization of North America by several millennia. The word has its root in the Latin *silvaticus,* meaning "in a state of nature," "of a woodland," or "wild." (*Silvaticus* itself is linked to *silva,* "wood" or "forest." In Spanish, the Latin word became *salvage,* in French, *sauvage.* Closely related words that are instructive in this context are *pagan,* from the Latin *paganus,* "villager," "rustic," not of the city; "*heathen,*" from an Old English word meaning "of the heath," "a person of a vast wasteland"; and "barbarian," from a Greek root meaning "one whose language and customs differ [from the speaker's]."

"Noble savage" is an idealized concept of uncivilized man; it symbolizes the innate goodness of one not exposed to the corrupting influences of *civilization.* The glorification of the noble savage is a dominant theme in the Romantic writings of the eighteenth and nineteenth centuries (*Encyclopedia Britannica* online). In French, the word *sauvage* does not have the pejorative meaning it has in English but signifies more someone unexposed to Western civilization or culture—in a primitive state of existence; a mythic conception of people belonging to non-European cultures as having innate natural simplicity and virtue uncorrupted by European civilization; also: a person exemplifying this conception (Merriam Webster Dictionary).

[5] Manifest Destiny is a nineteenth-century belief that the *United States* had a mission to expand westward across the North American continent, spreading its form of *democracy, freedom,* and culture. The expansion was deemed not only good, but also obvious ("manifest") and certain ("destiny"). Many believed the mission to be divinely inspired while others felt it more as an intrinsic right to expand the territory of liberty (*New World Encyclopedia* online).

eventual integration into the dominant Euro-American society.[6] Unfortunately, the Catholic Church of its time approached evangelization with the assumption that acceptance of Western culture and rejection of native culture were essential to becoming Catholic. However, these attitudes coexisted with a genuine desire to share the Gospel message, to proclaim the love of God, and to share a relationship of friendship with the people they served. As educators, the Religious of the Sacred Heart (RSCJ) saw their educational work as a way to help their students develop their full potential as children of God. Their Constitutions urged them "to see in the children entrusted to them souls redeemed by the Blood of Jesus Christ."[7]

The RSCJ who served at the mission were on the fringe of the frontier, and their community life developed in response to the needs of the people. It was obvious that the rules of cloister, regulations for community life, and customs that developed during this time both in France and in other houses in more settled areas of the United States were not practical here. The community was small; living space was crowded and primitive, and the culture of the people with whom they lived and ministered was very different from their own. There appears to have been a certain freedom to take up tasks based on the person's abilities and gifts rather than community status. Not all the superiors who supervised the houses of the Society were sympathetic to the special circumstances of life on the frontier.[8]

Much of the basic history of the mission is well-covered in Chapter IX of Louise Callan's *The Society of the Sacred Heart in North America* (1937) and her biography of Philippine Duchesne (1957). These published works and her unpublished research were depended upon heavily in writing this project.[9] They trace the beginning of the mission to the Potawatomi back to the initial call that Philippine Duchesne felt to work with native peoples

---

[6] Belfrey, "Savage and Savagism." *Encyclopedia of North American Indians* Over time, the equation of Indians with savagery became formalized into a philosophy scholars now refer to as *savagism*. According to the tenets of this outlook, Indians are (1) emotional rather than rational; (2) morally and culturally deficient; (3) uncivilized; (4) genetically inferior; (5) untrustworthy (although individuals have the potential to be "noble"); (6) generally lazy and indolent; and (7) often immorally sensual in their nature. The logical outcome of this array of traits was the belief that Indians belonged to a vanishing race, one that must necessarily perish in the face of civilized "progress." The succession of savagery by civilization also served as an additional justification for "civilizing" (that is, dismantling) native societies. From this perspective, converting "savages" to "civilization"—, which often entailed destroying their ancient traditions—could be understood as humanitarian. Invaders could thus recast themselves as civilizers dedicated to the salvation of native barbarians. The internal logic of these concepts required non-Indians to be seen as rational, civilized, moral, trustworthy, hardworking, and triumphant.

[7] *Constitutions* of the Society of the Sacred Heart, 1815, § 175 VII.

[8] See admonitions of superiors who visited in the sections of this work on 1856-1870. In all fairness to them, most of whom had never lived on the frontier, they were trying to fulfill their mission of assuring unity in life and practice within the Society in the United States.

[9] Another invaluable source was the research gathered by Marie Louise Martinez, RSCJ, who hoped to compile a history of the mission with the Potawatomi and left copious notes in RSCJ Archives XII Martinez Collection, Box 10.

in North America. This call led her to take the Society of the Sacred Heart to the Louisiana territory in 1818. She initiated work with the native people who were remaining in Florissant, Missouri, from 1825 to 1831, but she soon realized that the frontier settlements were pushing natives farther west. Finally, in 1841, she was able to fulfill her dream of working with native people in the Sugar Creek Potawatomi mission. Although she was forced by age and health to leave in 1842, the mission continued there with other RSCJ until 1848, when the Potawatomi and the RSCJ were forced to move to another location in Kansas territory. Education of Potawatomi girls continued in Saint Marys, Kansas, until almost the end of the RSCJ involvement in 1879.

This new study seeks to explore, through more recent material and deeper understanding of native culture, how the natives might have regarded the religious and why the pioneers were successful in their ministry in spite of their limited understanding of native culture and their own cultural biases. It will look also at the way community life, with a two tiered membership system of choir religious and coadjutrix sisters, evolved during the time of the mission.[10] During the early days of the Society in the United States, this system was still undergoing development in France. There were two classes of members: choir nuns and lay sisters (called coadjutrix) in the Society. This was a remnant of monastic structures required by the church of this time. Choir nuns in a monastery were bound to recite the Office, (in the case of the Society, to teach) while the lay sisters were not so bound and did the manual work of the monastery. The family's economic status sometimes influenced the status of the member, since choir nuns brought a dowry, but lay sisters were not required to do so. Because of the Society's work in schools, previous education and the ability to teach also determined a woman's status as choir or coadjutrix.

Because of the small number of RSCJ in the mission community[11] for most of its existence and the demands of ministry, the traditional separation of duties and separate lives of the choir religious and coadjutrix sisters[12] could not be maintained. The community developed a more egalitarian relationship, which is evident from the resulting friendships, the sharing of duties, and the comments of superiors who visited them. This relationship was a response to the needs of the ministry and to unique demands that were quite different from those of the Society in both France and other parts of the United States.

This work suggests that the spirit of *cor unum*, "one heart," developed within the community was an important part of the ministry to the native peoples. With native people the "heart" communication was much more educative and effective than the head. This was noticed even by the commissioners for Indian affairs who

---

[10] Phil Kilroy, *The Society of the Sacred Heart in Nineteenth-Century France, 1800-1865* (Cork, Ireland: Cork University Press, 2012) describes the evolution of the two-tiered system in the Society during this period, especially pp. 9-84, "One musical ensemble: The evolution of a community."

[11] The seven religious buried in the prairie grave reflect the same size as the average community of RSCJ throughout the history of the mission 1841-1860. Only between 1860 and1879 would the size increase.

[12] Kilroy, *Society in 19th century France*, pp. 31-34, 51-54, 72-79.

visited the mission, who were usually not Catholic. One of them observed of the RSCJ that "It was plain to me that their hearts are in the work."[13]

This work will outline the inspiration for the work with the native peoples that impelled Philippine Duchesne and her companions to accept the call to begin a mission in Kansas. It will give some of the historical background of the Potawatomi people they served. Within the story of the development of the mission both at Sugar Creek and Saint Marys, this study will look at the behavior of the natives and what that might reveal of their attitudes toward the RSCJ. It will also explore how the RSCJ were able to achieve a relationship with the Potawatomi that overcame their own unconscious stereotypes of native people. It will also look at the ways their ministry influenced the life of the community and allowed it to develop in ways that differed from fellow RSCJ communities in other parts of North America. The biography of each of the women buried in the prairie grave in Saint Marys, Kansas, will be situated within the context of the history of the nearly four decades that the mission existed.

---

[13] William Elsey Connelley, *The Prairie Band of Pottawatomie Indians* (Jackson County, Kansas: History of the Reservation; Secretary of the Kansas State Historical Society). Material available online quotes reports of various Indian agents, commissioners and the Jesuit superiors. Manuscript at the Kansas Historical Society.

Prequel to the Mission with the Potawatomi 1806–1840

The person most identified with the mission of the Society of the Sacred Heart to the Potawatomi is Rose Philippine Duchesne. Although she spent only one year at the mission before she was withdrawn because of health and age, her influence was potent even when she was not physically present. It was her desire to work with native people that brought the Society of the Sacred Heart to the United States in 1818. During the next twenty years, her desire remained strong, and her persistence was instrumental in the foundation of the mission. Of the three original Sugar Creek religious with Philippine Duchesne in 1841, Lucille Mathevon had lived with her in Grenoble before either of them came to America, and Louise Amiot and Mary Anne O'Connor had been admitted into the Society of the Sacred Heart by Philippine. All three would remain at the Potawatomi mission until their death. Others who lived in Saint Mary were admitted to the Society by Philippine and had also lived with her in Florissant, Saint Charles, and Saint Louis. Even those who came later were influenced by her accounts of life there.[14] In 1852, the year of Philippine's death, she wrote to Madeleine Sophie Barat, her superior general, giving a glowing account of the work at Saint Mary's Mission, thus showing that her interest had not wavered. She was still trying to get more recruits and resources for this work so close to her heart.[15]

This chapter will indicate the centrality of Philippine Duchesne's call to work with native peoples and her influence on those who eventually staffed the mission at Sugar Creek and Saint Marys, Kansas. Long before the mission to the Potawatomi was a reality, it was a seed nurtured by Rose Philippine Duchesne. Philippine, a native of Grenoble, France, born in 1769, was inspired by the stories she heard as a child of the missions in North America. It might even be said that her childhood is the true origin of the mission's inspiration. Missionaries made fund raising trips to France and promoted the work with stories of their adventures.

---

[14] Including Mary Layton and Bridget Barnwell. Others who served at the mission either lived with Philippine or had listened to her and Lucille's letters read at recreation or in the refectory: Marie-Rose Monzert, Bridget O'Neil, Catherine Thiéfry, Ann Haggerty, Margaret Cornelius, Susanna Lalor, Margaret Knapp, Julie Bazire, Mathilde Hamilton, and Julia Deegan. (Compiled from the annual *Catalogue* of the Society of the Sacred Heart and notes of Marie Louise Martinez in RSCJ Archives). Even after her death, she drew people to the mission. Elisabeth Schroeder, who arrived in 1856, promised to volunteer for the mission if she was cured of an illness through the intercession of Philippine Duchesne—she was and she came.

[15] Jeanne de Charry, ed., *Saint Madeleine Sophie Barat, Saint Philippine Duchesne: Correspondence.* Trans. J. Sweetman et al. Vol. II-III, Letter 335 (22 April 1852) describes the boarding school with sixty students in vivid detail. In 1852, Lucille Mathevon visited Saint Louis and might have had a chance to give Philippine a personal update on life at the mission.

Some had given their lives among the tribes of North America. She herself notes, "My first enthusiasm for missionary life was roused by the tales of a good Jesuit Father who had been on the missions in Louisiana and who told us stories about the Indians."[16]

Philippine was born to Rose Euphrosine Perier and Pierre François Duchesne, a prominent lawyer in Grenoble, in 1769. She was the eldest surviving daughter of the family and named for the apostle Philip and the South American saint Rose of Lima. Educated at home and in the nearby Visitation monastery of Sainte-Marie d'En-Haut, she grew up in an upper middle class family that valued learning and service to the poor. She was known for her strength of will and stubbornness. This was exhibited when, in 1787, at eighteen she decided to enter the Visitation monastery without the knowledge of her family. The advent of the French Revolution and its dissolution of monastic foundations brought her home while still a novice. During the troubled times of the Reign of Terror, she spent her time working with prisoners, especially priests, helping the poor and children in need of catechesis.[17] After an unsuccessful attempt to reestablish her local Visitation community, she joined the Society of the Sacred Heart in 1804, only four years after its foundation. She was received by the young founder, Madeleine Sophie Barat, ten years her junior, with whom she developed a lifelong friendship.

Philippine had heard of the work with native peoples on the western frontier of the United States. In 1806, the convent in Grenoble, where she was very busy working in a boarding school, was visited by a Trappist abbot on a begging tour in Europe. He told her about the journey of twenty-five Trappists from Switzerland to the United States in 1802. Later, she wrote that she heard about "the migration of the Trappists to Kentucky where settlers were numerous and land plentiful and cheap, but missionaries were lacking for work among the pioneers and Indians."[18] Philippine learned about the Louisiana Purchase[19] and the spiritual needs of its inhabitants. She was told about the Indians who lived there, some of whom had been catechized by French missionaries. So inspired

---

[16] Louise Callan, RSCJ, *Philippine Duchesne* (Westminster, Maryland: Newman Press, 1957) p. 23. Father Jean-Louis Aubert lived in Grenoble during her childhood. He and other missionaries from Louisiana and Illinois territories spoke of the missions there to both settlers and native peoples.

[17] A summary of her life is available at http://sofie.org/files/pages/attachments/lifelived.pdf. France, after a period of unrest caused by economic crisis and social inequities, erupted the year after Philippine entered the Visitation. A revolutionary government was set up to transform French government totally. Part of this reform was to suppress monastic establishments throughout the country. The Reign of Terror, 1793-95, was known for violent suppression of dissent and execution of many aristocrats, including the king and queen, clergy and religious, as well as former revolutionaries who fell out of favor.

[18] Callan, *Philippine Duchesne*, pp. 112 f. Much of the material in this section about Philippine's remote preparation for her mission comes from this work.

[19] The sale of this territory by France to the United States in 1803 immediately doubled the size of the country.

was she that she was ready to give up even her beloved house in Grenoble to go to these far-flung mission lands.[20] When she shared this missionary desire with Sophie Barat, she received encouragement. Sophie revealed that she, herself, had had a similar desire but had received the answer in prayer: "No, you are destined for France, you will never leave it. That is your battlefield." This answer was only partially true, since Sophie did leave France eventually to go to Italy, Spain, and even England, but she never left Europe. For now, however, Philippine needed to remain in France. The Society was too small and did not have sufficient personnel prepared to expand to the New World. But Sophie did not discount Philippine's own desire for mission. She wrote to Philippine, "Give me time, I cannot answer you yet. But I say, instead: Hope on, foster these desires and sentiments, try to grow more worthy of the signal favor you long for."[21]

Philippine learned many administrative skills during her time at the school in Grenoble as well as skills in caring for the sick. She had not stopped thinking about the missions; and as one of her students told, she asked them, "Now, children, which of you wants to go with me to America to convert the Illinois?…Every child in the group held up her hand…."[22] In 1815, she participated in the Second General Council of the Society in Paris. At this meeting, she was appointed secretary general and subsequently moved to Paris. While in Paris, Philippine developed other skills that would prove valuable in her work in America. She took an active role in getting the new Society house in rue des Postes ready by "scrubbing and polishing floors, cleaning walls and directing the workmen who were remodeling the house; she frequently picked up a trowel to speed a mason's job or a brush to finish up some painting or whitewashing."[23]

Only eleven years after joining the Society would she see some possibility of her dream coming true. Louis William Valentine Dubourg, bishop of New Orleans in the missionary territory of Louisiana,[24] came to France in 1816 seeking funds and recruits for his vast territory. Philippine met the bishop when he visited Paris in 1817.[25] She had heard of the bishop through Sophie's brother, Louis Barat, who had encouraged Philippine in her desire. Louis had already suggested Philippine to Bishop Dubourg as a possible candidate for this work. Sophie was

---

[20] Callan, *Philippine Duchesne*, p. 113: "I resolved to offer myself for the foreign missions, to reach the pagans of China or any other distant lands." This resolution occurred after she had experienced the attraction to the native peoples of the Americas during her time in Grenoble in 1806 after a visit from Dom Augustin Lestrange, who spoke of the Trappists in America.

[21] *Ibid*, p. 116, letter from Sophie to Philippine.

[22] *Ibid*, p. 145, One of these children was Lucille Mathevon who would be the heart and soul of the Mission to the Potawatomi and in the second group of RSCJ after Philippine to come to the new world.

[23] *Ibid*, p. 186.

[24] This vast territory stretched from the Mississippi to the Rocky Mountains and from New Orleans in the south to the Great Lakes in the north – over 828,000 square miles of territory.

[25] Appointed Bishop of Louisiana and the Floridas in 1815. Responsible for bringing over many clergy to the new world including his successor, Joseph Rosati, who succeeded him in 1827.

concerned: "Philippine is always thinking about her missions overseas, and my brother has almost smoothed the way for her. In spite of the terror such a venture causes me, we shall, perhaps, see it carried out. I tremble to think of it."[26] Although Louis had no authority, he had already been meddling in the affair. He even told the bishop that Philippine's superiors had already approved her plan. He then wrote to Philippine that the bishop had agreed and "so the matter is arranged. There remains only to decide on the time of your departure and the means of accomplishing the project."[27] On January 14, 1817, Bishop Dubourg arrived in Paris and visited Sophie, who described many years later what had happened. Philippine was the one who opened the door for the visitor. When she went to call Sophie to come to the parlor, she used the opportunity to lobby her for a positive response to his request "She implored me not to let such an opportunity slip. God's hour had come, she assured me, and I had only to say the word. I did not let her see that I shared her conviction but only answered that if the bishop brought up the subject, I might discuss it, but I should want a year to eighteen months to prepare."[28]

Sophie bidding farewell to Philippine as she is about to embark for North America.

Original icon by Patricia Reid, RSCJ • Photo by Susan A. Sibille

Icon: "The Mission to America," Patricia Reid, RSCJ

The next morning Sophie and Bishop Dubourg finally had a discussion about the mission, and Sophie admitted that she was in favor of a foundation. She proposed Philippine as a possible candidate to lead a group to Louisiana. Naturally, when she was called in, Philippine was filled with joy as she knelt for the Bishop's blessing. However, Sophie's closest advisors were not in favor of the projected expansion but most especially the sending of Philippine as its leader. They believed it was essential to the Society and its founder that she remain in France. So Sophie informed the bishop and Philippine that the approval had been withdrawn. He visited them again on May 16, just before a return to America after his fund raising tour. He was disappointed, and as Sophie walked him to the door, Philippine suddenly appeared, knelt in the doorway and pleaded with Sophie, "Your consent, Mother! Give your consent!"[29] And Sophie did.

With Philippine went two other choir religious, Eugénie Audé and Octavie Berthold, and two coadjutrix sisters, Marguerite Manteau and Catherine Lamarre. Eugénie and Octavie were volunteers, and Marguerite and Catherine were chosen by Sophie. All knew they would probably never

---

[26] Callan, *Philippine Duchesne.* p. 192, letter of Sophie to Therese Maillucheau, October 1816.

[27] *Ibid*. pp. 192-93. Louis goes so far as to suggest how many and what type of companions she might need.

[28] *Ibid*. p. 194. The discussion occurred only the next day during his breakfast conversation with Sophie after the bishop had come to offer Mass. Philippine must have been dying with suspense!

[29] *Ibid*. p. 195.

see France or their loved ones again. Only Eugénie would return to France, when she was summoned back to community leadership in 1834, dying there in 1843. All the others would die and be buried in the United States.[30]

Philippine, now forty-eight years old, arrived in the new state of Louisiana[31] with her companions in May 1818. On the voyage up the Mississippi from the port of New Orleans, she had her first glimpses of the Native Americans she longed to serve. She could also see the rapid population growth on the river banks and the cultivated fields. Although they had hoped to settle and found a school in Saint Louis, they wound up in the village of Saint Charles in Missouri Territory. There they started a school, not for Native Americans but for the Creoles[32] and American settlers, since the native population was being pushed farther west. The town was the jumping off point to the West, and it was where Lewis and Clark had begun their expedition in May 1804. From 1821 to 1826, it was briefly the capital of the newly formed state of Missouri. Besides receiving boarding students, the religious opened a free day school with a small group of students who included Creoles and some of mixed race.[33]

The school lasted only a year in Saint Charles and was moved to Florissant on the other side of the Missouri, where there was property to build beside the parish church. In Saint Charles and Florissant, Philippine had her first experience of an alien culture—not that of Native Americans but of the French-speaking Creole girls. She was shocked by their frivolity and their attention to fine fashion. They confronted her with an independent and rebellious spirit she had not found in her students back in France.[34] She was also introduced to the Métis people, children of a European immigrant and an American Indian. In a letter to the community in France she wrote,

> I do not know how to describe the place in which we live. Its population is made up of a mixture of American emigrants from the East, French and Canadian Creoles, German, Irish and Flemish settlers, along with half-breeds,[35] who seem to inherit the worst faults of both Indian and white parents. As for real Indians, we never see them because the Americans from the East are pushing them out and making war with them. They are withdrawing farther away.[36]

---

[30] Interesting to note that all, much younger than Philippine, would predecease her, some by more than twenty years.

[31] Established in 1812. The rest of the Louisiana Purchase was now known as Missouri territory. All or part of fifteen U.S. states plus portions of two Canadian provinces were included in the Louisiana Purchase.

[32] Creole is a term used to describe those born in the territory, of both French and Spanish parentage.

[33] *Ibid.* p. 275 gives a detailed and very descriptive account of the first year at Saint Charles.

[34] De Charry/Hogg et al, *Correspondence* 2-1, Letter 114 (29 July 1819). Philippine describes the independent spirit of the Creole girls—they are not docile French children and have no desire to be. "Children here command or make themselves equal to their parents.... They drink in independence from their mother's milk."

[35] It is ironic that Philippine would eventually wind up working with the Potawatomi who had many "Métis" or mixed French and Indian families. Her judgment here reflects the prejudices of her contemporaries.

[36] Callan, p. 283. She hopes for Jesuits to bring the Indians to them but remarks, "We would attract them more quickly with liquor than with sermons...but in conscience no one should give it to them seeing what a state it puts them in."

Almost from the beginning, there was tension in the community because of the two classes of members: choir religious and coadjutrix sisters. Working class women who entered the Society of the Sacred Heart as coadjutrix sisters did not recite the Office; many could not read. They were in charge of the domestic duties in the convent and its grounds. The Constitutions of the community saw the coadjutrix candidates as having the same call and needing the same interior spirit of generosity as the choir religious, but without formal education.[37] Over the next twenty years in France, the role of the choir and coadjutrix religious would be developing.[38] In America, with its focus on egalitarianism, this system could be considered foreign. Louis Dubourg thought that having two classes of religious was not acceptable and opposed it. Even Philippine doubted that the two-tiered system was practical after she had been in America for only a year. "It will be impossible to have two ranks of religious when everything must be equal."[39] The original pioneer group had three choir and two coadjutrix sisters.

Complicating the situation was the culture of slavery existing in the territory. Domestic work was often performed only by slaves. From their arrival in Louisiana, the culture presented problems. Catherine Lamarre, assigned to help in the laundry while the RSCJ were staying with the Ursulines in New Orleans, learned quickly that whites and blacks did not mix in this kind of work.[40] Although a coadjutrix sister, Catherine, who had some education, was eager to be assigned to teach and assumed that Sophie had agreed to that. She had taught in a Society free day school in France and was encouraged at first in this dream in America by Bishop Dubourg.[41] She and her companion coadjutrix, Marguerite Manteau, were not always willing or able for health reasons to fulfill the duties traditionally given to lay sisters in the kitchen and laundry, and Philippine was forced to hire outside help for both tasks. They served from time to time as teachers and monitors of study halls.[42] Marguerite Manteau was given responsibilities that she evidently performed satisfactorily, since she was considered a possible assistant to Eugénie Audé in 1823.[43] Of the five original RSCJ, the two coadjutrix sisters were the ones who expressed

[37] *Constitutions* of the Society of the Sacred Heart, 1826, §20.

[38] Kilroy, *Society,* discusses this development in chapter one.

[39] De Charry/Hogg, Letter 114.

[40] Catherine M. Mooney, *Philippine Duchesne, A Woman with the Poor* (Mahwah, New Jersey: Paulist Press, 1990) pp. 128-30. Philippine sharply corrected her and reminded Catherine that if she had no intention of working with the blacks of the area that there was a ship in the harbor that she could take to return to France. Initially open to both women of color as candidates as well as students, Philippine quickly learned that the racial climate of the country would not accept either. Perhaps, she dreamed, an auxiliary branch of coadjutrix formed of black women would be possible.

[41] Callan, *Philippine Duchesne,* p. 293. In Kilroy, *Society,* pp. 39-40. The latter notes that Catherine had entered as a choir novice but was professed as a coadjutrix sister. From the beginning, most of the complaints about conditions in the foundation come from the two coadjutrix sisters. Philippine attributes most of their problems to health both physical and mental.

[42] De Charry/Hogg, 2-1, Letter 114 (29 July 1819) has a number of examples.

[43] *Ibid*. 2-2, Letters 170 and 175 (see notes also). Philippine is considering making Marguerite a choir nun so she can be Eugénie's assistant. She asks for a replacement cross (the coadjutrix sisters' cross was different from that of the choir religious).

the most unhappiness with life in America.[44] It is difficult to know if this dissatisfaction was due to personality, temperament, and the two-tiered system of membership or the contact with the new culture.

American applicants would come and inquire about the Society, but they had a sense of equality and independence that did not allow them to accept the role of lay sister. Some prospective American vocations had assumed that the chores, such as cooking, would be shared by all on a weekly rotation, each taking a turn.[45] Although some Americans entered the Society as coadjutrix sisters,[46] often seeking what was presented as a contemplative life of prayer and simple manual labor, their number diminished by the dawn of the twentieth century. Coadjutrix sisters from Malta, Italy, the Caribbean and Latin America came to the United States, but the number of coadjutrix sisters entering in the United States was always small.[47]

In 1819, the school and the sisters moved to a property in Florissant where a bigger house was being constructed with more room for the school and students. The story of the move and the initial simple dwelling, a small frontier cabin that awaited them, is detailed in Philippine's letters and journal of the time.[48] It was here that a limited ministry to Native Americans would exist and where the first novices of the Society in the United States would enter and be trained. By 1823, a foundation of Jesuits was close by and included some of their men in formation. Here Philippine first met the Jesuit novice Pierre De Smet, who would become the quintessential "Blackrobe" and would urge her to make a foundation among the Potawatomi. Their friendship would continue throughout her life, and from him she was able, if only vicariously, to follow the progress of the ministry with native peoples.

Lucille Mathevon, who would later be called by one of the religious the "golden thread of unity" in the mission, deserves her own biography. She held the operation together and was much loved by the Potawatomi whom she served to the end of her life. Except for two years, she was the superior of the Sugar Creek and Saint

---

[44] *Ibid.* 2-2, Letter 189 and 2-1, Letter 114 among others, for example.

[45] *Ibid.* Letter 114 notes also that they were applying to be coadjutrix sisters.

[46] Few American-born women would apply to be coadjutrix sisters. Many of the women who entered as coadjutrix sisters would be immigrants, mostly from Ireland. In the nineteenth century, immigrant Irish women were often the stereotypical domestic servant, "the Bridget," and such work was a step up from the heavy farm labor of their homeland. Going into service was one way illiterate immigrant Irish women, who had had no opportunity for education at home, were introduced to American culture and society. They soon aspired to acquire education and its rewards. Most religious congregations founded in the United States never had a two-tiered system, making them attractive to prospective vocations. Other congregations founded in Europe later abolished or adapted the system to suit American culture. See: Margaret Susan Thompson, "Sisterhood and Power: Class, Culture and Ethnicity in the American Convent," *Colby Library Quarterly* 25:3 (September 1989): 149-175, which addresses the issue of the two-tiered membership system brought from Europe to America and its demise here as well as the conflicts it brought.

[47] *Ibid.* p. 160, footnote 36, notes that the Society had to recruit coadjutrix sisters from other countries to try and fill the shortage of American vocations, first from Ireland and then from Latin America.

[48] Callan, *Philippine Duchesne*, pp. 309ff. She struggled with finances as well as the rugged frontier life.

Marys RSCJ community until 1868.[49] As the superior, she set the tone for the community and was responsible for forging a unified mission among all the religious regardless of their occupations or rank in the Society. A lover of music with a beautiful voice, she cheered others with her singing. She had a good sense of humor and brought the gift of laughter to the community, especially in difficult times. Her smile was remarked on to the end of her life.[50] She, like Philippine, nurtured a call to work with native people from her childhood.

Lucille Mathevon, a native of Rive-de-Gier near Lyons, France, was born in 1794.[51] She was the daughter of Jean-Marie Mathevon and Catherine Savoie. When the school in Grenoble administered by Philippine Duchesne opened, she was one of the students. Undoubtedly she was inspired by Philippine's stories of mission work in America during her time there. She entered the Society in Grenoble in 1813, when Philippine Duchesne was still in the community, and made her first vows there in 1815. She was professed in 1818 in the new Society that existed after the general council of 1815.[52] In a letter to Philippine in 1818, Sophie mentions Lucille, who by this time was working in the Society as a class mistress in the day school.[53] Sophie remarks that Lucille "is burning to join you; she is a person of solid virtue, she holds the day school very well, but how can she learn English?"[54] English was to remain a challenge for Lucille even after twenty years in the United States.

In 1821, Sophie praises Lucille as a person who "will be useful to our Society," capable of being "in charge of all domestic employments: infirmary, kitchen, and poultry. She can do anything and her health is good. The only money for the voyage comes from her."[55] Another letter mentioned that Lucille had no living family but appeared

---

[49] Sent back to Saint Charles, Missouri in 1868 because of her health, she was able to return in 1871 and lived at Saint Marys until her death in 1876.

[50] RSCJ Archives, Martinez Collection. Ellen Craney, *Memoir of Lucille Mathevon*. Although she had health problems, Craney says that Lucille never had a toothache and had good teeth to the end of her life – a blessed asset on the frontier. Ellen helped care for Lucille and is the source of details about her and the mission that she heard directly from her.

[51] De Charry/Hogg 2.1, p.76 (21 August 1818) has a letter from Sophie that refers to her origin in Rive-de-Gier, department de Loire, Saint Etienne. The 1865 Kansas census taker wrote Lion, for Lyon, France. She probably named the nearest city for the census taker. In the Saint Mary register, her parents are John Marie and Catherine Savoie.

[52] Now with the approval of the 1826 Constitutions under the official name of the "Society of the Sacred Heart." For political reasons the title "Sacred Heart" could not be used at the beginning of the community.

[53] Day schools were founded in partnership with Society boarding schools for working class girls who could not afford boarding school tuition and needed skills that would enable them to support themselves as adults. There were always many more students in the day or poor school than there were in the boarding school. It was called the "poor school" in France and in the Society Constitutions but Philippine discovered that was not an attractive name to Americans. She also had to institute tuition in the day school or American parents would not send their daughters.

[54] De Charry/Hogg, 2.1, p. 76 (August 21, 1818).

[55] *Ibid*. p. 275. Sophie had none since she had just purchased the Hotel Biron but hoped that the benefactor who was donating Grand Coteau might reimburse the cost of the voyage and thus Philippine could use these funds for the Louisiana mission.

to have some family property at her disposal, since she brought six thousand francs from her own resources to Louisiana.[56] In the letter announcing her arrival, Sophie praised Lucille as a person with leadership potential: "She has virtue, judgment, and understands economy and order. Also, she is a strong-minded person; she has greatly edified us since she has been here."[57]

Lucille left for America on November 14, 1822, accompanied by a postulant, Anna Murphy (later Anna Xavier Murphy), who was an older vocation, an Irish woman fluent in English. Sophie sent Lucille off to do work among the Native Americans.[58] Anna wrote back to Sophie an account of the turbulent sea voyage, during which Lucille was terrified and "invoked every saint in the calendar."[59] The sea journey included the experience of being becalmed off the Canary Islands, being chased by a pirate ship and the delay waiting for a steamboat to get up the Mississippi. When she arrived in America, Lucille would join Philippine and learn that the people she wished to minister with were diminishing rapidly in Missouri. Her first contact with native students was to come only with the opening of a short-lived native school in Florissant in April 1825.[60] She wrote to Sophie: "One evening, whilst we were saying office, the Father Rector arrived with two frightened little savages who were hiding themselves under his cloak, and he asked to see the superior. He had sent a cart to bring them and he left them with us. So now we have begun our class for the natives. This is the work, dear Mother, for which we have been pining. Each of us is longing to be employed in it."[61] Philippine Duchesne was well pleased when she wrote: "Our school for the little Indians is at last beginning. We have given the care of it to an Irish sister, Madame Mary O'Connor, who has just made her first vows." The Indian seminary provided an education for the teachers as much as for the children; in it they studied the characteristic traits and language of the Indians.[62] It is probable that these children were Osage, since at this time the Father Rector, Felix van Quickenborne, was focused on bringing children of the Osage to a boarding school at Florissant. He felt only by removing the children from the family could introducing them to Christianity be accomplished. His vision included the Sacred Heart school for

---

[56] This appears to have continued since in the 1850's she is selling her interest in a coalmine in France.

[57] De Charry/Hogg et al, 2.1, p. 275 (23 November 1821).

[58] RSCJ Archives Series II A Interprovincial Affairs, United States, Packet 1, folder 1 #12 "Comers and Goers," "Statistics on Missionaries to and from North America" compiled by M.L. Martinez. Lucille and Anna were the second group of RSCJ to sail for North America. Over the years close to one hundred RSCJ would be sent from France to the foundations in the United States and British North America.

[59] Callan, *North America*, p.126, quoting a letter from Anna to Sophie on their arrival in New Orleans.

[60] The Jesuits also had a school for native boys at Florissant – neither school had a big enrollment and both closed by 1832.

[61] *Ibid*. pp.109-110. Unlike the Mission at Sugar Creek and Saint Marys, this school did not receive any government subsidy even though the Jesuit superior wrote to Washington asking for aid.

[62] Thomas Kinsella, *The History of Our Cradle Land: A Centenary of Catholicism in Kansas* (Kansas City: Casey Printing Company, 1921, pp. 18-19. Transcribed by Sean Furniss online at http://skyways.lib.ks.us/genweb/miami/kinsella/kinsel04.html. Part I, quoting from Father Hoecken's diary. The Indian School continued until about 1831.

girls producing young Christian women who would be suitable wives. Then the Christian couple would be a seed sent home to develop the faith within the Osage nation.[63]

Community dormitory, Florissant, Missouri

Mary Anne O'Connor was born in Ireland, possibly in the area around Tralee, County Kerry, about 1784,[64] and immigrated to the United States alone or with other members of her family.[65] Her parents are unknown, and she could have immigrated with one of the many Irish settlers coming into the new Louisiana territory. It would have

[63] Willard H. Rollings, *Unaffected by the Gospel* (Albuquerque: University of New Mexico Press, 2004) pp. 140ff.

[64] Society records do not agree, giving 1783-1794 as possible birth dates but the earlier is the most probable as she was said by Philippine to be about forty in 1825 and is reported to be around eighty when she died in 1863.

[65] Descendants of Charles O'Connor have an oral tradition that Mary Anne O'Connor was his sister. Given her age, she might more likely have been his aunt if related at all. Charles was born about 1823, based on U.S. census records. He and his wife Catherine Flynn were married in 1847 in Tralee, both residents of Ballyvelly townland.

Some of his children were baptized in Castleisland and Milltown, County Kerry. The family emigrated because of "reversal of fortunes" in 1868 from residence in Audley Place, County Cork, long after Mary Anne had died. After landing in New York and briefly stopping in Pennsylvania, the family is in Council Bluffs, Iowa, in the 1870 U.S. census. None of the extant Society records lists Mary Anne O'Connor's parents. Charles' daughter, also named Mary Anne, entered the Society but died young. There is no mention of this relationship in her death notice in 1882.

been unusual for a respectable single woman to travel alone at the time. Did she come with a brother or other male relative? What did she do before she entered at age forty, and how did she learn of the Society of the Sacred Heart? There certainly was no scarcity of Connor families in Missouri. Mary Anne could have lived in Saint Louis, since by 1820 the Irish were the largest population in the Saint Louis area.[66] She also could have lived in one of the predominately Irish settlements in Missouri, notably *Bois Brulé* Bottom[67] or the Murphy settlement. Both were established in the late 1790s.[68] Unfortunately, there is no record of where she came from or how she was introduced to the Society of the Sacred Heart.

Mary Anne was received and trained as a novice by Philippine, making her first vows on Sunday, April 17, 1825, and her final profession on September 4, 1829. Mary Anne probably knew enough French to communicate with Philippine, Lucille Mathevon, and the other RSCJ who must have used French as their common language.[69] She had some education, since she was received as a choir nun and was able to teach. If she was resident in the area in any of the early settlements, she might also have learned French that way since most of the area's Creole residents were French speaking.[70]

Mary Anne O'Connor was trusted by Philippine, who remarked in a letter to Sophie that "her solid virtue makes her the best person for this work, which will keep her part of the day and the whole night separated from us." She related well to the children in the native school. They "call her Mamma and run and jump about her wherever she takes them, to the cows, the poultry yard, the garden."[71] Mary Anne seemed to have understood

---

[66] Louis Houck, *A History of Missouri from earliest explorations and settlement* (Chicago: R.R. Donnelley and sons, 1908) online through Google Playbooks, 2.316. One local O'Connor who knew Bishop Dubourg and others connected to the Society was Jeremiah O'Connor, who was born in 1773 in Ireland and died in Saint Louis in 1823. Jeremiah was a cofounder, with John Mullanphy, of the Erin Benevolent Society in 1818. When Bishop Flaget, of the diocese of Bardstown, Kentucky (later Louisville), visited Saint Louis before the arrival of Bishop Dubourg that same year, Jeremiah contributed to a fundraising campaign with a generous contribution of one thousand dollars toward the repair of the bishop's residence. With Auguste Chouteau, Bernard Pratte, and many French residents, he signed a document setting aside land for the new bishop to use for educational purposes. He also donated additional land to Dubourg to be used for a future educational purpose. Mullanphy, Chouteau, and Pratte all knew the Society of the Sacred Heart.

[67] Michael O'Laughlin, *Missouri Irish*, 1984.

[68] Houck, p. 43f. Some of these Irish settlers had migrated down the area of the Illinois territory that borders Missouri.

[69] De Charry/Hogg 2.1, Letters 108 and 118. Octavie appears to have had a good grasp of English. Philippine lamented her lack of English and was unable to communicate with a young Irish postulant who entered (but did not stay) in 1820. Anna Xavier Murphy would have been a fluent English speaker.

[70] Charles Van Ravenswaay, *Saint Louis: An Informal History of the City and Its People, 1764-1865* (Missouri Historical Society, 1991), p. 176. There was conflict in Saint Louis among Catholics over which language to use for the sermon at Mass, especially the popular Sunday High Mass. When the preacher decided to preach in each language on alterative Sundays, people would walk out. In 1842, the church stopped using French for sermons, much to the discontent of the Creoles.

[71] Letter of April 23, 1825. The Indian school at Florissant was in a separate cabin near the stream, not in the main house.

that the girls needed activity and were not happy being confined to a classroom. The little girls were timid with strangers and would scramble up trees to hide until they left. The girls appear to have been luckier than the boys. Father van Quickenborne was a harsh taskmaster. He forced the boys to observe a strict horarium, and they were moved to tears when forced to farm, in their eyes, women's work. He used physical punishment and shocked novice Pierre De Smet with his severity.[72]

The Osage did not want to be separated from their children, and the expected boarders did not increase in number. Van Quickenborne blamed the children for their unwillingness to "bend under the yoke of discipline."[73] The Indian schools, Jesuit and Sacred Heart, did not survive. The students did not like school life, and the boys often escaped and had to be pursued. Both boys and girls missed their parents and the freedom of the Indian camp.

Mary Anne O'Connor would be one of the four pioneer RSCJ at Sugar Creek, going there in 1841 with Philippine, Lucille and Louise Amiot. She would spend most of her religious life in Saint Marys, dying there in 1863.

Ten years after the original founding of Saint Charles in 1818, it was reopened in 1828 with Lucille Mathevon and Mary Anne O'Connor, who would later work together at Sugar Creek with the Potawatomi. On October 10, 1828, they went from the convent in Florissant, to Saint Charles, accompanied by Philippine Duchesne and Octavie Berthold. They found themselves in very poor circumstances, living in what had been a shelter for animals. Four days later, Lucille and Mary Anne were left to fend for themselves when Philippine and Octavie returned to their work in Florissant. They "immediately went to work to fulfill the functions of carpenters, painters, masons, etc., and by dint of industry in fifteen days the house was finished."[74] On October 24, classes opened for five day students, and their number steadily increased to reach fifty in a few months. Certainly, the skills they honed in this foundation would prove useful in their future life as two of the founders of the Indian mission at Sugar Creek. They lived together until the mission to Sugar Creek was started. The Saint Charles community was always small, reaching the grand number of eight only in the two years before Lucille and Mary Anne left for Kansas.

Mary Layton, the first American-born woman who entered and persevered to make her vows, applied to enter

[72] Rollings, *Unaffected by the Gospel*, pp. 140-42.

[73] *Ibid.* p. 12 and p. 140f. Van Quickenborne was a failure at missionary work with the Osages. They asked that he not visit them and when he went on to work with the Kickapoo tribe, he had a similar experience. A difficult man, his community was reluctant to assign him to work with native peoples despite his desire to work in this ministry. There were complaints by his colleagues of his "bad temperament," and gloomy and secretive nature. He was not an easy man with whom to work.

[74] *Missouri Pioneer Families History, 1876* [database on-line]. Provo, Utah, USA: Ancestry.com Operations Inc., 2004. Original data: Bryan, Wm. S., *A History of the Pioneer Families of Missouri, with Numerous Sketches, Anecdotes, Adventures, Etc. Relating to Early Days in Missouri*. Saint Louis, Missouri: Bryan, Brand, 1876, pp. 437-38. Also Layton family history posted on *ancestry.com*.

the Society in 1820.[75] She was born July 2, 1802, in Washington County, Kentucky, of a Catholic family that had its roots in Saint Mary's County, Maryland, and was led by her grandfather John to Kentucky in the 1790s.[76] She was living in the frontier settlement of the Barrens, about sixty miles from Saint Louis. Her grandfather, John Layton, may have been born in England, but most of his children were born in Maryland. Together with three of his sons, Bernard, John, and Ignatius, he had secured a land grant from the Spanish authorities before the Louisiana Purchase and moved there in 1803. The 1805 Missouri territorial census lists John and his sons, John and Ignatius, as residents. Two of his other sons, Joseph,[77] Bernard and Zechariah, while not getting a similar grant, later went to Missouri. Although some Society records[78] list her father as Bernard Layton, the register of the RSCJ community at Saint Mary's identifies her father as Joseph and her mother as Mary Ann Downs. In the same register, she is identified as Mary Josephine Ann Layton.

Mary's mother died July 2, 1802, giving birth to Mary and her twin brother Joseph. Her father, who doted on Mary, dedicated her to her patron Mary Immaculate[79] at an early age. Joseph, left with several small children, quickly remarried in 1803,[80] had two more children, and lost that wife in 1805. With perhaps six children under ten years old, he was married again that August 5, 1805, to Theresa Yates,[81] who gave the family two more children. Joseph planned to take his family to the Missouri territory, but he died on October 9, 1809, in Washington County, Kentucky, and was buried there. Only after his death would Mary, her step mother, Theresa Yates, and other siblings move to Missouri where both she and her stepmother had family. These deaths were a lot of loss for

---

[75] The first choir novice to persevere, Emilie St-Cyr was a student in the school at the time Mary Anne was received, as were the Hamilton sisters. Kilroy (p. 44) notes that Eulalie Hamilton entered as a coadjutrix sister but was professed as a choir sister.
[76] John and his sons were all listed in tax records in Washington, Kentucky, in 1800. Some of his sons were married in Kentucky in the late 1790's, as is attested by Kentucky marriage records. Joseph Layton is listed as a "spy" for the military after 1784. National Archives and Records Administration (NARA); Washington, D.C.; *Compiled Service Records of Volunteer Soldiers Who Served from 1784 to 1811*; Record Group: *94, Records of the Adjutant General's Office, 1762 - 1984*; Series Number: *M905*; Roll Number: *15*.
[77] Joseph is listed in Kentucky tax records in 1800. *Ancestry.com. Kentucky, Tax Lists, 1799-1801* [database on-line]. Provo, UT, USA: *Ancestry.com* Operations Inc., 2006. Original data: Clift, G. Glenn. *Second Census of Kentucky, 1800.* Baltimore, MD, USA: Genealogical Publishing Co., 2005. This "second census" of Kentucky is an alphabetical list of 32,000 taxpayers and is based on original tax lists on file in the Kentucky Historical Society.
[78] Louise Callan has Bernard as her father in her books as does the house register at Saint Charles. However, the information in the house register at Saint Mary's Mission was likely given by Mary herself. Genealogical records also indicate that Bernard's wife was not Mary Anne Downs but Mary Yates.
[79] July 2 at that time was the feast of the Visitation of Mary to Elizabeth.
[80] Dodd, Jordan. *Kentucky Marriages, 1802-1850* [database online]. Provo, Utah, USA: Ancestry.com, Operations Inc., 1997. Original data: Electronic transcription of marriage records held by the individual counties in Kentucky.
[81] *Ibid.* Names given as Joseph Leaton and Tracy Yates.

Mary, who would have been around seven when her father died and the family was uprooted and moved from Kentucky. She had already experienced the death of her first stepmother in 1805 and her twin brother in 1807.[82]

Society tradition is that Mary had many brothers, which would have been true only if Joseph was her father. There were at least seven boys of the fifteen children born to Joseph and his wives.[83] Joseph's brother Bernard, who had married Mary Yates in 1799 in Kentucky, had no boys but four small daughters all around Mary's age.[84] Mary Yates was the sister of Theresa Yates, Joseph's third wife.[85] It was probably in Bernard's home that young Mary Layton was raised or in the home of one of her married brothers. Her two oldest brothers were already married, Wilfred when Mary was two and John Walter when she was five. Both of them lived in Missouri.[86] Their grandfather John provided land for Joseph's orphan children in 1820 just as some of the children were of the age to be married.[87]

When the Layton family settled on land grants in the Barrens (Perryville), Missouri, there was no Catholic church. The nearest church was twenty miles away in the settlement of Sainte Geneviève where family marriages were performed, but baptisms were usually performed privately at home. Her grandfather signed a letter with other early settlers petitioning for a parish. This petition led to the foundation of Saint Mary's church in the Barrens. The Layton family and other pioneers donated 640 acres to Bishop Dubourg to build a seminary there in 1818. The founding rector at the time Mary lived there was the future bishop of Saint Louis, Joseph Rosati. At some point, probably after moving to Missouri, Mary made her First Communion. She then first felt a call to greater

---

[82] Layton family history on line has Mary Layton, b. July 2, 1802 d. 1876. There are several trees posted on *ancestry.com* of uneven quality for both Bernard and Joseph. What they all agree on and what seems borne out by Kentucky marriage records are that the husband of Mary Downes (Downs or Downes?) was Joseph Layton, not Bernard. An example of one tree can be found at http://trees.ancestry.com/tree/32819767/family?fpid=19948339355.

[83] He and his first wife had eleven children: Wilfred, b. 1795, John Walter, b. 1786, Mary Anne Aloysia, b. 1790, Anne, b. 1791, John Baptist, b. 1795, Jane, b. 1797, Rosanne, b. 1799, twins Barnard and Zachariah, b. 1800, and another set of twins, Joseph and Mary, b. 1802. Two girls were born from his second marriage, Elizabeth in 1804 and Priscilla in 1805, and there were two children from his third marriage to Theresa Yates, Charity in 1806 and Ignatius in 1807. At least four of Mary's uncles moved to Missouri: Bernard, Zachariah, John and Ignatius.

[84] They may have later had two other girls, Christina b. 1821 and Martina b. 1818.

[85] *Parish Census of Saint Mary's Parish, Perryville, Missouri, 1823*. Original data: Timothy J. O'Rourke, *Parish Catholic Families of Southern Maryland: Records of Catholic Residents of Saint Marys County in the Eighteenth Century* (Baltimore, Maryland: Genealogical Publishing Co., 2003). Also available as typewritten copy and on www.ancestry.com and http://files.usgwarchives.net/mo/perry/census/stmarys.txt.

[86] Parish census notes that Mary's stepmother Theresa married Christopher Hines two years after Mary left home. Theresa's two sisters Jane and Charity were married to men in the Barrens settlement.

[87] *Ibid*. Land Plat record posted on same website.

love and service of God but had no idea how to fulfill it.[88] It is perhaps thanks to the influence of the priests at the seminary, that her vocation was directed to the Society of the Sacred Heart. "The child felt a strong desire to give her life to God, but she did not know where to turn until she learned from her pastor that some nuns had come to Missouri from France.[89] Mary arrived at Florissant accompanied by Father Rosati and two other priests and was received by Philippine. When they arrived, the priests told Philippine about a visit Bishop Dubourg had had from a delegation of Osage Indians. The chief asked the bishop to visit his people, and he was making plans to do so the next month. The bishop gave the chief a crucifix,[90] which the man so prized that he would not exchange it for a saddle, liquor, or money offered by a merchant. One of the priests predicted that Philippine too would go to the Osage "just as surely as I would go to bed tonight."[91]

Philippine wrote to Sophie that "she [Mary Layton] is certainly the best we have had so far, but she can only be a coadjutrix sister."[92] Mary received the habit of a coadjutrix sister on November 22, 1820, just two years after Philippine Duchesne brought the then-young Society to North America. There is a rare note of triumph in Philippine's journal entry: "On this happy day those of the pupils who have a talent for music sang the Mass, and very well, too. We celebrated in a becoming manner the first religious clothing that has taken place in Upper Louisiana since the beginning of the world, and great was our joy to see another soul entirely consecrated to the Sacred Heart."[93] The children were impressed by the ceremony; in time some of them, Émilie Saint-Cyr and Eulalie (Regis) and Mathilde (Xavier) Hamilton would follow Mary Layton's example. Eventually "native born Americans would outnumber those from France."[94]

Mary found religious life difficult at first, but she was determined to overcome these difficulties. She was commended by Philippine for persevering in humility. Friendly and open, she adjusted to her strange new life, guided by Eugénie Audé, her novice mistress, whom Mary in turn helped to learn English. Despite her lack of domestic skills, she was getting some harsh basic training in them. Philippine wrote to Sophie: "You can form no

[88] *Annual Letters*, Society of the Sacred Heart, 1877, p. 279.
[89] Frances Gimber, RSCJ, "Builders of the US Province" on Mary Layton: www.rscj.org. Shortly after Mary entered the Society, the Sisters of Loretto established a foundation at the Barrens.
[90] Rollings p. 132. The Osage chief was Sans Neuf who probably had no idea what the crucifix represented and would have found the concept of someone dying for his sins incomprehensible, since the concepts of sin and redemption were foreign to his spirituality. But it is probable that he would have been familiar with tribes that tortured enemies and admired this tortured man's bravery.
[91] Callan, *Philippine Duchesne*, p. 327. It would be interesting to know if Mary was present for this conversation.
[92] De Charry/Hogg et al. 2-1, Letter 131 (30 October 1820), p. 222. Several other Americans had entered as postulants but either had no vocation or aptitude for the life. Most entered as coadjutrix sisters. Philippine never explains why Mary could enter only as a coadjutrix sister.
[93] *Ibid.* p. 222.
[94] www.rscj.org, Gimber.

idea of all this novice suffers in tending the cows in the mud, snow, ice, often wet to the skin or numb with cold. One day we had to chop the milk in her pail with a knife and hammer, as one cuts loaf sugar."[95]

Philippine mentions that Bishop Dubourg approved Mary's acceptance as a coadjutrix sister even though he had opposed the system as not suited to the American way of life. Philippine herself also wondered whether this system would ever work in the United States. The only hint Philippine gives as to why Mary was accepted as a lay rather than a choir religious is in a reference comparing her to another possible candidate "who has more education."[96] Philippine had problems with the attitudes of the Americans and found them too independent for her tastes. Was she taking her time with Mary? Several women who later were received as coadjutrix novices were professed as choir sisters when Philippine had a chance to assess their talents. Sometimes she used this time as a way of testing out a prospective member. In one instance, Philippine mentions another postulant with ability and intelligence, bilingual in French and English, who "might do well at studies, were it not better for her spiritual formation to keep her a little in obscurity."[97]

Mary Layton, while still a novice, was sent with Eugénie Audé in 1821 to found a Sacred Heart school in Grand Coteau, Louisiana. There she continued her formation, made her first vows in 1822 and her profession in 1825. Although Mary was a coadjutrix sister, whose main task was domestic work, she seemed to have been lacking in some basic skills, such as cooking and housework. Eugénie Audé had to instruct her in these necessary domestic duties and wound up cooking herself until Mary learned.[98] She remained at the convent in Grand Coteau for seven years, during which time it never had more than eight community members. Until Mary left that community, there was only one other coadjutrix sister. In 1828 she was at Saint Michael's foundation in Convent, Louisiana, a much larger community with twenty-two members, including nine novices. She joined Lucille Mathevon and Mary Anne O'Connor at Saint Charles in 1829, sharing the challenging mission there. During that time, she would get to know these two RSCJ with whom she would live for many years in the mission to the Potawatomi. She was in Saint. Louis from 1831 to 1837.

While there, she would have met Louise Amiot, who would be her companion and coworker for many years

---

[95] Callan, *Philippine Duchesne*, p. 332.

[96] *Ibid.* p. 222; also see the 1870 U.S. census. Mary could both read and write so had at least some education.

[97] *Ibid.* p. 333, letter to Sophie. In France at this time, there were coadjutrix novices with ability who were professed as choir sisters but as is noted in Kilroy, (pp. 50-51), it was difficult to suggest an opposite move when a choir novice showed no promise or ability as a teacher. So perhaps Philippine was just being cautious. Society writings give little indication of Mary's personality, and she left no writings of her own. Later in life at Saint Mary's she would receive a negative assessment from Amélie Jouve who would visit the community in 1856.

[98] RSCJ Archives, Marie Louise Martinez, Series XII, Box 9 #63 item 39, Data from RSCJ who knew Philippine. Also mentioned in Callan, *North America* (p. 122) in the history of the foundation at Grand Coteau. Callan suggests that Mary was unfamiliar with cooking Southern food with its dependence on corn.

at Sugar Creek and Saint Mary's. When she was again assigned to the community at Grand Coteau in 1838, it would have grown to twenty-three members. That was the largest community in which Mary would live until the end of her life. There she would remain until she joined the Sugar Creek community as its second coadjutrix sister in 1845.

By 1833 Philippine was once again pursuing the idea of an Indian mission. She mentions that Pierre De Smet, pioneer Jesuit missionary, was preparing himself for that work. She seems impressed that he was forcing himself to speak English by living in a community that used that language exclusively.[99] Unfortunately, since the Society in Missouri and Louisiana at that time was French-speaking, Philippine could not avail herself of a similar opportunity.

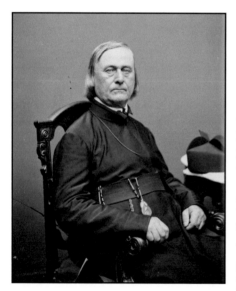

Pierre De Smet, SJ, in the 1870s

In October 1833, Philippine received a cautious response from Sophie about starting an Indian mission. Sophie expressed concern that their community resources would be stretched too thin:

> As to a request to move to the Indians I am afraid I have not the means. You would need two or three reliable people with you, not too young and English speaking. Where can I find them? And what would you live on? You would have absolutely no income. I can see nothing but the difficulties and would not dare to give my approval.[100]

But she did give Philippine a glimmer of hope when she continued: "Speak of this to me again should you find this enterprise to be feasible…Tell me the bishop of the tribe and what would be your spiritual and material supports."[101] Philippine sent a letter in December of that year to Sophie in Rome to be hand-delivered by the missionary De Smet himself. In it she tried to answer some of Sophie's objections. Philippine was anxious that another congregation might seize the opportunity to go to the mission ahead of the Society. She assures Sophie that the proposed Indian foundation is in a different place (from Florissant) and could not be started for a year or more, and the Society was third on the list after the Sisters of Charity and the Sisters of Holy Cross. Philippine answers Sophie's question about the bishop of the tribe reassuring her that the Indian missions in the United States for those natives living outside an established diocese would be under the care of the Jesuits and the Society

---

[99] De Charry/Hogg et al, 2-3, Letter 289 (23 June, 1823). He was urging her to send sisters to the mission.

[100] *Ibid*. De Charry/Hogg et al, 2-3, Letter 293 (16 October 1833), letter from Sophie to Philippine.

[101] *Ibid*.

for the Propagation of the Faith. The Jesuits would be settling in the same place, providing spiritual support, and as to finances, the Jesuit superior was petitioning the government to arrange a subsidy to support the work with the Indians.[102]

Philippine knew the foundation would need mature religious, with both experience in religious life and leadership ability, and those were few. After the foundation at Florissant in 1819, between 1820 and 1828, there had been five other foundations, which limited the available number of women who could qualify as mature religious. Because of her experience at Florissant with the short-lived Indian school, she knew that the Society needed to move farther west to minister to the native peoples. Letters from the Jesuit Charles Felix van Quickenborne in 1837 about the failed mission to the Kickapoo tribe kept Philippine's desire alive. When the Jesuits abandoned that mission, they were invited by the Potawatomi to serve them. Her desire to serve was further fueled by the news in 1838 of the forced march of the Potawatomi people[103] from their home in Indiana to the opposite side of the Mississippi in the territory set aside by the United States government, where they were supposed to make a permanent new home. Philippine was inspired by the heroic priest, Father Benjamin Petit, who accompanied the people on the "Trail of Death" on which many of the tribe died and who himself, broken in health, died soon afterwards.

Eventually Sophie gave her approval for the mission, moved perhaps by the personal appeal of the new bishop of New Orleans, Joseph Rosati, while on a trip to Paris. Bishop Rosati even secured the approval of Pope Gregory XVI for the mission school on a trip to Rome and informed Sophie of the Pope's desire that the Society of the Sacred Heart would go to work among the Indians.[104] How could Sophie say no? Philippine was elated and began to prepare, though she was not sure if she herself would be in the number to go because of her age and poor health. She had just been relieved for those reasons of her position as superior of the Society in the United States.

---

[102] The unfortunate tie in with government aid made the missionaries much more open to the project of "civilizing" the native peoples and more cooperative with some government policies such as allocation of land to private ownership instead of common tribal ownership.

[103] Garraghan, *The Jesuits of the Middle United States,* 2, p. 203. Jesuit Christian Hoecken who returned to Florissant in 1839 for recovery from bad health probably was the person that gave Philippine a firsthand account of the arrival of the band from Indiana.

[104] Callan, *Philippine Duchesne,* pp. 628f. Philippine shared Bishop Rosati's letter with Pierre De Smet in January 1841, which concluded, "If I did not know you well I would say it is too much for you. But knowing you as I do, I say: Go! Follow your attraction or rather the voice of God."

THE PEOPLE CALLED "KEEPERS OF THE FIRE"

The people Philippine wished to serve, the Potawatomi, were a tribe of the Algonquin culture and language, related to the Ottawa and Chippewa people. According to Potawatomi tradition, the Odawas, (Ottawas) Ojibwas (Chippewas) and Potawatomi were initially a single tribe, known as "three fires" or "three brothers," because of their similar way of life. Their name for themselves "Bodewadmi" means "the People," but in the alliance of the three brother tribes, they were called the "Keepers of the Fire."[105] Their original ancestral lands were in southern Michigan near the Great Lakes, where they had migrated over the centuries from farther east near the Saint Lawrence River. They first encountered French explorers in the seventeenth century, when they had been pushed farther northwest into Wisconsin by conflict with the Iroquois. The French were fur traders and the Potawatomi soon became middle men in the trade and allies of the French. The French traders cemented alliances with the tribes by intermarrying with native women. Many traders had a native wife as well as a French one back in Montreal.[106] While tribes accepted mixed race children as members, those children formed a hybrid culture called the Métis. The Potawatomi with whom the RSCJ would work would have a subculture of Métis members as a result of almost 150 years of contact with the French. Among the Potawatomi, they served as the bridge with the white world and became important tribal leaders. By the eighteenth century, the tribe had migrated again into a large area from present day Milwaukee to Detroit and Chicago and south into Indiana.

The Potawatomi had bad luck in their choice of allies in two wars: they sided with the French against the British in the war ending in 1763 with the French defeated. While remaining neutral in the War of Independence, they chose to side with the British against the Americans later in the War of 1812. Having chosen the losing side in both instances, they suffered by being forced to migrate from the Great Lakes after the first conflict and to settle in Indiana after the War of 1812, forfeiting their lands to the north. After a series of treaties, they had lost

---

[105] *Encyclopedia of the American Indian,* "Potawatomi." In the traditional roles of the "three brothers," the Ottawa were the keepers of trade, and the Chippewa were the spirit keepers, which refers to their roles in the alliance of tribes: commerce and spirituality. The Potawatomi were the keepers of the fire or the hearth uniting the three tribes. This article is the source of this part of the history of the Potawatomi nation.

[106] Nicholas Perrot (1644-1717) was one of these explorers. In 1712, he wrote a book about his experiences that is one of the earliest accounts of the customs and religions of the Potawatomi and other Great Lakes tribes. He also had a Potawatomi wife and one of his direct descendants lives today on the Potawatomi reservation in Michigan. The author of this history is descended from Nicholas and his French wife Madeleine Raclos. See appendix of Shirley Willard and Susan Campbell, *Trail of Death 1838,* Fulton County Historical Society, Rochester, Indiana, for information on Nicholas Perrot of Michigan, a Potawatomi who claims to be a direct descendant of the explorer through his Indian wife.

more than six million acres of land to white encroachment, including much of what is now the city of Chicago. Because of their alliance with the British and their fierce defense of their homes, especially during the battle of Tippecanoe, they were perceived as "enemy combatants" by the settlers.

Like many native tribes, the Potawatomi were governed by consensus. They were divided into many bands and were loosely organized along clan lines, a federation of blood relatives living in a band or village. They had traditional alliances and also enmities with other tribes but had no overall central authority. At a time when European governments were authoritarian and hierarchical, the Potawatomi organization was based upon principles of freedom and mutual respect. A clan leader had only as much authority as he was given. Disputes within the village were settled by the dissenting parties' moving to another village. The position of clan leader was familial and dealt with issues of daily life. Colonial powers often defined the relationship with native peoples as a "familial" one—the king was their "father" and they his "children." However, the definition of family for the colonists was patriarchal and authoritarian, while the natives did not see the relationship through that lens.

> Traditionally, in northeastern North America parental authority was much less coercive than in Europe. In agreeing to call the governor their father, the native leaders required that he be a provider and defender, allowing him to play a role much like that of an Indian chief. In other words, they expected him to be a leader who could rally everyone around him and yet act non-coercively. The French did not see things in this way. Their goal was to use the *father* title to impose upon their allies the European patrilineal kinship system, whereby the father had absolute authority over his children. Their attitude caused a great deal of friction, with one governor after another trying to give his "children" orders and the latter seeing these orders as proposals to be first debated and then agreed to or turned down. Throughout the French regime, the Amerindian interpretation largely prevailed over the European one.[107]

Negotiations with tribes often were made with the clan leader. But many tribes also had a war chief whose position was not hereditary but was based on skill and personality. He could not order his tribe to do anything; rather he governed by persuasion. There was a sense of equality in the authority he wielded that was not understood by the French, the British, or even the Americans.[108]

Both the European and the American authorities constantly misunderstood the leadership systems of native peoples, providing labels, such as King or Prince, categories that the natives did not have. They sometimes selected a tribal member and negotiated with that person to attain their ends, as if with a king who could validly speak

---

[107] Hoxie, *Encyclopedia of North American Indians,* pp. 281f.

[108] Early U.S. experiments in government such as the Articles of Confederation were based on observation of native governing practices among the Iroquois of New York. For more information on tribal government and its influence on that of the U.S., see Bruce F. Johansen, *Forgotten Founders: How the American Indian Helped Shape Democracy* (online at: https://ratical.org/many_worlds/6Nations/FF.html) or Jack Weatherford, *Native Roots: How the Indians Enriched America* (1992).

for the tribe.[109] In wartime, natives would fight fiercely and just as abruptly retreat when they felt finished. The Chief could not command his warriors to follow him or support him. This must have been frustrating to militia captains or regular army generals used to commanding troops. Not all bands of Potawatomi necessarily supported the same alliances. While most supported the French and then the British, individual bands chose to support the other side. The United States government found the band structure especially difficult and between 1787 and 1867 negotiated and renegotiated over forty-four treaties, as it became apparent that no one band could speak for all the Potawatomi. Frustrating to government authorities on all sides, it also must have confused the missionaries, as they were used to a hierarchical church with clear lines of authority.[110]

Many bands of the Potawatomi had accepted Catholicism during the French period. They also had a substantial tribal population of mixed blood or Métis people who were at least nominal Catholics. After leaving their former territory in Michigan and Wisconsin, they settled in Indiana after the War of 1812. Although they had little contact with clergy,[111] they kept the faith alive through private prayers and devotions, such as the rosary and services led by native leaders.[112] In the 1830s, they asked for and received a "black robe" for their tribe, a Belgian diocesan priest, Louis DeSeille.[113] He became aware of the encroaching settlers who eyed the native lands with envy. The tribe had become more agricultural and had established prosperous farms, despite their previous hunting culture. When Louis DeSeille attempted to become an advocate for tribal rights, he was forbidden to

---

[109] Jeffrey D. Schultz, *Encyclopedia of Minorities in American Politics: Hispanic Americans and Native Americans*, (Westport, CT: Greenwood Publishing Company, 2000): pp. 699ff. Explains how different tribes had a variety of government structures and gives examples of various treaties that were negotiated with leaders who could not speak for their people. He also explains the role of the Indian Agent.

[110] For example, when the Potawatomi signed treaties promising to vacate their land to move west of the Mississippi, some of the clans refused and remained where they were. Today there are five Potawatomi bands still occupying their ancestral lands in Michigan, Wisconsin and Indiana as well as the Citizen Band in Oklahoma and the Prairie Band in Kansas who were displaced in 1838.

[111] They were visited sporadically. One of the first priests ordained by John Carroll, Stephen Badin, visited the Potawatomi in Niles, Michigan, and later when they moved down to Illinois and Indiana.

[112] An interesting study of the use of leaders, especially native and Metises women to evangelize can be found in Susan Sleeper-Smith's *Indian Women and French Men* (Amherst, MA: University of Massachusetts Press, 2001). These bands always had a shortage of clergy and depended on laity to lead prayers, baptize, and catechize.

[113] Andrew Ditlinger, "The History of the Catholic Church in Indiana: Indiana Saints," *Saint Meinrad Historical Essays*, 2:3 (March 1932). Available online at http://indianacatholic.mwweb.org/st_deseille.html. This article gives the details of the dispute with the U.S. government Indian agent that led to DeSeille's being banned from the native village. DeSeille was originally a novice in a religious community but became a member of the secular clergy in America.

enter the tribal areas by the local United States Indian agent, who feared his influence.[114] The agent accused him of violating the Indian Trade Act of 1834, which designated the United States government as sole agent to deal with tribal peoples. Although Louis DeSeille stayed nearby and tried to continue his ministry with the Potawatomi, he fell ill after seven years of exhausting ministry and died at the age of forty-two, a few months after being banned from the native territory.

Potawatomi Indians at Crooked Creek, Indiana, George Winter (TCHA)

In 1837, a young, newly-ordained French priest, Benjamin Petit, went to minister with the tribe. He had been a successful lawyer in France before becoming a priest. Like Philippine he had felt a strong call to work with the native peoples and was sent to the Midwest despite his poor health. The natives, without a clergyman or the sacraments for several years, were delighted when he arrived and declared, "We were orphans, and as if in darkness; you appeared among us like a great light and we live."[115] He got involved with helping the chief Menominee fight for his people's rights against those attempting to annul their treaties and seize their lands. Father Petit helped Menominee write a petition to Washington and was influential in advocating for the tribe. For this, he also incurred the wrath of the local Indian agent, who both threatened and tried to bribe him.

The priest was not impressed by the Americans, although some of the surrounding Catholic settlers also sought

---

[114] Indian agents served as an intermediary between the U.S. government and the local Indian peoples. They promoted government policies, distributed goods or money promised tribes in treaties, and tried to keep peace between white settlers and the tribal peoples around them.

[115] Shirley Willard and Susan Campbell, *Trail of Death 1838* (Rochester, Indiana: Fulton County Historical Society, 2003) reprint of a 1941 collection of Benjamin Marie Petit's letters with new notes and appendix. The older source can be found on line at the Indiana Historical Society website.

his ministry. He observed the contrast between the natives and the Americans: "How little savage [the natives] are at heart…while the Americans have hearts dry as cork and their whole thought [is] land and money; [they] fail to appreciate [the natives] and treat [them] with so much disdain and injustice." [116]

Benjamin Petit wrote to his bishop defending his advocacy, saying the Indians "have so often been deceived by lawyers and interpreters and they had so often been made to say what they do not mean."[117] Fearing his bishop may think him too much a lawyer rather than a priest, he eloquently tied his priestly ministry in with the work of protecting those oppressed who had no "other defense other than a priest's voice."[118] Petit's heart was with the native people, and his letters cite examples of the natives' response to this love. He testifies to feeling "an inconceivable tenderness for them at the bottom of my heart."[119] Perhaps because of his legal background, Petit's letters and questions to Bishop Bruté and his vicar general also give some idea of the complications that conversion to Christianity brought to the native culture, especially in the area of marriage, multiple wives, and previous liaisons. He supports the cause of Chief Menominee, who took his sister-in-law as a second wife at his brother's death because of cultural obligation. When he wished to become a Catholic, Petit supported his dispensation to marry the sister-in-law, since his first wife was now deceased.[120]

The United States government in 1830 had adopted a policy of moving all native peoples west of the Mississippi.[121] It succeeded in making a treaty to that effect with some of the Potawatomi chiefs during a visit to Washington. Menominee did not sign the treaty, and many in the tribe were considering refusing to move. The Potawatomi tribe agreed to move to land guaranteed them forever in the so-called Indian Territory

---

[116] *Ibid*, p. 42.

[117] *Ibid*, p. 42-43.

[118] *Ibid*. p. 43 Letter to Bishop Bruté.

[119] *Ibid*. 45.

[120] *Ibid*. pp. 53f. Probably the man who had been evangelized by a Protestant missionary and had refused to set aside his sister-in-law, who had nine children out of a sense of duty to her and his dead brother. When the man wanted to become a Catholic Father DeSeille had made the same request and the man refused citing injustice to the woman and her children. Later the man had evidently asked Father Petit for baptism. (He was baptized and married in the church to his sister-in-law and went on the Trail of Death in 1838).

[121] Oklahoma State University Digital Archive of government printing office, 1904: Indian Affairs: Laws and Treaties, Vol 2 Treaties, edited by Charles L. Kappler, Washington, DC, gives the terms of 39 treaties negotiated with the Potawatomi people over the years, which guaranteed them land that would be theirs "forever" and a cash or food subsidy in return for moving. Indian removal to land west of the Mississippi became policy under President Andrew Jackson.

(Kansas–Nebraska–Oklahoma).[122] It is not clear that all those signing really understood what the treaty implied, and some of those who signed later signed the protest document that Petit wrote and sent to Washington. The Potawatomi had been stockpiling arms in their cornfields and woods, which were discovered by the soldiers sent to remove them from their land. General Tipton, the Indiana agent assigned to remove the tribe, remarked that they were "sullen" and blamed them for planting their corn in June, which they would now be unable to harvest. He felt the guns alone justified their removal, although Judge Polk, federal agent in charge of the removal, who was more sympathetic to the Indians' plight,[123] took the guns with the idea of returning them, for hunting and defense, when they reached their new home.[124]

Despite Petit's efforts at advocacy with the government, the removal was set for September 1838. His heart was broken, and he wanted to go with the Potawatomi, but his bishop refused permission. The Indian agents, General Tipton and Judge Poole, were nervous about the Indians' resisting and persuaded the bishop to allow Petit to go, thinking he would help keep order. Since by then he was fluent in their language, he served as an interpreter on the journey. From his diary of the journey, as well as from those of both Tipton and Poole, it is possible to get a vivid account of the journey. The procession, as described by eyewitnesses including Petit, included as many as eight hundred natives led by a soldier with a U.S. flag. There were two hundred and fifty to three hundred horses ridden by men, women, and children single file. Included in the lineup was a jail wagon where Menominee and some dissenting chiefs were confined.

---

[122] William Connelley, *The Prairie Band of Pottawatomie Indians* (Kansas State Historical Society, 1917). In February 1837, the United States agreed by treaty to convey to the tribe a tract of land on the Osage or Marais des Cygnes River in Kansas, sufficient for their needs. The Pottawatomies [*sic*] of the Woods, and what was then known as the Mission band, settled on this tract, in what became Miami and Linn counties, Kansas, the same year. See text http://www.kansasheritage.org/PBP/books/kshsroll/kshs_01.html.

[123] *Ibid*, pp. 251f. Both Tipton and Poole had bad experiences with natives: Tipton's father was killed in an Indian raid and Poole had been captured as a child and adopted into an Indian tribe, becoming accustomed to Indian culture and language before finally being rescued.

[124] *Ibid*, p. 224.

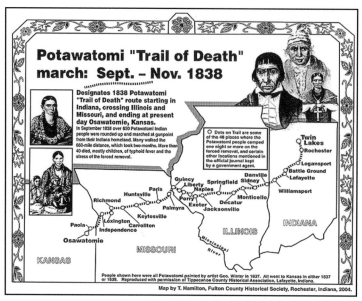

Map of Trail of Death, (Fulton County Historical Society, Indiana)

Forty baggage wagons with their goods also carried those too sick to walk as well as some of the women and children. These were "rudely jolted, under a canvas, which far from protecting them from the dust and heat, only deprived them of air, so that they felt that they were buried under the burning canopy."[125] Passing through towns, the caravan attracted curious onlookers. Soldiers and one hundred civilian volunteers hastened the stragglers on with severe gestures and bitter words.[126]

General Tipton and most of the soldiers left the group at the Illinois line, leaving only about sixteen soldiers to keep order. Judge Poole, who represented federal authority, took over and released the captive chiefs from the jail wagon. When they passed through Springfield, Illinois, he asked the people to dress in their best regalia for the march through town, which they did, putting on a brave show of pride watched by residents who enjoyed the spectacle but rejoiced at their departure. Poole allowed the group to spend each Sunday as a day of rest. Petit was able to celebrate Mass, give instructions, and pray Vespers as the Indians had done back in Indiana.[127] The Judge only refused to stop when they got closer to their destination, and scarce provisions and colder weather made haste more necessary.

---

[125] *Ibid.* pp. 98-100. Contemporary newspaper accounts said the procession was three miles long and settlers triumphantly lined the road or overlooking hills to watch the Indians leave.

[126] Willard and Campbell, p. 98. The diary of General Tipton denies that this happened.

[127] When they were near white settlements those settlers often came to join in since most had not seen a priest for years.

The heat abated when they crossed over the Mississippi, but the damage had been done, and many children and frail elderly had died and were buried along the road. The Potawatomi were able to hunt along the way but noticed that game became scarcer as they traveled—a bad omen for their new homes. Another problem on the way was the sale of liquor, both by and to the soldiers and to men of the tribe, which led to drunkenness and fights. A sense of doom and despair was natural as they neared the end of their long journey.[128]

Christian Hoecken, SJ, was waiting to greet them as they approached the Sugar Creek mission, where he and his companions had arrived earlier at the request of other migrant Potawatomi.[129] They had first considered another site farther north but had settled on this one as more secure. They had begun to build shelters and a chapel. [130] Benjamin Petit, ill and exhausted by the journey, left his people and planned to return to his bishop in Indiana as he had promised. However, on his way back, after taking refuge at the Jesuit seminary in Saint Louis, he died on February 15, 1839, just two months short of his twenty-eighth birthday.

With the arrival of the procession from Indiana, the mission now had a total of 1200 natives, about half of whom were Catholic. This number was augmented by at least two other groups of Potawatomi who moved into the area, over 500 in October and over 800 in November 1840.[131] By Christmas of 1840, the community had dedicated its church. The Potawatomi were probably heartened by the many sugar maples that lined the creek. They were fond of sweets, and maple sugar was highly prized. The land, however, was not as fertile as what they had left behind. Neither the missionaries nor the tribe realized that this would not be the last destination on their migration.

Philippine, who had been superior of two different houses since 1819, was relieved of her leadership role in 1840, as she had been requesting for years. She then moved to Saint Louis, where she became seriously ill. None of these events seemed to dim her desire for the mission, though in September of 1840, she expressed doubts that she would be able to go, both because of her age and because of the mistrust she felt as to her own abilities.[132] Her own health concerns seemed to vanish when it was clear (on account of the pressure of Jesuit Pierre-Jean Verhaegen) that she would be part of the mission. "Even though ill and surrounded by opposition, my old fire is

---

[128] Willard and Campbell, pp. 99f.

[129] Kinsella, Fr. Hoecken's Diary in appendix to *The History of Our Cradleland*, indicates that about 150 Indians had arrived and Chief Nesfwawhe had requested the Jesuits. Fr. Hoecken and Fr. Verreydt arrived in January 1838 and May 1838 for temporary visits from their station with the Kickapoo. After the second visit, the Jesuits allowed Fr Hoecken to return permanently.

[130] The other site was closer to territory of other native peoples who were hostile to the incoming Potawatomi such as the Osages and the Pawnee.

[131] R. David Edmunds, *The Potawatomis: Keepers of the Fire* (Norman, Oklahoma: University of Oklahoma Press, 1978). Many of these groups were from Michigan. The second group came willingly, but the first were marched at gunpoint from Michigan and at Illinois, put on steamboats to journey to Westport and from there to the Osage River Agency where Sugar Creek was located.

[132] De Charry/Hogg et al, 2.3, p. 332, Letter 320 (Sept 30, 1840).

rekindled. I saw that it would be possible."[133] Since she had just been relieved as superior, she attributed her illness to this switch from an active to a more sedentary lifestyle.[134] In the same letter, she writes at length on why the mission is so "precious, so necessary, so easy." She explains that it is easy since they are being asked for, by both the other missionaries and the natives, stressing that these are "good tribes" who present no danger to the sisters. Philippine has a sense of urgency about the necessity of the mission, knowing (perhaps from her conversations with the Jesuits, especially Father De Smet) that Protestant missionaries are pushing into the frontier, receiving the government subsidy,[135] and using it to educate and evangelize. She adds that their wives will educate the girls and "give the children to Satan." In turn, she asks, "Will the Sisters of the Sacred Heart shrink from giving them at all costs to Jesus Christ?"[136] Finally, she refers to the image she has received from the Jesuits of the natives living as the first Christians in a community modeled on the Paraguay Mission "reductions." She felt this atmosphere would make the work easy.

The Paraguay Reductions (1610–1767)[137] were a missionary experiment by the Jesuits to allow the native tribes to develop without interference from the colonizers' greed. In these settlements the Christianized natives lived apart, were educated in art, music, and agriculture. While they were introduced to European culture, their own was also studied and in some aspects preserved. Native languages were respected; missionaries studied them and produced grammars and dictionaries. Native crafts were promoted, and a trade relationship was set up between the settlements. The people were gradually introduced to the concept of having their own plots of land. The goal was to create an idealized Christian community free of the vices of the Europeans, who were banned from the settlements.

The early Jesuits in the United States were inspired by this example, and Father De Smet carried a history of the Reductions on his journey to the Oregon territory to establish a similar native settlement. He often referred to the Jesuit missions as "reductions," although that particular model was not practical on the rapidly changing American frontier. De Smet estimated that if the two cultures could be kept apart and missionaries worked with

---

[133] *Ibid*. Letter 323, pp. 339-40.

[134] *Ibid*. De Charry/Hogg et al, 2.3, Letter 321, pp. 333-36 (15 January 1841).

[135] Missionaries, both Catholic and Protestant, received a government subsidy to help them promote the adoption of Christianity by the natives, a goal the government saw as a "civilizing" influence on the tribes. The government paid a subsidy in goods, services such as education, and cash to the tribes according to the terms of various treaties made with them in return for ceding their lands. Philippine's negative view of Protestant missionaries would be typical of a Catholic of her time who would see them as competitors preaching error. They would have been seen that way by the Jesuits, who influenced her view of the missionary work.

[136] Letter 323, January 1841.

[137] The movie *The Mission* has dramatized the Reductions and their destruction.

the native people, they would need about twenty years to achieve evangelization of the tribes.[138] The model of the reduction would shape the attitudes of both the Jesuits and the RSCJ in the policies that guided the work at Sugar Creek and Saint Mary's.

Eventually, however, both RSCJ and Jesuits realized the "reduction" model was not practical because it was impossible to keep the natives isolated from the influence of mainstream culture. Ironically, both the United States government and the church saw the missionaries' task as "civilizing" the natives and assimilating them into the mainstream Euro-American culture. Both assumed that this dominant culture was superior to that of the natives. The missionaries recognized the evil influences in mainstream culture but never questioned that, purified of those tendencies, its art, music, literature and religious expressions were superior to that of the natives.[139] This basic flaw doomed the reductions model from the beginning.

Although Philippine may have had a somewhat romanticized view of the natives and their life she was well aware that the mission would require some practical adaptation in the sisters' lifestyle. The Jesuit community in Florissant would have informed her of the challenges of the life among the Potawatomi. In a letter to Sophie, Philippine listed a number of situations in which they might have to be dispensed from their rule of life. She asked if they might mitigate cloister. They would have no chapel and would need to attend Mass in the common church of the mission. They would need to travel around the mission, but she assures Sophie that they will not leave the property, not realizing how vast that might be. A shorter veil and a cap made of a coarser material would be needed, since they would be unable to obtain starch for the caps of the religious. According to what she has learned from the Jesuits, it might sometimes be necessary to eat meat on Friday. One of them had informed her that he had only "wild cow"[140] to eat and no bread. She asks that they not use a summer choir cloak.[141] As time would tell, there would be more informal adaptations of rule and lifestyle as a result of their frontier adventure than Philippine could have imagined.

In the same letter Philippine speaks of Mary Anne O'Connor's work with the native children at Florissant as qualifying her for the mission. She also mentions another sister, "a strong orphan who was at Saint Ferdinand and would go voluntarily and knows two languages and can easily learn the native tongue."[142] The editor of

---

[138] Robert Carriter, "Admiring Advocate of the Great Plains: Pierre-Jean De Smet, S.J. on the Middle Missouri," *Great Plains Quarterly* (Fall, 1994): 243-252. DeSmet had ministered to the Potawatomi at Council Bluffs without much success and his thinking about how to present his message to native people evolved. He admired and loved the native culture and was seemingly unaware (as were the RSCJ) of how his work would destroy that culture.

[139] George Tinker, "Missions and Missionaries," *Encyclopedia of Native American Indians,* pp. 381-84, analyses both the American and the Native reasons for promotion and cooperation with the process of "civilization," much to the detriment of native culture.

[140] What the missionaries called buffalo.

[141] De Charry/Hogg et al, 2.3, pp. 333-36, Letter 321 (15 January 1841).

[142] *Ibid.*

Philippine's letters does not identify this woman, but might she be the fourth member of the company, Louise Amiot?[143] Louise was born in Canada on February 18, 1818.[144] Her parents are not identified, but the area around Saint Louis, Florissant and Saint Charles was full of French Canadian and Métis families. An Amiot (first name not given) received three Spanish land grants in 1805. Eustache Amiot dit Peltier[145] received an early land grant under the French authorities. If Louise's family used the Peltier/Pelletier name, there are over thirty entries in the Saint Ferdinand parish register in Florissant for Pelletier, and over eighty in the early records of both Florissant and Saint Louis.[146] Did Louise come as a child? It seems likely, since she was fluent in both English and French by the time she entered religious life. Based on the comment of Philippine, she may have been the orphan living at Saint Ferdinand and connected to one of those Pelletier/Peltier (fur trader) families. In a reference to Louise, Philippine wrote to Mother Galitzine, January 25, 1841: "In this house there is Sister Louise (Amiot)...She has lived among the Indians, knows them, longs to go to teach them and she has all the qualities to succeed."[147] No further details of where Louise lived among the Indians, but it is possible she was the daughter of one of the many fur traders who lived in or near the many forts that traded with the Native Americans.

She was only seventeen when she entered as a coadjutrix sister in Saint Louis in 1835. She made her first vows September 28, 1837, also in Saint Louis, where she remained until leaving for Sugar Creek. Her time there gave her a chance to meet Mary Layton, with whom she would live and work until her death. The early days in Saint Louis were fairly primitive, and the house (whose site today is in downtown Saint Louis) was removed from town.

---

[143] Name spelled Amiotte in other records and Amyote on her gravestone in Saint Marys, Kansas, I have chosen to use Amiot as the most common way she is mentioned. Since the letter mentions possible recruits it is quite likely this is Louise since she is the only one not mentioned by name by Philippine and the description fits her.

[144] Several records close to this date have been found for a Louise Amiot in Canada but without her parents' names, it is impossible to know which is hers. In the reconstructed 1776 census of Saint Louis, an Auguste Amiot, 29, Fur Trader, is listed. Auguste died in Saint Louis in 1788. No Amiot families occur in U.S. census for 1830-50 or in the parish census for the Barrens 1823 or the Territorial census of 1805.

[145] "Dit" names were nicknames adopted by French Canadian families derived from a soldier ancestor or picked up to distinguish between families of the same name living in the same area. This name spelled Pelletier was an occupational one meaning "fur trader" in old French. On coming to the U.S., French Canadian families often chose to use either name as their surname. There are no Amiot/Amyote families in the registers of Saint Ferdinand or Saint Louis published in the Drouin collection on ancestry. com (see next citation).

[146] Original data: Gabriel Drouin, *Drouin Collection* (Montreal, Quebec: Institut Généalogique Drouin). Available on *ancestry. com*. In later American records the name morphs into "Pelkey." Florissant, Saint Louis, Detroit and early Illinois records have many Pelitiers. The French Canadian genealogy collection of Abbe Tanguay notes a wedding of a Charles Fontaine in 1815 to a Pelitier that took place in Florissant.

[147] Philippine Duchesne: Complete Writings, letter 565, L 3 to Mother Galitzine, January 25, 1841.

An RSCJ commentator, Henriette de Kersaint,[148] describes the house as being in the middle of the woods and isolated with poor roads. One room served for both refectory and community room and was so dark that the religious assigned to read during meals needed a light. The religious were too poor to afford sugar for their coffee. They were in habits that were in need of replacement, patched and re-patched. Evidently, Lucille Mathevon had brought replacement material from France, but that had all been used to clothe the Jesuits whose baggage had been lost in transit. In 1834, the house had eighteen boarders, twenty orphans, and one hundred day students. That same year the school had to be closed briefly because of illness; students were sent home while the RSCJ were sent to Florissant. The year Louise entered in Saint Louis, Catherine Thiéfry was superior and may have been responsible for her formation.[149] Later Catherine would be superior at Sugar Creek in 1843 and 1844 and live again with Louise there.

Louise, at twenty-three years old, was the youngest of the Sugar Creek religious. She made her final profession at the Indian mission in 1852[150] and spent nearly all of her religious life there. Her delicate health was mentioned a number of times, and in 1852 it was serious enough for Lucille Mathevon to take her on the long trip back to Saint Louis to seek medical treatment. It was called "lung illness," which might indicate tuberculosis.[151] Despite her ill health, Louise served as cook and was their seamstress. She taught needlework, was in charge of the boarders' clothing, helped with teaching in Potawatomi, and oversaw the infirmary for many years. She became fluent in Potawatomi, working closely with the children, and at her death in 1857 was greatly mourned by the tribe. The Potawatomi felt that she "loved their children like a mother."[152]

Lucille Mathevon would remain in Sugar Creek, and then in Saint Mary's when the mission moved, until nearly the end of the foundation, dying in 1876. Mary Anne O'Connor would labor at the mission until her death in 1863.

All three RSCJ community members would be buried together in Kansas sharing a common grave in the current Calvary cemetery with four RSCJ who would arrive later.[153]

---

[148] *Memories of Mother de Kersaint*, papers of Marie Louise Martinez, RSCJ Provincial Archives.

[149] Callan, *Philippine Duchesne*, p. 668. In a letter she notes that Catherine was happy at Sugar Creek, and the small community was happy to have her, although she was ill at first. She also mentions that Louise is now ill.

[150] In a revision to the Constitutions made in 1839, coadjutrix sisters would make their final vows only after ten years. Louise had to wait fifteen.

[151] Unpublished paper "Notes on the Life of Mother Lucille" written by M. R. Monzert, RSCJ, who later lived in Saint Marys. It refers to the long trip when the two religious slept in the wagon under the stars, and Lucille attempted to keep Louise warm through the night (see later reference in section on 1850s).

[152] *Annual Letters* 1856-57, p. 379.

[153] The first to die, Louise was probably buried in the mission cemetery near the church. The body was moved to a cemetery just for the missionaries and the bodies from that cemetery, both RSCJ and Jesuits, were moved to the Catholic cemetery early in the 20th century to allow the college to expand.

SUGAR CREEK INDIAN MISSION, 1841–1847

Philippine Duchesne
(RSCJ Archives)

Philippine never abandoned her desire to work with Native Americans. Two events spurred her to greater advocacy for such a mission: the decision of the Jesuits to abandon an unsuccessful mission with the Kickapoo tribe in 1837, which released personnel to begin work with the Potawatomi, coupled with their March of Death in 1838 and the death of Father Petit shortly after. Both she and Lucille Mathevon had expressed a desire to work in this mission in letters to the bishop of Saint Louis, Joseph Rosati. In 1840, he visited Mother Barat and expressed the desire to have her religious work with indigenous Americans. He spoke also with Pope Gregory XVI of Philippine's desire that her sisters begin such a work; the pope agreed and wrote to Mother Barat supporting the bishop's request. Elizabeth Galitzine, on her way to America as Mother Barat's emissary, carried a letter from Bishop Rosati to Philippine about his visits to the Pope and to Sophie Barat. Despite papal approval, Elizabeth Galitzine[154] needed some persuading about the feasibility of the Indian mission. Father De Smet, who was a successful fundraiser for the missions, surprised her with five hundred dollars in gold, which he had just raised to start the mission.[155] Elizabeth Galitzine agreed, after receiving a letter from Sophie Barat confirming her approval. She asked for volunteers for the mission to the Potawatomi. There was a double strain on personnel, since she was also planning foundations in New York and Pennsylvania. Both Lucille Mathevon and Mary Anne O'Connor volunteered. Lucille wrote to Mother Barat: "There are already more than a thousand Catholic Indians in the tribe. The Jesuit Fathers are obliged to teach even the girls…These are civilized savages. They resemble the first Christians in fervor and have been begging for three years to have religious come and teach these children…Oh,

---

[154] This entire section depends heavily on the work of Louise Callan: her biography of Philippine and *The Society of the Sacred Heart in North America* (Longmans, Green and Co. London/New York/Toronto, 1937). Because of the same author, the subsequent references will include the title as *Philippine* or *North America*. Elizabeth Galitzine was sent to the U.S. as Sophie Barat's personal visitor in 1840. She became superior vicar on Philippine's retirement.

[155] Callan, *Philippine* p. 630. This was the fruit of a begging tour to New Orleans and the planters of the Gold Coast of the Mississippi. The Gold Coast—the current River Road between New Orleans and Baton Rouge—was a line of prosperous sugar cane plantations on the Mississippi River. Ironically, profits from the labor of hundreds of slaves enabled the donations that initially funded the Sugar Creek mission.

how much good we could do, how many souls we could save…"[156] There was still some doubt about Philippine's ability and health for the mission. When the personnel were announced, Philippine's name was not on the list. Jesuit Pierre-Jean Verhaegen, who was to accompany the religious, visited Saint Louis and Philippine to discuss the details of the voyage. When he learned that she might not go, he was indignant, insisting that Philippine must go even if he had to carry her. He was unconcerned that she could not work, defining her ministry there as one of prayer that would be essential to the success of the venture.

On June 29, 1841, on a Missouri river packet boat, Lucille Mathevon, Mary Anne O'Connor and Louise Amiot set off with the aging Philippine Duchesne, accompanied by two Jesuits, Pierre-Jean Verhaegen and Jean Baptiste Smedts, and a diocesan priest named Renaud. Also with them was a black slave, Edmund,[157] a skilled carpenter. They had a grand send-off at the levee by friends who included the newly appointed bishop of Natchez, Jean-Marie Chance. Lucille left a detailed and colorful account of the voyage and their reception by the Indians. She described the many towns along the way and Philippine's seemingly miraculous recovery of health and energy. The journey included a celebration of Independence Day, July 4, with prayer, preaching, and a glass of iced sherry. After a four-day trip, they reached the river town closest to Sugar Creek, Westport.[158] Westport, founded in 1831, was by this time a popular jumping off point to trails farther west[159] and had a population of about 700. It was where native people came to spend their government annuity and where travelers stocked up on provisions. It was also the nearest post office to Sugar Creek. There they stopped at the home of a French settler, where two Indian scouts met them. They were guided on the next eighteen miles of their journey by scouts posted every two miles. When they were a mile away, they received a tremendous and colorful welcome. Five hundred men met them dressed in ceremonial attire—colorful blankets, "plumes and feathers, and moccasins embroidered with porcupine quills. Their faces were painted black, with red circles around the eyes."[160]

While Lucille appears to have found the display a bit frightening, Philippine gloried in it and greeted them

---

[156] Callan, *Philippine*, pp. 631-32.

[157] A male slave is listed at the Sacred Heart house in Saint Louis in the 1830 U.S. census, age 10-23. In 1840 census, a male slave age 24-35 is listed. In 1831 records of this house, a slave named Joseph is mentioned, but he was sold before 1840. Philippine refers to "the Negro from Saint Louis" in De Charry/Hogg et al, 2.3, p. 342, Letter 324 (July 1841), who is called Edmund in Sugar Creek records, so it is unclear if they are the same man. However, he is mentioned by name by Catherine Thiéfry, local superior, in letters from the late 1830's.

[158] Now a part of modern Kansas City, Missouri. It is also referred to as Westport Landing. It was at a bend in the Missouri River and a rock landing place made it a convenient spot for riverboats to disembark passengers and cargo.

[159] The Santa Fe, Oregon and California trails would start here and the town would almost triple in population by the time the mission would move to Saint Marys, Kansas.

[160] Callan, *North America*, p. 637.

like "a mother her long lost child."[161] What really impressed Lucille was what came next: a thrilling and skillful display of horsemanship with such precision that she remarked it rivaled the skill of the armies of Napoleon.[162] One of the Métis tribal leaders, Joseph Napoleon Bourassa,[163] made a speech expressing the tribe's welcome and gratitude that they had come to educate their daughters. Philippine was presented to the tribe as a woman who had been waiting for thirty years for this moment. She was introduced as the "woman of the Great Spirit."[164] Then the tribe commenced what the religious would learn was a traditional greeting (practiced well into the late 1860s at the mission), in which each native would shake the hand of the visitor.[165] The greeting of each sister must have taken a long time, as it was estimated that there were seven hundred people gathered. Philippine embraced all the women and girls and seemed not tired at all by the long ritual of welcome. After the ritual greeting, they had a feast at the home of another Métis leader, Joseph Bertrand.[166]

One shock at their arrival was that there was no house for them, despite the money set aside for it. One of the natives hospitably vacated his home for a tent and lent it to the religious. The house was small, 12 by 15 feet, and had two chairs, boards across stumps for sleeping benches, and some bedding. It was shared with insects that attacked the religious. Given Philippine's reputation for austere living, she must have been in her glory living in this simple accommodation. While Lucille remarked that both the beds and the food were good, she noted that cooking was done outside, which must have been challenging in bad weather. Their final dwelling place would have five rooms—a veritable palace in contrast—with its own fireplace for cooking and warmth inside.

In a letter to Mother Barat, Philippine writes enthusiastically about the journey and the tribe. She describes the life at Sugar Creek as an ideal reenactment of the early church and the natives as honest, sober, and prayerful.[167] From the beginning, the natives crowded the small cabin sitting in silence to observe this strange group of women, saying nothing and departing as quietly as they came. They were fascinated by the bell used by the religious to

[161] Lucille Mathevon, "Years among the Potawatomi," Martinez Collection, RSCJ Archives: Series XII Ministry Files Box 11, #10, 14.

[162] Ibid. Martinez.

[163] By an odd coincidence, Joseph Napoleon Bourassa was a fourth cousin of the author. He was a well-educated man bilingual in English and French who would be a strong leader for the Potawatomi here and in Saint Mary. His name appears on treaties he helped negotiate with the federal government. His father, stepmother and siblings were part of the Trail of Death march.

[164] O'Connor, p. 23.

[165] Callan, *North America,* p. 278 – Lucille refers to the hand shaking ceremony as "penitential," so not all were as enthusiastic as Philippine.

[166] Joseph Bertrand, Jr., was a prominent Métis leader, a first cousin to Joseph Napoleon Bourassa and fourth cousin also to the author. His wife, Elizabeth Ann Jackson, is described as "an American from Michigan, a very lovable woman." Both spoke French and English. She was a former Holy Cross sister from Maryland.

[167] Nicholas Perrot and others who visited the Potawatomi before they became Christians also describe this group as placing a great value on living in harmony with each other, so the culture and the influence of Christianity appear to have worked together.

signal prayer times, the community's clock and Philippine's watch. The sisters adapted to this being observed, learning to show no astonishment.[168]

The religious were given two cows and had at their disposal a pair of oxen, a horse and carriage. Food does not seem to have been a problem at first, although the cook had to contend with thieving prairie dogs stealing their provisions. The first order of business was to construct a house for the religious to live in and eventually have students. Edmund proved useful in training natives to help with the building of the house.[169] Eventually a small log house was constructed with a loft for sleeping, reached by a ladder, and a wood stove. Each corner was designated for a different purpose: kitchen, refectory, and superior's room with the center space for parlor and classroom.[170]

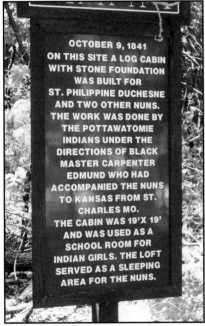

OCTOBER 9, 1841
ON THIS SITE A LOG CABIN
WITH STONE FOUNDATION
WAS BUILT FOR
ST. PHILIPPINE DUCHESNE
AND TWO OTHER NUNS.
THE WORK WAS DONE BY
THE POTTAWATOMIE
INDIANS UNDER THE
DIRECTIONS OF BLACK
MASTER CARPENTER
EDMUND WHO HAD
ACCOMPANIED THE NUNS
TO KANSAS FROM ST.
CHARLES MO.
THE CABIN WAS 19'X 19'
AND WAS USED AS A
SCHOOL ROOM FOR
INDIAN GIRLS. THE LOFT
SERVED AS A SLEEPING
AREA FOR THE NUNS.

Sugar Creek marker for convent

The Jesuits wanted the natives taught in their own language, thinking that it would insulate them from the evil ways of the Americans. That meant that the RSCJ needed a crash course in the native language. Two Métis women were appointed to help teach Potawatomi to the religious, although Philippine, who had never even mastered English, found this impossible. In about two weeks, older students who knew French were employed as interpreters. Lucille, with a gift for music, soon memorized without understanding some Potawatomi hymns and prayers and was able to teach them. Mary Anne O'Connor was in charge of teaching in English. Louise Amiot was the quickest to learn the language and soon was able to teach sewing and manual crafts, while Lucille often took over the cooking.[171]

Philippine was a prayer-filled presence, something the natives, who had their own spirituality, immediately recognized. She spent long hours in prayer in the mission church or in the small cemetery. The Potawatomi noticed this. Later they named her "the Woman who prays always." Her age also would have endeared her to them as a revered grandmother. She

---

[168] *Ibid*. Callan, *Philippine*, p. 645; also Callan, *Society of the Sacred Heart*, p. 281.

[169] Edmund is never mentioned again in letters or mission records. Did he marry into the tribe or strike off to claim his freedom? The mission was close to the Santa Fe Trail leading into Mexico. Until the Mexican War in 1847, slavery did not exist in Mexico and would be established in the captured territory of Texas only after the war. Lucille appears to have decided to keep him in ignorance of his free status when in Indian Territory. She writes in "*Notes sur nos Fondations de Sauvages de Sugar Creek et Saint Mary's*" in a letter of August 1841: "I am careful not to tell him he is free here, because however happy he is and perhaps too pious to take advantage of it, it is nevertheless surer to leave him, if possible, in ignorance."

[170] Callan, *North America*, p. 183.

[171] *Ibid*. Callan, *Philippine*, p. 648.

was unable to master the native language but made herself useful with sewing, visiting the sick and consoling the dying. The natives showed their respect for her by bringing the best they had, corn, prairie hen eggs, wild fruit, and clean straw for her bed.

By July 19, just ten days after their arrival, the religious started a school, with twenty-four girls and some women who were learning to knit and sew. By the next month there was double the number of students, "all very good and easy to manage."[172] Prayers were learned in Potawatomi and some in English. This may indicate who was teaching, since only Mary Anne O'Connor and Louise Amiot were fluent in English. Edmund was doing some teaching also, sharing his carpentry skills with the natives. "He is teaching the Indians carpentry. They are naturally skillful and easily imitate what they see others do. They built a pretty fence around their cemetery, but did not know how to find the center of one side, in order to locate the gateway correctly. Edmund helped them out of the difficulty and so brought the work to a happy conclusion."[173]

The work on a bigger house was begun in August, but the first room was not ready until October. Lucille wrote that the larger cabin was built by thirty Indians in three days who "refused all payment for their services, except a hearty dinner each day of squash and navy beans cooked in lard." Philippine wrote letters back to Sophie Barat and to her benefactors describing the mission, plans for a bigger house, and the difficulties of building when the old growth forest logs were so heavy that it took ten to twelve oxen to transport them. During the winter, Edmund and the few Indian men not out hunting continued to work on expanding the one room cabin and added a second story loft. The loft was reached only by a precarious ladder, and the religious could not stand up in it, but it served as a dormitory. The lifestyle at Sugar Creek was as primitive as the initial months at Saint Charles, perhaps even more so. It was impossible to follow a regulated monastic life with only one room. The cabin was next to that of the Jesuits, and the Indian church served as the chapel for both communities. Forty to sixty students came during the day, using a makeshift shed for instruction. Finally, when the second story loft was added, there were five to six students who boarded with the sisters and shared their daily life.[174]

Philippine remarks that the girls were learning to spin and knit but also that some knew how before they came. "They are, on a whole, rather interesting children, but they find it difficult to stay at the same work for any length of time."[175] This was a constant complaint of both the RSCJ and the Jesuits. They did not realize how

---

[172] Callan, *North America*, p. 279, from the account of the mission's early days by Lucille Mathevon.

[173] *Ibid*. p. 284. She mentions that the Indians respected him and that they were almost "as dark-skinned as he."

[174] One of those children was Theresa Slevin (nee Lavia or Living), an orphan of the Trail of Death, whose descendants are still living in the vicinity of Saint Marys today (Janet Reberdy: Notes of Jubilee Trip 1999, Provincial Archives, Pottawatomi Mission, Box 2). Theresa, who died in 1876, is buried in the same small cemetery as the Religious of the Sacred Heart in Saint Marys. In the 1870 census a native child with this surname is enrolled at Saint Marys, perhaps a daughter of this woman (she had one daughter Mary E. Josette Slevin).

[175] Callan, *Philippine*, p. 546.

strange their methods of teaching must have appeared to the native people. Potawatomi children were prized and treated with great respect. They were allowed to learn at their own pace, playing at adult roles while young, imitating their elders, especially grandparents, who were the main child care providers. It was not usual to punish the children, and they were taught their obligations in a non- coercive way. When they wanted to eat they did, when they wanted to sleep or play they did.

The missionaries were attempting to enforce a kind of work discipline on the natives who were accustomed to a more leisurely way of life. Time in the native world was linked to the movements of sun and moon and seasons. Measuring out the day in hours and minutes was a foreign concept. This must have been puzzling to the Potawatomi, both adults and children, who worked when they needed to and did not understand the need for the artificial work schedules of the missionaries. Throughout the history of the mission, there are accounts of children disappearing into the woods or deciding to take some days off and going to visit their parents. This continued up to the 1860s, when a fairly fixed schedule of classes and manual work was part of their days. Parents, for the most part, were undisturbed at this behavior and would bring their children back without comment when they turned up at home. Only in one case, mentioned by Lucille, did they suggest the children be punished for running away. Philippine also learned from the experience of other missionaries that teaching methods must be adapted to the native culture. She quotes the advice of an unnamed missionary priest who said they needed to first gain the affection of the girls before attempting to teach and to use methods "entirely different from those used with white children. He says that [they] never forget a refusal or a reprimand and that the superiors at a distance cannot make regulations for them."[176]

The mission school grew to around thirty to fifty and sometimes included adult women who wanted to learn sewing. The RSCJ seemed to have either overcome the difficulty they first experienced in keeping the students focused or learned how to work around it. Mary Anne O'Connor taught catechism, prayers, reading, writing, and some math. They also learned carding, knitting, and sewing (perhaps from Louise or even Philippine, who were both skilled seamstresses). Lucille gave lessons in singing, told Bible stories (perhaps in French or memorized Potawatomi), and gave practical household instruction in cooking and washing. Since Louise was also a cook, she may have assisted in some of this instruction. Lucille was under the impression that the natives did not know how to cook their meat and ate it raw. In reality, there was a number of native ways to cook that they probably had not noticed. Most families had a pot of stew simmering over a fire, and members ate when they were hungry rather than at a specific time of day.

Food was plentiful and good when they arrived, and Lucille writes enthusiastically of their varied diet, which

---

[176] De Charry/Hogg et al, 2-3, Letter 327 (28 February 1842). The priest was Jesuit Christian Hoecken who became very fluent in Potawatomi, sensitive to the native culture, and was superior of the Jesuit community for some years at Saint Marys.

included vegetables, dairy products, rice, cornbread and even bread from wheaten flour.[177] The sisters appeared put off by the custom of not washing the wooden bowls they used (perhaps cleansing them with sand) and the use of dog meat as a prized delicacy for special feasts and guests. The summer plenty seemed to energize the missionaries. Philippine wrote to Sophie in September that both Mary Anne and Lucille were enjoying better health. Mary Anne is no longer plagued by migraines and Lucille "seems to be indefatigable and has a good appetite; lard has become like chicken for her."[178]

In contrast to the pleasant summer, winter was another story; the cold was penetrating; and despite their stove, wind swept through the cracks in the logs, making the canvas covering the walls billow like sails. The church was unheated even during daily Mass, and Lucille, as superior of the group, had to forbid Philippine to go back to it during the day on the bitterest days of winter.

The enlarged house with five rooms was completed by March.[179] During the construction the RSCJ got Philippine out of the way by sending her to the church, which probably delighted her. When Elisabeth Galitzine made a surprise two-day visit to the mission, they had procured a bed for her by some means so she did not have to sleep in the loft. Their visitor arrived on Palm Sunday weekend, so they could not show off the students to her, since class was not in session. She did have the experience of a full native welcome with horsemanship and a parade of the tribe in full colorful regalia and face paint. She also endured the "dreaded, but indispensable ceremony of shaking hands."[180] While Elisabeth did not urge Philippine to return, she noticed her poor health; that, combined with the primitive conditions, must have given her cause to worry. Bishop Kenrick from Saint Louis visited some months later and was equally concerned.

Philippine, on the other hand, seemed to feel that her health had improved at Sugar Creek. In a letter written to Sophie Barat on February 28, shortly before Elisabeth Galitzine's visit, she describes her daily visits to the little cemetery and her desire to stay with the natives and be buried with them in Sugar Creek. But in the same letter, she betrays that she is thinking that she might go to the Rocky Mountains, where she has heard people live to be over a hundred. "My health is restored and being only seventy-three I think I shall have at least ten years of work."[181] She was accurate in her assessment of how long she would live: Philippine would die ten years later, but it would not be with the Potawatomi or in the Rocky Mountains. As a result of both visitors' observations, Philippine was recalled after only a year with her beloved Indians. She left on June 19 for Saint Louis, escorted

---

[177] This was not grown by the natives but from the government subsidy of goods or purchased with cash subsidy.

[178] De Charry/Hogg et al, Letter 326 (22 September, 1841).

[179] De Charry/Hogg et al, Letter 327 (28 February, 1842) says that they are still in the one room with loft cabin in February but other sources, including the historical marker, say the cabin had five rooms and was finished in March.

[180] Callan, *North America*, p. 285.

[181] De Charry/Hogg et al, 2-3, Letter 327. She had heard that Elizabeth Galitzine had been recalled to Rome but evidently did not know she planned to visit them in March before leaving in April 1842.

by Pierre-Jean Verhaegen, and arrived in Saint Louis on June 29, 1842.[182] She settled in Saint Charles, accepting the will of God and renouncing her beloved mission, but still she could not forget her people. She continued to lobby for financial support for the mission and was still writing about it in one of her last letters in 1852, the year of her death.[183]

Members of other tribes would visit and asked the religious to come and educate their daughters. It was then that the religious realized the utility of a boarding school to take in some of these girls. It is possible that the native scholars of the mission always included not only Potawatomi girls but also mixed-blood Métis and members of other tribes. In the small quarters at Sugar Creek, it was impossible to have more than a few boarders. Indeed the Jesuits had only a day school until they moved to Saint Marys.

The religious found the native children adept at learning, and they quickly mastered some of the basic lessons. In a letter to Sophie Barat, Lucille notes proudly that the children knit, crochet, wash, iron, "care for the cows, bake bread, churn and make candles. In fact, we train them in all that can be useful to them as wives, mothers, and housekeepers. The docility of their character makes them very easy to handle and teach, and the parents uphold us in all we do."[184] Very early in the mission, on the feast of Saint Ignatius, July 31, in 1844, the custom of awarding prizes was instituted using "pretty and useful" items sent by their religious in France. Benefactors in Saint Louis sent bolts of brightly colored cloth with which to make dresses that delighted the girls. She describes the prize giving witnessed by a large gathering of Indians called together by the mission's bell. At the end, Louise Amiot treated each child to an apple tart made of apples sent from Saint Charles, since the mission had no fruit trees yet.[185]

[182] Callan, *Philippine*, p. 657. Other records say July – she appears in mission records as godmother on July 10.
[183] De Charry/Hogg et al, 2-3. Letter 335, (22 April 1852). She writes Sophie that Lucille has told her news about Saint Mary – perhaps on her visit to Missouri that year with an ailing Louise Amiot.
[184] Callan, *North America*, p. 290.
[185] *Ibid*. Lucille just mentions that the tarts were made by "Sister," but since Louise was the only lay sister there that year it must have been her work.

D-Mouche Kee-Kee-Awh, George Winter (TCHA)

The community at Sugar Creek would remain small. Lucille would be superior at Sugar Creek 1842 to 1868 except for 1843 and 1844 when Catherine Thiéfry was appointed superior. She and Anne Kavanagh, an aspirant, were added to mission staff in 1843.[186] Perhaps the intention was to relieve Lucille, but Catherine was in poor health herself and left May 23, 1845. In that year, the first American-born novice who persevered until vows, Mary Layton, age forty-three, joined them. She would spend the rest of her life at the Indian mission, dying shortly after Lucille in 1876.

The house at Sugar Creek, although quite as primitive as the experience of the religious at Saint Charles, had another element—that of the Indian settlement that surrounded them. Totally immersed in Indian life, they dealt with what must have been culture shock for themselves as well as the aftermath of trauma in the native

---

[186] One wonders if this change was the result of Elizabeth Galitzine's official visit to the mission. Catherine was a contemporary of Lucille. The aspirant, a religious in first vows, does not appear again in Society records and probably left shortly after her experience here. She is referred to in Father Hoecken's diary as Madam Xavier. They both left the mission in May 1845 leaving behind a Sister Mary according to Father Hoecken: Mary Layton.

population.[187] The Indians had experienced the "Trail of Death" in 1838 when forty to fifty [188] of the original eight hundred or more had died during the walk south. Students had parents and grandparents who told them of the experience, even if they had been too young to have been a part of it. The Potawatomi had been treated as "enemy combatants"; men, women, and children were rounded up and forced to travel far from their traditional homeland and the bones of their ancestors. For native people, who felt that nature and place were full of spiritual power, this was a cultural wound that would be hard, if not impossible, to heal. For many of the mission population who were already Catholic, the familiar prayers and rituals may have served as a comforting link back to their lives before they were forced to move. It is amazing that despite these hardships, so many were able to lay down new roots, establish new hunting grounds, and cultivate land to sustain themselves.

The atmosphere in the settlement is described by Lucille as almost monastic. She remarks on both the many devotions of the natives but also on the silence. In a letter to Sophie she says: "Here we live in perfect silence and recollection, and so do the Potawatomi among whom we dwell. They are by nature a quiet people; they all speak in a low tone of voice, and the children are never noisy at their games or in the classroom. The little boys stand in silence watching a game, or draw their bow-strings in silence at the birds. On Sundays, however, the women allow themselves the relaxation of singing nearly all day long at the doors of their huts or in the church."[189] Another observer described his visit to a Potawatomi village before the move to Sugar Creek. He wrote that "… no sense of hurry exists. A great deal of the time is spent…eating, smoking, and talking…scattered fires glimmering through dark foliage, blanketed forms stealing from hut to hut, low murmuring voices accented with random peals of laughter [and] the tinkling of bells on ponies…."[190] It is similar to the scene that a visitor to Sugar Creek might have experienced and what Lucille described.

In the descriptions of the way of life of the Catholic Indians, emphasis is placed on their devotion to Mass and to the sacraments.[191] Daily prayer for those close to the mission chapel was part of their order of day in the

---

[187] Culture shock was not new, as the original French sisters experienced it with the Creole inhabitants of Louisiana and Missouri who, although French speaking, had very different ways. They had some experience also with the American culture norms and the slave-owning culture of the South. The natives seem to show signs of depression and the addiction to alcohol only makes this worse. What is interpreted as "laziness" on the part of the natives may also be a sign of the trauma of uprooting they had gone through and the lack of hope for the future.

[188] Sources vary in number 41-47 and it is possible that some deaths were not recorded. The elderly and children were most likely to die. By the time they left Sugar Creek there were 500 burials in the graveyard there.

[189] Callan, *North America*, p. 289-90.

[190] *Trail of Death* p. 270.

[191] Callan, *Philippine*, p. 654ff for description of life at the mission during her time there.

morning and evening. The rituals of Catholicism and its prayer had captured their hearts.[192] They were untutored in doctrine, and the missionaries made efforts through sermons to close that gap. Catechism was a priority in the educational mission and was taught in Potawatomi. The RSCJ taught not only the children but also adult women. During the years leading up to 1847, there were many conversions among the natives, swelling the number of Catholics in the mission. Saying the rosary as a family in homes and in larger gatherings continued to be popular, a tradition that had developed during the days when the tribe had no resident priest in Indiana.

The main evangelization tools of the missionaries for the adults, besides the Sunday worship and instruction, were various confraternities that were formed and the celebrations they promoted. Philippine served as godmother to some converts, and the parish register shows her as sponsor to Jean Francis Regis (called) Tokapowi, twenty-six years of age, whose baptismal name may have been influenced by Philippine's devotion to that saint. "Mother Duchesne also assisted in the capacity of godmother at the baptism (on succeeding days) of Josephine Rose, *dicto* Anwamkc, fifty-five years old, and of Marie Akogue, sixty years old."[193] She also witnessed both the baptisms and the marriage of another convert and his wife, April 10, 1842, when Father Hoecken baptized and then joined in wedlock Pierre Droyard and Therese Rose Kuese.[194] The years of the highest number of adult conversions were from its foundation up to 1847. After the move to Saint Marys, the conversions would continue but diminish in number. Although conversions were abundant in the earliest years, it seems that the main task of the missionaries was pastoral care of the Catholic population of the village, one half of which was Catholic, some for several generations. Mass, administration of the sacraments, especially confession, and the anointing of the sick and dying as well as catechesis of the children of the congregation would not allow much time for evangelization and outreach to natives who were not Christian. Pastoral care of the Catholics, including natives, Métis, and later the American settlers, would consume more and more time.

---

[192] Rollings, p.14f compares the efforts of Catholic and Protestant missionaries and attributes the success of the Catholics to many parallels between native culture and spirituality and that of the Catholic Church. Although he is speaking specifically of the Osages many of his examples such as the elaborate rituals of Mass and sacraments, apply equally to the Potawatomi.

[193] Garraghan, *Jesuits of the Middle United States,* 3, p. 228, quotes from the Baptismal Register in the notes. However he has the baptism of Jean Francis dated July 10, likely one of Philippine's last times as a godmother, as she left on July 19.

[194] *Ibid.* p. 230, footnote from parish register.

In the Potawatomi culture, the men were the hunters and warriors while the women tended to the children, made clothing, and grew what food they planted. Because of these gender roles, the Jesuits appear to have had a difficult time teaching the boys farming. The RSCJ were teaching the girls skills that fit their culture's gender roles. Even the adult women wanted to learn some of the sewing skills the RSCJ were teaching their daughters. During the next years, the U.S. government, assisted by the missionaries, would attempt to make the men farmers as the hunting grounds shrank, and settlers encroached upon Indian territories. "The missionaries were asking people to give up a successful and satisfying way of life to adopt an alien way of life ill adapted for the prairies."[195] The role of the warrior for the men continued to be important through the mid-nineteenth century as the hunters encountered warriors of other tribes during their search for game. In pushing the Potawatomi into Indian Territory, the government was forcing them to come into conflict with other peoples, such as the Pawnee whose traditional territory was in this area of the Great Plains. Some of those people were traditional enemies of the Potawatomi. Jesuit accounts of this period mention raids on the mission to steal ponies, a staple of the native warrior culture.[196]

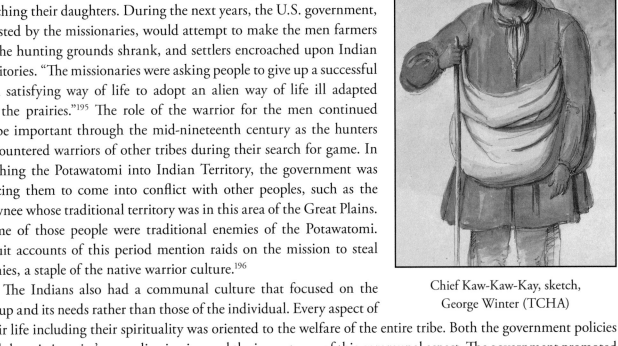

Chief Kaw-Kaw-Kay, sketch, George Winter (TCHA)

The Indians also had a communal culture that focused on the group and its needs rather than those of the individual. Every aspect of their life including their spirituality was oriented to the welfare of the entire tribe. Both the government policies and the missionaries' evangelization ignored the importance of this communal aspect. The government promoted weakened tribal ties by forcing the acceptance of a land allotment by individual tribal members and discouraging any communal ownership. The Catholic missionaries had some sense of the importance of a communal culture, but it was a sectarian one with the people divided into Catholic, Protestant and "pagan" (traditional).

The official government policy at this time was to move the native peoples of the eastern and southern United States to a new "Indian Territory" west of the Mississippi. But this policy did not envision the flow of settlers to the West through Indian Territory along the Santa Fe, California, and Oregon Trails. The natives were viewed more as wards of the state than as sovereign nations. The annual government subsidies they received in return

---

[195] Rollings, p. 14, commenting on the lack of success of missionaries with the Osage people.
[196] Charles O'Connor, SJ, *Jesuits in the Kaw Valley*, 1925 unpublished, Jesuit Archives, Saint Louis, pp. 94, 141.

for ceding their lands made them dependent on the changing whims of U.S. policy. Schools such as Sugar Creek and Saint Mary's were supposed to "civilize" the natives, teaching them the values of the Euro-American culture. Eventually the government hoped the Indians would assimilate into the mainstream culture.[197] When this process was too slow to keep up with the rapid westward expansion of the United States government, policy would change with a goal of eradication of native culture and total assimilation into the dominant society.

The Jesuits and the Religious of the Sacred Heart, while they supported the effort to "civilize" the natives, also had a love and respect for the native people. From the teaching of the Gospel they knew the natives had a God-given dignity as children of a common Creator. They valued education and saw it as a tool to enable the natives to survive in the dominant culture. The RSCJ and the Jesuits sought to convince them of its value rather than coerce them into accepting its tools. Throughout the life of the mission, visiting chiefs from neighboring tribes were treated to meals from the locally grown produce in an effort to convince both guests and hosts that farming would provide all their needs. Unlike later policies toward the end of the nineteenth century, the promise of education was a part of the treaty promises, and the natives were not forced to send their children to the schools.[198]

Until the early 1870s, when the Mission Potawatomi moved from Saint Marys, their communal lifestyle would also influence the RSCJ, affecting the rules such as cloister.[199] Even as late as 1868, an account written by one of the sisters described that "when the parents came to see their children...they entered into our midst without even knocking at the door, and it seemed that we must submit to this or we would otherwise hurt them."[200] It is interesting that the Jesuits and the RSCJ did not recognize that the communal culture of the natives worked against their and the U.S. government's attempts to make the natives part of the individualistic culture dominant in the United States.

Nicholas Perrot, one of the first French trappers to contact the Potawatomi, was impressed by their lavish

---

[197] Eugene Provenzo, Jr., and Gary N. McCloskey, "Catholic and Federal Indian Education in the late 19th Century," *Journal of American Indian Education,* 21:1 (October 1981) pp. 10-18, discusses the development of this concept.

[198] Government run residential boarding schools located in territory far removed from their people became the policy in the late 1870's. Children were forcibly removed from family, language and culture up until the mid-20th century.

[199] Elisabeth Schroeder (Schrader), RSCJ (*Notes*) writes a memoir of her time at Saint Marys composed about 1879 describing life in 1850-1865. She describes how the children who lived far away would spend the weekend with their friends and wind up sleeping all over the convent wrapped in their blankets. RSCJ Archives, Saint Louis Province K Box 2 folder 1, item f.

[200] Marie-Rose Monzert, RSCJ, *Notes on the life of Lucille Mathevon,* RSCJ Archives, IV K Potawatomi Mission.

hospitality and the harmonious relationships with one another.[201] He had experienced this hospitality himself when he encountered the tribe in the mid-seventeenth century. Perrot writes that they would welcome strangers and spend all their means to entertain them with the best food. He also suggests that long association with the French weakened that trait, although the Potawatomi of the mission still appeared to practice it. The accounts of the RSCJ of their arrival and lodging in Sugar Creek bear out that this trait was still a characteristic of the Potawatomi in the 1840s.

Like most others of their time, the RSCJ did not attempt to understand the spiritual beliefs of the natives. In this, they were little different from other settlers who considered the natives' religious beliefs, if they thought they had any, uncivilized, barbaric, pagan or even demonic. Some even thought that the natives had no "religion," since native spirituality was so integrated with their everyday life. Most of the Jesuits, although they shared the same cultural biases as the RSCJ, made the effort to try to understand (and occasionally misunderstand) the religious practices of the people they served. These men had a big influence on the thought of the women who formed the Sacred Heart community. They were spiritual advisors but in addition brought the religious into contact with the broader native culture. Jesuits Christian Hoecken, Maurice Gailland, and Pierre De Smet were true students of the native culture, even if they did not fully understand it. They felt that their aim was "to know what an Indian is, his character, his mode of being, judging and activity, the different traditions of the people… their ceremonies, practices, and customs."[202] However, elements of native religious belief and spirituality they perceived were sometimes misunderstood and even labeled "demonic."

The declared philosophy of the U.S. government was, as much as possible, to wipe out the native religion and culture and to replace it with Christianity and mainstream American culture. Some of the later Jesuit superiors, notably John Baptist Duerinck, appeared also to accept this philosophy. These missionaries, despite their appreciation for native culture, felt that the only way Native Americans could become Christians was to

---

[201] Nicholas Perrot, *The Indian Tribes of the Upper Mississippi Valley and Region of the Great Lakes as Described by Nicolas Perrot, French Commandant in the Northwest; Bacqueville de la Potherie, French Royal Commissioner to Canada; Morrell Marston, American Army Officer; and Thomas Forsyth, United States Agent at Fort Armstrong,* Volume 2 (Google eBook) Nicholas Perrot, Bacqueville de La Potherie (Claude – Charles Le Roy M. de), Morrell Marston, Thomas Forsyth, Paul Radin, Gertrude M. Robertson Vol 2 (Google eBook). Translation of French published ca. 1864: The Arthur H. Clark Company, 1912, pp. 141ff. Among the vices according to Perrot were those of vanity and concern for appearance, pride and vengeance. But he does admit these are vices of the French as well.

[202] O'Connor, p.6.

totally abandon their native religious traditions. This attitude increased the divisions in the Potawatomi people by dividing the Catholics from the Traditionalists.[203]

Unlike Protestant missionaries, who were sent by the often anti-Catholic officials of the U.S. government to proselytize among the native tribes, the Jesuit "blackrobes" and the Religious of the Sacred Heart were invited by the people themselves to come and minister among them. It was the natives who built the chapels and the missionaries' dwellings. They welcomed and participated enthusiastically in the liturgy and other devotions introduced by the missionaries. They saw the benefit of their children's being introduced to the English language and the learning the missionaries brought. The influence of the Métis families, descended from French traders, was strong in the Sugar Creek Potawatomi people. They had Catholic roots and wanted the presence of the missionaries among them.

The Jesuits and the Religious of the Sacred Heart tried to preserve a valuable anchor to their culture: the Potawatomi language. Several of the Jesuits and at least two of the original RSCJ mastered enough Potawatomi to teach the children. Lucille declared that the natives "sang like angels"[204] and described the language as musical and pleasant to the ear. She enjoyed the Potawatomi musical ability and first learned the language by learning their songs.[205] Although Mass was in Latin at the time, hymns, sermons and other devotions were in Potawatomi. The natives, like members of many oral cultures, had prodigious memories. Missionaries would give long instructions that would be exactly translated from memory by native interpreters at the end. Whole catechetical instructions and biblical stories were committed to memory. Maurice Gailland, who would join them at Saint Mary's mission and spend his whole missionary life there, composed both a dictionary and a grammar of the Potawatomi language. He was fascinated by it, comparing its intricacies and some of their customs to those of the ancient Hebrews. He and Christian Hoecken preached and heard confessions in Potawatomi, and Gailland was so worn out by his labors that his superiors feared for his health.[206]

The missionaries had respect for the innate dignity of the Potawatomi as children of God, an attitude that differed from most others of their time. They considered the native congregation as equal to any congregation of Catholics anywhere else. The United States government tended to treat the natives as hopelessly backward wards of the state who were unable to make decisions for themselves. Only by becoming "white" would they be able to survive. Indeed some government decisions were designed to ensure that the natives would not survive. While

---

[203] Rollings. In a study of what he perceives as a way of "passive resistance" among the Osage people, the author sees that the keeping of traditional ways, even when combined with a veneer of Christianity, enabled them to maintain much of their culture. He also sees some of the success of Catholic missionaries as due to the natives' seeing connections with their own rituals and spirituality in the message they brought.

[204] *Account of the Mission*, Lucille Mathevon, RSCJ Archives, Potawatomi Mission, Box 1

[205] Callan, *North America*, p. 302.

[206] Garraghan 2, p. 229.

the missionaries agreed on the benefits of adopting certain aspects of the dominant culture, they did not feel the natives were inferior to other Americans. They even felt that they surpassed some of their American Catholic congregations in morality and spirituality. Philippine raised the question of native vocations and felt that native women would be as good candidates as any other women.[207] The RSCJ learned from the natives and often were inspired by them.[208]

It is possible that some of the native spiritual beliefs had already been altered by their long relationship with the blackrobes and by the presence of mixed blood families.[209] At least half the people at Sugar Creek were Catholic, some more catechized than the others, and they may have lost touch with some of their native spiritual heritage by the time the mission was founded. It is hard to know whether they continued some of their cultural practices, such as the sweat lodge or the vision quest, since the missionaries do not mention them. However, the same visitor who described the atmosphere of the camp of the Potawatomi in the 1830s also described a sweat lodge as does a documentary made in the 1930s.[210]

From some hints it appears that they still practiced some of the healing rituals and dances.[211] The Potawatomi spiritual life, even after conversion to Christianity, persisted and adapted itself to the missionaries' norms. They were a people whose beliefs were expressed by simple rituals that pervaded their daily lives. Rituals involved enclosing circles and clockwise movements. They used fire, tobacco, and water in their rituals. Healing herbs were part of native medicine. It is possible that the native love of ritual and music made Catholic rituals particularly attractive to them. Fire and water were used in their own rituals and also in Catholic ones, and the use of smoke was similar to Catholic use of incense.[212]

Lucille Mathevon noted that they used the expression *Gitchi-Manitou* for the Spirit of life, the power behind

---

[207] De Charry/Hogg et al, Letter 335 (April 22 1852), letter from Philippine to Sophie, pp. 364-66. She asks, "Must good people be deprived of religious life because of their native blood?"

[208] Garraghan 2, p. 226, quotes from a letter of Felix Verreydt indicating the Jesuits also were inspired by their flock: some they felt never committed a deliberate sin.

[209] A drawing of a Potawatomi conception of the afterlife (undated) on the website of the Kansas Historical Society shows influence of Christian missionaries since the drawing depicts both a cross and hell as well as heaven.

[210] O'Connor, p. 277.

[211] A film documentary made in the 1930s and posted in three parts on YouTube shows that many of the traditional customs and religious rituals persisted. http://www.youtube.com/watch?v=ctvBYTCQ-SE It is possible that a copy of this film is part of the Prairie Band archives in Mayetta, Kansas. It is not listed with any archive information and a search of the WPA archives in Washington does not have it listed in their database. It also appears on the website of the Citizen Potawatomi Nation Cultural Center http://www.potawatomiheritage.org/history/kansas/ which notes that it was taken in the 1930s and voice over added in the 1970s.

[212] *Encyclopedia of the American Indian*, articles on Potawatomi and other aspects of native culture such as child rearing, death, and religion influence this section.

creation. They felt a kinship with nature and natural spirits, respecting the presence of spiritual power in animate and inanimate creation. Their clans were named for a totem animal. They counted on the spiritual powers to guide them to good hunting. The Euro-American insistence of the human being as the apex of creation and their domination of other creatures must have been incomprehensible to the Potawatomi. Their religious beliefs equally confused the French observers because they did not connect them to any doctrines or ethical concerns.[213] The Indians' insistence that all creation has spiritual power, including plants and animals, led Lucille to think they had many lesser gods. This same native belief may have made the Catholic devotion to the saints attractive. There is no indication in the RSCJ writings that the missionaries were able to understand the possible connection between the natives' attraction to Catholic beliefs in the use of sacramentals,[214] the symbols of the Sacraments[215] or the veneration of the saints and their own native spirituality.

Medicine bundles were very important to the tribe and were kept in the custody of clan leaders as well as individuals. These bundles were prized and guarded since the tribe felt they were a gift from heaven. Seldom shown to outsiders, they were considered sacred. The rare glimpse of their contents revealed a mix of natural objects: owl and other bird skins and feathers, bones of animals, stones, shells, medicinal roots and plants.[216] Observers called them "medicine" bundles, since they were used in healing ceremonies. They had power to guard the clan and its members and were used to insure success in the hunt and communicate with the spirit world. Individual bundles could have some connection to the owners' vision quest or be inherited. Giving them up, as the missionaries demanded, endangered the clan's and natives' livelihood and health.[217] Priests insisted that they be surrendered when a native became a Christian. The Potawatomi were surprised when missionaries assumed that they would abandon their own religious practices when adopting Christianity rather than simply adding to them.[218] One of the causes of division in the mission in the future would be the choice of some to keep their traditional ways rather than convert and the choice of others to abandon them as a requirement to become Christians.

A sense of place was extremely important to the natives, although owning land was a concept foreign to them. They "belonged" to a place rather than the place's belonging to them. Space rather than time governed

---

[213] Perrot, 1, p. 47; 2, p. 264 He felt they had no religion although he described in detail their belief about creation and the meaning of rituals.

[214] Blessed objects such as medals, statues, rosaries used in Catholic devotions.

[215] Sacraments use tangible objects such as water, oil, bread, and wine. Natives would have also used chants and songs in their religious rituals, as did the missionaries.

[216] Perrot, 1, p. 50 describes a bundle that he saw and the ritual around it.

[217] Although some were allowed to keep those herbs meant for healing, since the missionaries recognized the natives' knowledge of herbal medicine. Bundles contained bird and animal skins, bones, and shells. They were in the possession of the clan leaders; hence giving them up endangered the entire clan.

[218] *Encyclopedia of the American Indian*, p. 383.

their lives. Tribal territory was where the bones of the ancestors were buried, and special features in the landscape were connected to creation myths. They had a traditional hunting territory, and each tribe appeared to know which was theirs and what other tribe was allowed to share it. They held this territory in common for the good of the whole tribe. The Potawatomi had learned to move from place to place because of the past migrations of their tribe, but these had usually taken place over long periods, not abruptly like more recent moves.[219] In their sojourn in Indiana, they had cleared land for farms and set down roots successfully, but this life was interrupted by the forced abandonment of their hard work and the march to Kansas.

The Potawatomi had the experience of many deaths during the forced march and the periodic epidemics of diseases such as small pox, measles, and typhoid. Already the Potawatomi had been disconnected from their sense of place by the movement from the Great Lakes, through Indiana and then to Sugar Creek. Buried nearby were the bones of their people who had perished since the journey south.[220] Perhaps, given their displacement and the many deaths they had experienced, the idea of death was something that was foremost in their minds. This must have made them receptive to the focus of the missionaries on the "end time" and the promise of heaven.

The Potawatomi did have the concept of a human immortal "soul" or spirit and eternal life. Writing over one hundred fifty years earlier, the explorer Nicholas Perrot described in detail their belief about the journey the soul took after death. It involved passing through many obstacles, suffering hardships, and crossing a perilous river; but, once successful, the spirit would enjoy a land that was an extension of this life, although better. There was no connection between reaching the land and the person's moral life. He describes the drumming, feasting, and dancing that would welcome the traveler into the heavenly realm.

> They find there innumerable viands of all flavors, everything of the most delicious taste and prepared in the best manner. It is for them to choose whatever pleases them and to satisfy their appetites; and when they have finished eating they go to mingle with the others—to dance and make merry forever, without being any longer subject to sorrow, anxiety, or infirmities or any of the vicissitudes of mortal life.[221]

The description almost parallels Isaiah 25:6-8: "The Lord of hosts will provide for all peoples a feast of rich food and pure, choice wines…he will destroy death forever…wipe away all tears." The explorer was nevertheless unable to see any connection with his own Catholic belief.

---

[219] Their ancestors may have originated around the area of the Saint Lawrence River, moved to the southern Great Lakes, then to Wisconsin and back south to the southern Great Lake area over a period of 300-500 years.

[220] RSCJ Archives, Saint Louis Province: K Potawatomi Mission, box 2 folder 1. Catherine Tardieu, RSCJ, "Account of the founding of the Mission," written about 1872 but drawing on Lucille's memories, since the author was not an eyewitness. She mentions the difficulty the Potawatomi had in giving up ancestral religious practices and how Lucille considered some of those demonic.

[221] Nicholas Perrot, *Indian Tribes of the Upper Mississippi Valley and Region of the Great Lakes*, Vol 1, pp. 90-91.

The Potawatomi compared the journey of the spirit to following a path, which they saw symbolized by the sky path.[222] Although the path could involve difficulty and obstacles, there was no real connection with what the person had done in this life. The only exceptions were murderers' spirits, who in some instances were condemned forever to wander aimlessly. The traditional native belief did not seem to have any idea of hell or eternal punishment.[223] The missionaries seized on this opportunity to promote the aspects of Catholic eschatology that focus on purgatory and hell.[224] The emphasis on sin and punishment and on the need for penitence followed the missionaries' own spirituality which, for the French,[225] was influenced by the negative Jansenist theology of their times. The seventeenth century spiritual movement of Jansenism, with its rigorous moral theology, emphasized sin and the unworthiness of humans before God and influenced how frequently people received communion. Although condemned by Catholic Church authorities in the eighteenth century, it persisted as an influence in French spirituality well into the twentieth century.

The missionaries were appalled by the native practice of polygamy, branding it immoral. Culturally this practice addressed the problem of men lost in battle and the imbalance in the number of men and women in the tribe. It was a voluntary practice with women having the choice of a spouse and of being a second wife. Second wives were sometimes blood sisters. There was a cultural obligation, much like that of the ancient Hebrews, for a man to marry the widow of his brother and care for her. The missionaries branded as sinful the unwillingness of the natives to adopt what would come to be known as the "Protestant work ethic": a belief in the moral benefit and importance of work and its inherent ability to strengthen character. They could not understand why the native men did not feel the need to work in the fields, preferring to obtain their food by hunting. To the missionaries' credit, they did equally condemn as sinful the conduct of fur traders who used alcohol to cheat the natives and who had introduced natives to the practice of binge drinking. These same traders sometimes formed alliances with

---

[222] Charles N. Clark, "The Ritual of the Dead" *HozoNikau*, 29:7 (August 2008), p.5 for a more modern account of Potawatomi practices around death. See also Encyclopedia *of the North American Indian,* articles on death and religion.

[223] Callan, *Philippine*, p. 626 quotes a letter of Father Verhaegen about the Kickapoo who had similar beliefs to the Potawatomi. He notes that "they call God the Great Spirit and every morning pray for his blessing. If they feel sad or guilty they blacken their faces and fast for an entire day…When a brave dies they bury his horse beside him so that his soul may ride to the palace of the Great Spirit, which they think is far away from their village beyond the Western prairie."

[224] De Charry/Hogg et al, in a postscript to a letter of September 14, 1825 to Sophie, Philippine requests that she send brightly colored pictures for the Indians of the death of sinners and hell, perhaps in preparation for the Indian school in Florissant.

[225] French seminaries were influenced by this rigorist interpretation of the administration of the sacraments and moral theology long after Jansenism as a movement had been condemned by church leaders. Irish priests were sent to France for training during times when the Irish church was not allowed seminaries (seventeenth and eighteenth centuries) and were also influenced by this movement, which in turn influenced nineteenth century American Catholicism with its heavily French and later Irish clergy. Sophie herself admitted that her family had a strong Jansenist influence, and RSCJ spirituality was influenced in spite of the emphasis on the devotion to the Sacred Heart.

native women but then abandoned them when the man returned to mainstream society.[226] The traders also used the natives' delight in gambling games that were part of their culture to introduce them to compulsive gambling and rob them of their goods.[227]

The concept of sin, eternal punishment for sin, and the need for redemption were pervasive in the Euro-American theology of both Catholics and Protestants. For the native peoples these were utterly foreign concepts. Often the missionary misinterpreted the acceptance of Christianity as signaling the integration of these concepts. One Jesuit wrote about how much he admired many members of his flock: "I can say that the piety of many among them and the innocent life they lead often touches me. It is true we have some who are weak, but I know several who can be compared with the first Christians. I am convinced that they never commit serious sin, yes, sometimes one has difficulty in giving them absolution for lack of matter"[228] (if they had committed no sin, they did not need absolution in confession). He may have been correct in his assessment of their virtue, but their lack of confession material might also have been due to inability to grasp the missionaries' concept of sin.[229]

The Potawatomi used fasting and the reception of a vision to make decisions, and dreams and fasting often played a part in their lives after their conversion.[230] They would ask the priests to give them a list of fast days during Lent before leaving on a spring hunt. They came to the Jesuits, not only with spiritual but also physical problems. For the natives healing and religion were intimately connected, and the healer was often the religious leader as well. Since the Jesuits often had some medical knowledge,[231] they were perceived as healers as well as religious leaders.

The Potawatomi were probably as mystified by these black robed women as the religious were by the Potawatomi. Women religious were scarce on the frontier, and it is likely that they were puzzling out these female "Blackrobes." It almost seemed as if the natives were trying to understand these women who seemed to

---

[226] Exceptions to this were those who stayed with their Indian wives and became integrated into the tribe.

[227] Articles on French-Native relationships and Intermarriage with Non-Indians, in *Encyclopedia of the North American Indian*. See also Susan Sleeper-Smith's study of "Indian Women and French Men" which indicates that the alliance with a native woman was an advantageous one for the trader because of her kinship connections with those who trapped the furs.

[228] Garraghan 2, p. 226.

[229] Later mission records note that confession was popular but natives preferred to go in their own language. When there was no priest who spoke Potawatomi present, they would use an interpreter but they disliked that practice.

[230] There are accounts in O'Connor's *History of the Kaw River Mission* of Indians, especially children, experiencing visions and prophetic dreams and also in sources cited in Garraghan, *The Jesuits of the Middle United States*.

[231] Jesuits Christian Hoecken and Brother Andrew Mazzella both had medical training. Later at Saint Marys, Maurice Gailland was called upon to treat sicknesses but admitted he relied on the knowledge of his grandmother's remedies.

have alighted like a flock of black birds among them.[232] They came to the sisters' house without any notice, sat wrapped in their blankets around the small room that served as community room, refectory, and school room, and watched the sisters without speaking. Whatever they saw seems to have convinced them that, even though verbal communication was difficult, these women lived in harmony with one another and wanted a genuine relationship with the native peoples. They could be trusted with their children. Within their culture the upbringing of children was often the task of grandmothers of the family. With the exception of Louise Amiot, the religious were older. From later accounts the love of the RSCJ for their charges was described as that of mothers. The Society did not practice corporal punishment—something that the natives too did not usually use with their children. Some of the orphan children from the "Trail of Death" appear to have been the first boarders, and natives from other tribes expressed a willingness for their daughters to be educated by the RSCJ after visiting the school.[233] They do not appear to have used fear as motivation for the girls' cooperation. Instead the girls were motivated with rewards and praise. They built on some of their students' strengths, such as a gift for music, facility for needlework, and a love of color and activity.

In a letter to his superior asking for more missionaries to help with the work, Jesuit Felix Verreydt remarked on the natives' nonverbal ways of communication. He noted that anyone who comes needed to appreciate the native style of communication.

> It seems that those who have never lived among the savages are unwilling to believe they are men like ourselves. But their black and piercing eyes show that they are. If a stranger comes among them, they don't need much time to know him thoroughly. In a short time they give him a name that fits him exactly. It seems that when they look at a person they penetrate to the depths of his soul. An Indian is perfect master of his passions. I have never seen him in anger. His eyes rarely indicate the movements of his soul. You can heap on him the greatest insults; he is unmoved. His eyes are fixed on you, but without emotion. Everything remains hidden in his heart until an occasion presents itself for vengeance.[234]

This silent evaluation and the native response of acceptance or sometimes violent rejection of the stranger often led to the charge that the natives were treacherous and unpredictable since they did not verbally communicate their intentions and emotions.

---

[232] Hickman, Laura, "Native Daughters: Saint Mary's Mission School among the Potawatomi," paper, U. of Nebraska at Omaha, p.1, suggests that the Indians who "regarded them as beings come down from the sky" were thinking less of angels than of a flock of crows. RSCJ Archives Saint Louis Province K Potawatomi Mission box 2 Folder 4 #14.

[233] The Pearl family of Kansas and Ohio have a strong family oral tradition that their Potawatomi great grandmother Theresa Slevin (1837-1876) was one of those children. (Interviews with Virginia Pearl, CSJ, and family).

[234] Garraghan 2, p. 227: Verreydt to Roothaan, April 23, 1847.

Shrine to Philippine
Duchesne, Sugar Creek

The two RSCJ who had the most impact on the natives were Philippine Duchesne, who never could speak their tongue, and Lucille Mathevon, who initially could only sing in Potawatomi. While each shared the misconceptions of their time about the natives, the RSCJ's prayerful presence and willingness to share the life of the tribe seemed to enable them to overcome the stereotypes they had of natives. Philippine who, of necessity, used nonverbal communication, was a woman of deep prayer and spirituality, and she was austere in her own personal habits and lifestyle. The Potawatomi spirituality saw spiritual power in all beings, and they fasted to gain spiritual guidance. She willingly, even joyfully, shared the privations of the native settlement, spending long hours in prayer in the primitive, cold church. Her prayer vigils involved fasting. She showed reverence for the dead in their small cemetery, walking among the graves and praying for them. The Potawatomi gave her the name of "Woman-who-prays-always." Lucille was personally repelled by some aspects of native life: different standards of hygiene, for example. But she was able to adapt her own teaching methods to one that best suited her desire to share the Gospel with the native people and their children. The religious were hospitable and chose to forge bonds of friendship with the native people.

Lucille, Louise and Mary Anne O'Connor accepted the assistance of the Potawatomi in learning their language. They genuinely admired many of the qualities of the people they served. All come across as women of heart, whose genuine affection for the native people spoke directly to their hearts. The Indians responded by bringing little tokens of appreciation: special food and delicacies to the RSCJ, especially to the "old lady," Philippine. Even their less appreciated offerings, like the bloody scalps taken in skirmishes with native adversaries, were meant as gifts to honor the women. The RSCJ, in their turn, learned to accept the gifts, even the scalps, in the spirit in which they were intended—as tokens of friendship.

Some puzzling aspects of native culture worked against the establishment of a formal school with an academic year. The original school was started in July, but by fall whole families disappeared into the forest, as the men went to hunt and lay up venison for the winter, and their families went with them. In February the same thing happened when families went into the areas where there were sugar maples to tap the trees. Thus the number of students varied according to the rhythm of native life. Despite this, the Sacred Heart school consistently got high praise from inspectors and visitors for the accomplishments of its students.

Traditionally deerskins were used as clothing—a long dress for the women, breechcloth and leggings and decorated shirt for the men. However, by the time the Potawatomi settled in Sugar Creek, many items of European dress were mixed in with the native garb. The Potawatomi were known for their decorative quillwork. The description of the Potawatomi arrayed in traditional finery is very colorful, with distinctive hair arrangements for the men, face painting, and tattoos. An artist, George Winter,[235] visited the Potawatomi in Indiana and along the migration to Kansas. His sketches, later developed into paintings, are vivid depictions of the colorful, eclectic style of the people. These portraits are not the stereotypical ones of the Plains Indians that later became the image of Native Americans in art and film.[236] Rather they show a people whose dress was colorful, a mix of western and native. Men often had colorful turbans decorated with quills and feathers combined with western suitcoats and colorful cravats, leggings and silver nose rings and earrings. Earlier versions of the turbans were made of otter skin.

Mas-Sa, George Winter (TCHA)

The women were draped in colorful scarves and shawls as well as abundant silver jewelry and large blue cloaks. They dressed as colorfully and eclectically as the native men. Women wore tunics over wide skirts with leggings

[235] Sarah E. Cooke and Rachel Ramadhyani, *Indians and a Changing Frontier, The Art of George Winter* (Indianapolis, Indiana: Indiana Historical Society, 1993.) Winter, born in England in 1809, settled permanently in the U.S. in 1830 and became a U.S. citizen in 1841. He sketched the Potawatomi extensively in the 1830s with copious notes.
[236] *Ibid*. In fact, Winter did a sketch of the Potawatomi for the Indiana statehouse that was rejected as not looking "Indian" enough for American eyes used to the stereotype of the Plains Indian.

adorned with colorful ribbons. In one Winter sketch a woman sports a black top hat.[237] After seeing Winter's sketches and paintings, one has difficulty in understanding later comments of the RSCJ about the shabby dress, even rags, of the people around them. Was it possible that the natives did not understand how to mend these fabrics or had been prevented by the trauma of the tribal displacements from making or purchasing replacements?

Sewing materials appear to have been scarce. The native women soon exhausted the supplies of needles, thimbles, scissors, and thread of the religious.[238] One of the first educational ventures of the school was to teach European methods of sewing and knitting. The women of the tribe were fascinated and often accompanied their daughters to learn themselves. Lucille mentions the girls' delight in colorful clothing and the long blue cloaks that they made and ornamented. Winter also described the cloaks and said they were covered with silver ornaments. The traditional finery of the Potawatomi men is very festive, with distinctive hair arrangements, colorful face painting and tattoos.[239] This finery appears to have been especially on display when the tribe was welcoming visitors or celebrating feasts.[240]

Native culture was very flexible and adapted to new ideas and customs. In their contact with other tribes and with European explorers and traders,[241] the Indians were willing to adopt foreign technology, clothing, customs, and even religious beliefs, when they felt that they complemented or were superior to their own.[242] Originally mainly hunter gatherers, they had adopted some crop cultivation (beans, corn, squash, tobacco, and wild rice) from other tribes, as they moved from more northern territories. The horse, metal tools, glass beads, and silver ornaments were all incorporated into their own culture. They had no sense that any religious belief was the "right" or orthodox one. They valued spiritual power and probably saw the blackrobes as much like their own medicine men—not only as healers but also men with a powerful connection to the spirit world. Catholic rituals in the Tridentine Catholicism of the time used color, movement, music, song, chanting, incense, and candles. Various

---

[237] *Ibid.* Plate 46.

[238] Callan, *Philippine*, p. 654.

[239] Perrot writes of what he considered excessive vanity on the part of the men, always fixing their hair, changing styles, painting their faces, fascinated with mirrors.

[240] Philippine, Lucille and Jesuit accounts all mention these occasions as opportunities to display native finery. An example was the welcome given to Elisabeth Galitzine with natives in "full costume with feathers, and beads and paint" described by Lucille in a letter quoted in Callan, *North America*, p. 285.

[241] David Edmunds, "Indians and a Changing Frontier," pp .28-37, mentions the adoption of entrepreneurial activities as a sign of the influence of French traders and intermarriage.

[242] *Encyclopedia of the North American Indian*, articles on the influence of non-Indian culture. This worked also in reverse as the dominant culture adopted Indian technology, such as canoes, dwellings, snow shoes and hunting techniques, weapons, foods and words from different Indian languages. Many of our modern freeways and roads follow trails blazed long before white settlement by the various native peoples of the North American continent. The Potawatomi played the game we call Lacrosse as well as games of chance.

rites featured elaborate processions and devotional ceremonies, some in a language, Latin, that even most Catholics did not understand. What must have puzzled them was the missionaries' insistence that their spiritual ways could not coexist with native ways.[243]

Path near original cabin, Sugar Creek

Although the Jesuit missionaries wanted Potawatomi to be the main language, it was clear that English was necessary if they were to survive contact with the dominant American society. Many of the Métis families probably spoke both French and some English. Although Lucille's English was poor, Mary Anne O'Connor already had experience teaching it to Indian children at Florissant. Louise Amiot and Mary Layton were fluent in that language. While later there would be stricter division of labor between choir and coadjutrix sisters, as far as teaching was concerned in these early days, there seems to have been some flexibility.[244] The exigencies of the

---

[243] It was not until after Vatican II that missionaries did not insist that European culture and Catholicism were inseparable. Earlier prophetic experiments by Jesuits such as DeNobili in India and Ricci in China were condemned or not allowed to develop. However, the Mohawk and some other native people had Mass celebrated in their native tongue, long before the vernacular was introduced by Vatican II liturgical reforms.

[244] As late as 1865, Mary Layton is listed as an assistant teacher in the Kansas state census.

ministry allowed the religious to focus on what gifts each one could bring to the work rather than division of labor by class in the Society. The needs of the Potawatomi drove the division of labor.

A vivid description of a mission weekend and the colorful pageantry of devotions is found in Jesuit records. The weekend of the feast of Corpus Christi, June 20, 1843, began with a tremendous storm that hit just as the devotions started in the church. Gigantic trees were uprooted and lightning struck nearby, shaking the building violently. The natives seemed unfazed by the thunder and the rain. The missionaries heard the sound of drums in the distance and realized that the Osage tribe members were signaling that they wished to hold council with the Potawatomi. One of the Jesuits[245] tried to get close to the Osage camp to observe them, and he could see them dancing around the campfires. The next day the weather cleared, and the church was full with, not only the Mission Indians, but some Catholic Ottawa, some Osage, and a family of Miami. It was a high Mass (the missionaries also had an earlier low Mass) and the natives, especially the visiting Osage, were impressed with the splendor of the vestments, the songs, incense, and the ritual.

D-Mouche Kee-Kee-Awh,
George Winter (TCHA)

The Mass lasted two hours. The small children remained outside swinging in hammocks slung from the trees. A meal was provided after Mass by the Potawatomi. The usual Sunday Vespers followed at three in the afternoon, with alternate choirs of men and women for the psalms. A procession in honor of the feast day followed: two hundred warriors on horseback led with flags emblazoned with symbols of the Sacred Heart and the name of Jesus. Fifty girls from the Sacred Heart school followed, strewing flowers and dressed in their "richest attire"; sixty boys played drum and fife, and men fired salutes at intervals. The procession continued in two lines, single file, with six acolytes who also strewed flowers, and four of whom carried lanterns. The canopy over the Blessed Sacrament was carried by eight principal chiefs, followed by a squadron of lancers on horseback and women walking two-by-two reciting prayers. An elaborate repository was set up on a platform twenty-five feet long by six feet high in an area surrounded by seven high trees and flags.

---

[245] O'Connor, p. 28: the storm had made the ground very muddy but he got close enough to "observe some athletic naked fellows jump and kick about in a circle."

At the end, the horsemen dismounted and knelt. The visiting Osage were very impressed by this display of color and pageantry.[246]

According to the reports of the inspectors who arrived from the government, the RSCJ were doing an above average job. As early as 1844, the Commissioner of Indian Affairs, Thomas Hudal Harvey, praised the "five ladies"[247] of the Society of the Sacred Heart:

> …they have under instruction between fifty and seventy girls…the progress of the girls is extremely flattering. They are taught the useful branches of female education, and at the same time fashionable accomplishments are not neglected. A number of the girls are supported and brought up as the family of the ladies and their friends. It is to be regretted that they have not the means to enable them to enlarge their operations; they are extremely anxious to [have] room enough to enable them to put up looms. Too much praise cannot be given to these accomplished ladies for their sacrifice they have made in alienating themselves from society to ameliorate the conditions of the Indians.[248]

> I visited today the female school under the charge of five Sisters of the Sacred Heart of Jesus. The weather had been extremely wet for some time, and the scholars are, with a few exceptions, day scholars, that is, board with their parents. They are not as attentive as it is desirable they should be. Notwithstanding the unfavorableness of the day, I think I counted thirty-nine present. I examined a considerable quantity of their needlework, both fancy and for practical purposes, all of which would have been creditable to girls of their age in any society. The shirts, vests, stockings and spinning was well done, their fancy needlework was [sic] very pretty. Their recitations were highly creditable, their singing was very fine, nearly the whole school joining. Their singing was in four languages, the native, English, French, and Latin. It is much to be regretted that these ladies cannot carry on their works of charity on a more extended scale. It is only necessary to see them and their school to be convinced of their zeal and the happy effect which they are producing among the Indians at Sugar Creek. The single fact of teaching the girls to make the common articles of clothing will do much in civilizing the Indians. Induce the Indian to throw off the blanket, the leggings, and breech cloth, and his

---

[246] *Ibid.* pp. 28-31. One assumes the religious were also part of the procession or at least observers, but they do not leave any such vivid account. The Corpus Christi procession continued all through the time of the mission and at the end stretched through the streets of the village of Saint Marys. It was only discontinued in 1917.

[247] Five: this was the year that the three original pioneers were joined by a new superior, Catherine Thiéfry, and an aspirant.

[248] Potawatomi Mission collection, Box 1 RSCJ Archives Saint Louis Province, series K. Letter of his great grandson with quotation of Thomas Harvey's report of 1844. Most of the Indian agents reporting were not Catholic. The U.S. government paid the mission schools per student so good reports were essential. There was a preference by the government to fund Protestant schools rather than Catholic ones, but the Potawatomi never really supported the nearby Baptist mission.

civilization is half effected.[249] I will enclose an address from a little full-blood Indian girl about twelve years old delivered to me on visiting their school which very clearly sets forth their necessitous condition. Can the Government give them no aid?"[250]

In 1845, Agent Harvey continued his appeal for funds especially for the Sacred Heart School, pointing out that thousands of dollars were being spent to recruit Indian students for an academy in Kentucky that has no tribal support, while not one dollar was being given to this worthy school here, which the Indians supported.[251] The government agreed and promised yearly support of $500 to the girls' school but were slow in paying. Agent Harvey once again took up the cause:

> Five ladies who would be creditable to a school in any country devote their entire lives to the education of the females of this vicinity, boarding a number and teaching them all the useful arts of housewifery. Their school numbers about sixty and occasionally upwards. The happy moral influence which they have exerted among the Indians cannot be mistaken by the most casual observer (I speak from frequent personal observation). The Society, as I understand from those who know, cannot longer bear the entire expense of the school. I would view the removal or discontinuance of the school as a serious calamity to the Potawatomi in the Osage River sub-agency. I trust that I may be authorized to assure the ladies that the allowance will be continued.[252]

The sisters considered the native students equal to any other students—initially less educated, but capable of achieving the same level of education as other children. They remark that their students have equal intelligence and often surpass settlers in their moral and spiritual lives.[253] The natives' sense of time is so different from that of the missionaries, and it is the missionaries who must adapt to that.

> Good is being done here so slowly and only as the carefree moods of the natives allow…children are good and generally intelligent. They are able to learn easily but are not much inclined to it, and one must be careful not to reproach them but attract them with friendliness.[254]

---

[249] Harvey's comment gives voice to the American prejudice against Native culture: a "civilized" Indian dressed like a "white" person. He also ignores the fact that the Potawatomi had adopted articles of "white" clothing for some time while remaining Indian as could be seen in George Winter's portraits.

[250] Harvey to Crawford, May 29, 1844, quoted by Garraghan 2, p. 211.

[251] *Ibid.* p. 212. Evidently, a bounty was paid for each student recruited, and a recruiter had come to the mission but had no success since the Potawatomi believed the children they sent away would not return and preferred a school closer to home.

[252] *Ibid.* quoted Harvey to Medill, November 17, 1845, p. 2.212. The money came in the new year.

[253] De Charry/Hogg et al, 2.3, Letter 335, p. 365 (22 April 1852). Philippine suggests that there might be Indian vocations to the Society among four women who are helping Lucille.

[254] *Ibid.* De Charry/Hogg et al, 2.3, Letter 326, p. 345: letter of Philippine to Sophie (22 September 1841).

A visiting Episcopalian educator who heard of the school and the interest of the native girls in embroidery remarked on the wisdom of using this interest to draw the students into school work: "At one of the Roman Catholic Schools I…learned that the fondness of the Indians for embroidery is cultivated with success; by this one interest, so to speak, they may be led on to perfection. In some instances we have felt pained by a well-meant but most unwise crushing and quenching of Indian tendencies. Better to train and direct and make use of them for good."[255] This conflict over time and attitude to structured classroom learning would continue in mission life as long as the native children remained in the school. That the RSCJ were able to adapt made it difficult in later years to combine native and settler children in the same classes. When settler children started to come to the school in the late 1860s they would have spoken only English, and the native children were forced to adapt to an English only atmosphere. There would be a structured day following that of other Sacred Heart schools, which would not allow the same freedom of movement and casual visiting of parents.

The Natives were particularly vulnerable to the influence of alcohol. The missionaries and tribal leaders had attempted to banish alcohol from the settlement because they saw the detrimental effect it had on the life and wellbeing of the people. Unscrupulous traders, soldiers and river boat sailors would market alcohol to the natives. Tribal leaders tried to enforce an alcohol ban by fining or jailing native offenders, but the battle would continue all through the life of the mission.[256] Later in the history of the Potawatomi mission, alcohol was traded for the land allotments the natives received or for the cash payments they received from the government.

The missionaries continued the battle against the incursion of alcohol into the life of their ideal Christian community. The Jesuit fathers and brothers confiscated caches of alcohol that they found and destroyed them. Retreats were given and novenas made to renew the spirituality of their converts. The efforts did bear some fruit especially with those closest to the mission. Sugar Creek was relatively calm, and alcohol not readily available. Other Potawatomi who settled nearby struggled with addiction.[257]

From the records, however, it is clear that the struggle with alcohol would be an ongoing battle throughout

---

[255] Garraghan 2, p. 208 footnote 60 quoting a report by Felix Verreydt for 1844. The visitor was an Episcopalian official visiting schools of his own denomination in the area. A later note on p. 2.219 explains that he was prevented by weather from reaching Sugar Creek but heard of the school and the mission from meeting a catechumen at the mission. The man also told him of the generosity of the Jesuits who would give up their own bed for a sick Indian.

[256] *Ibid*. Garraghan 2, pp. 217-18 describes the problem as occurring throughout the history of the mission and goes into detail about the attempts to control it.
Callan, *North America*, p. 291, excerpt from the House Journal 1846, describes a recent murder with list of punishments imposed by tribal government for alcohol abuse.

[257] Jeanne P. Leader, "The Pottawatomies and Alcohol: an Illustration of the Illegal Trade," *Kansas Historical Society Journal* (Autumn 1979, pp. 157-161) traces the influence of the whiskey traders with the traditional Potawatomi people who came from Council Bluffs and settled at Potawatomi Creek near Sugar Creek. She notes that Sugar Creek had relatively few who were addicted to alcohol.

the life of the mission. The practice of giving some of the promised treaty annuities in cash was adapted to receive some in goods, with the hope of cutting down on the purchase of whiskey. When the Potawatomi moved to Saint Marys, the whiskey traders followed them; and when settler communities grew, alcohol availability grew also. Even Jesuit Maurice Gailland, who served the Potawatomi from 1848-1877, seemed discouraged by the relentless battle against the incursions of alcohol and its effect on the native population.

> As weeds will spring up in the best cultivated garden, so will vice sometimes make its appearance in places where virtue seems to reign supreme. This was the case at Sugar Creek especially, during the past years. Among the Christians of the mission was a band of drunkards, who, not satisfied with causing a great deal of trouble to the missionaries, determined to take a bolder and more menacing stand. Drunkenness, it must be said, is the most fatal means of corruption among the Indians, and there is not virtue sufficient left in them to withstand the temptation of the fire-water…once an Indian has drunk to excess, rage and despair seize on his soul.[258]

Unlike the sisters, who were bound by rules of cloister to the immediate territory of the mission, the priests ranged far from Sugar Creek serving both tribal bands in remote camps and settlers.[259] There was another settlement of Potawatomi nearby at the first settlement called Saint Joseph's on Potawatomi Creek, whom the missionaries also served. They received many requests to serve other tribes but were limited by their small numbers. Some of the Indians were motivated by these visits to come and join the settlement at Sugar Creek. The funding of the schools was augmented by the trips of the Jesuits to Saint Louis and to surrounding settlements, while the RSCJ did their appeals by mail for both money and donations of goods to use in the school. The mission life was not without its festive moments, such as the Corpus Christi feast day. Other feast days were also celebrated with public banquets, at which natives from other tribes joined the mission residents. The feast was held outdoors on rough tables made from the squared off trunks of trees, which were loaded with game provided by the hunt and other food donated by the missionaries. Visitors were served by the principal men of the tribe, and they also provided orations and prayers. On one Easter Sunday some of the visitors wished permission to dance but were told, "We pray the prayer of the blackrobes; we do not dance."[260]

---

[258] Garraghan 2, pp. 594-5 quotes Gailland who did not live at Sugar Creek since he arrived only in 1848; this is based on accounts of Jesuits Felix Verreydt and Christian Hoecken. He may also be referring to the band of Potawatomi who lived at Potawatomi Creek nearby. When they were at Council Bluffs Pierre De Smet commented on their addiction to alcohol.

[259] *Ibid.* Garraghan 2, p. 224. The parish register contains numerous baptisms and marriages performed by the priests for German, Irish and French settlers. (see notes) The same source describes p. 220-225 the distances covered by the Jesuits trying to stay in touch with different native groups. Visits to Catholic settlers on the Missouri side as well covered many miles of territory and stretched the Jesuit resources.

[260] O'Connor, p. 44 However on another occasion a visiting group of natives did dance without problem during a feast. Perhaps they didn't ask permission?

By 1847 the mission was just beginning to function well. The natives were getting settled in their new home.[261] That winter the hunting parties had great success, and the U.S. government had kept its promise to supply three thousand bushels of corn, a barrel of pork, and two hundred pounds of flour. Two hundred acres of arable land had been received from the Indian agent along with medicine, plus a promise of five hundred dollars a year.[262] Books arrived from Saint Louis and Cincinnati, which were distributed to the Potawatomi. Bishop Edward Barron came during Christmas time and confirmed eighty natives. A group of Peoria Indians were very impressed with the Christmas crib that had been set up. They wanted the Jesuits to come to visit them. A Kickapoo chief from the failed mission with that tribe arrived and requested Baptism. He was described as a "man of great soul, truthfulness and candor."[263]

> The mission plant of 1847 was well established. There was a large church, plainly but nicely furnished by the hands of the sisters and by contributions from distant cities. There were schools, well attended and efficiently taught. There was a priest's house, a sisters' convent and some workshops. There were horses, cattle, and farm implements. Hunting was still good in the locality; and elk, deer, and buffalo came along in due season; and, at times, fish was also plentiful. The yearly yield of maple sugar was quite an item, and nuts, berries, and wild fruit were in abundance. Father Hoecken deemed it an ideal spot for a Catholic mission. The land was poor, 'tis true, and malaria troubled them, as it did all early settlements along the creeks in Kansas; but it had other advantages that more than made up for these drawbacks. The harvest of souls was now ripening at Sugar Creek in 1847 when the clouds began to gather. Some wily agent or some secret influences were laying plans at Washington for the removal or rather the destruction of Saint Mary's Mission at Sugar Creek.[264]

In the previous June, 1846, a meeting was held in Council Bluffs, Iowa, with representatives of the U.S. government, the Potawatomi, and other tribes. On the 17th of June 1846, the government signed a contract purchasing the Indian lands on Sugar Creek and gave the Indians a reservation along the banks of the Kansas (or Kaw) River, extending westward from what is at present the city of Topeka fifty miles on both sides of the

---

[261] *Ibid*. pp. 37ff.
[262] The original allotment was three hundred dollars.
[263] Thomas H. Kinsella, *The History of Our Cradle Land: A Centenary of Catholicism in Kansas* (Kansas City: Casey Printing Company, 1921. Transcribed by Sean Furniss online at http://skyways.lib.ks.us/genweb/miami/kinsella/kinsel04.html Part I, quoting from Father Hoecken's diary.
[264] *Ibid*. Kinsella, p. 30.

Kansas River.[265] Therefore, less than ten years after settling at Sugar Creek, the Potawatomi would need to move once again.[266] They were reluctant to agree, but the Jesuit superior, Felix Verreydt, persuaded them that it would be in their best interest to do so. Maurice Gailland wrote,

> This treaty seemed to be very advantageous to the Indians, for it not only removed them from the poisoned springs of the fire-water, but also assured to each individual an annual pension for several years. Besides, the government offered to furnish them with a sufficient sum to support a school of 90 boys and 90 girls, and to erect mills, forges, etc.[267]

The news of the move plunged the tribe back into a sense of despair and desperation. What was the use of becoming farmers if they were constantly being told to move once they showed signs of success? They had the daily experience of contact with bands of native people from other tribes who, like them, had been moved from east of the Mississippi, some of whom organized into roving bands free of government control. They could also drown their sorrows in drink and gambling. It was easy to obtain liquor from "ruffian whites" who preyed on the natives' love of gambling to rob them of what they had.[268] Should they follow the example of other displaced tribal bands that had chosen to roam free and continue their traditional ways? This would mean they would have no recognized fixed territory and would put them in conflict with other tribes as they crossed into their hunting territory or with settlers suspicious of native intentions.

> The Pottawatomies [sic] have been more unsettled and more unsteady in their habits this year than formerly. This must, in some measure, be attributed to their contemplated removal to the Kanzas [sic] country. Some have planted and will raise a limited quantity of corn and succulent fruits; others again have not applied themselves to farming at all this year. Those who have planted, speaking generally, will not raise a sufficiency to carry them through this coming winter, provided they remain; but they have pledged themselves, in council

[265] http://www.pbpindiantribe.com/tribal-history.aspx, the website of the Prairie Band, Gary Mitchel tribal historian. After 1846 the tribe moved to present-day Kansas, a new region that was once called the "Great American Desert." Although the area lacked the beauty of the Great Lakes, the circumstances of removal left the tribal people little choice. It amounted to another period of adjustment for the tribe, just like so many times in the past. At that time, the reservation was thirty square miles, which included part of present-day Topeka. (His estimate of the reservation's size seems too small—it is described as extending 50 miles north and 50 south of the river.)

[266] *Ibid*. The U.S. Government, in its first treaties with the Indians, established boundaries for tribal land. In the numerous treaties that followed, known as "cession treaties," the Potawatomi agreed to sell land to the U.S. Government. Those early concessions soon led to more drastic policies.

[267] Garraghan 2, pp. 597ff. See also the words of Felix Verreydt giving the reasons of poor soil as reason for moving and the missionaries' inability to support the schools at that site. The Indian agent was amazed that the move was made peacefully.

[268] O'Connor, p. 48.

assembled, that they will remove this fall in the event of the payment being early enough for them to get off. I said the Pottawatomies [sic] have been more than usually unsteady. Drunkenness, and its dire companion, murder, have prevailed to a greater extent this year than for years previous. Even the hitherto exemplary Indians on Sugar Creek have not escaped the infection. I am, however, happy to state that a reaction is taking place. Some of the old and steady denizens of Sugar Creek have taken the matter in hand. They have called councils, invited the attendance of their brethren on Pottawatomie Creek, and mutually have pledged themselves to adopt rules, fines and penalties for the introduction of spirituous liquors within their limits.[269]

One of the reasons the missionaries supported the move was the hope that it might alleviate the alcohol problem.[270] Many of the Indians at Sugar Creek were reluctant to make the trek to the new location, and it was only the influence of the missionaries that would eventually persuade them to move.[271] They had just become accustomed to the new hunting territory, had built homes and a church, which they were planning to expand.[272] The bodies of almost five hundred of their dead, including those from the Trail of Death who were buried in the small mission cemetery, would have to be left behind. Much time and energy had been expended on the settlement, and they were laying down roots. There was a feeling of despair among the people, aggravated by mistaken reports that the land on which they would settle was barren and had no timber. This news greatly discouraged the Indians as well. They did not see the point of moving again to a place that once again they were promised would be theirs forever. Both the Jesuits and the Religious of the Sacred Heart felt the move would improve the life of the Indians and allow them to live in peace and tranquility. They perhaps had less reason to distrust the government promises. They seemed not to realize that what they saw as a lack of cooperation, even laziness, on the part of the tribe was a sign of desperation and depression. On the last pages of his diary, Christian Hoecken writes: "The decrease in the number of baptisms shows how the Indians were scattered in 1848. The baptisms for '46, '47, and '48 were 178, 142, and 48 respectively. The baptisms for the ten years (1838–1848) were 1,430, of which five hundred and fifty were adults."[273]

---

[269] From the report of Alfred J. Vaughan, Indian subagent at the Osage River agency, it appears that the Potawatomi there had not yet migrated to the Kansas River reservation. The report was made September 1, 1847. Some of them may have moved later in the year. www.kansasheritage.org

[270] Garraghan 2, p. 228.

[271] Garraghan 2, pp. 216-17. The land at Sugar Creek was not especially suited to farming – especially corn, which was their major crop. It was very shallow and rocky and hard to work.

[272] *Ibid*. 2.201. This was the third church they had built after the move from Indiana – one at their first settlement along Potawatomi Creek, the first log church at Sugar Creek and its expanded version. They had already selected a site in 1844 and begun gathering materials and were in process of working on the church when the news of the move reached them.

[273] Kinsella Part 1 quoting Father Hoecken's diary.

SAINT MARYS, KANSAS
THE GOLDEN YEARS: 1848-1860

After the decision to honor the treaty and move to a new location, the actual move was going to take much planning and exploration. It took several months and had a number of stages.

On November 21, 1847, Christian Hoecken performed the last baptism at the mission and set off with Brother Andrew Mazella and a few Potawatomi to explore a new location in Indian Territory, south of the Kaw (Kansas) River. They set up a winter camp at Mission Creek, about seventeen miles from the present town of Saint Marys, the future site of the Jesuit and Sacred Heart schools. Most of the natives and the RSCJ and their students remained behind. In March, April, and May other natives joined them, and there were plans to expand the camp and build a church. The natives found another site at Wakarusa Creek that they thought more suitable especially for a spring and summer camp. Some of the tribe went to this temporary settlement at Wakarusa, and some stayed at Mission Creek. They had started to plant and farm the land. But for various reasons the site at Mission Creek was not good.[274] Felix Verreydt and some of the Potawatomi explored the region on the north side of the river and found a more favorable site. By June 6, 1848, Joseph Bertrand, who was part Potawatomi, and Jesuit Felix Verreydt apprised the government Indian agent of their decision to resettle on what would be the site of Saint Mary's mission, north of the river, where there was good timber. Their only concern was that it was low lying land and near the river, with the chance of flooding; otherwise it appeared to have both good land and timber resources.[275]

The chosen mission site was approved by the Jesuit superior in Saint Louis, after Verreydt made a trip there in July and after sending two lay brothers back to Sugar Creek to help them prepare.[276] When he returned from Saint Louis, he brought Maurice Gailland with him. Gailland left an account of his arrival at Sugar Creek with Felix Verreydt and his travels with the band the ninety miles to their new home on the Kaw River. It was not until August 1848 that the RSCJ and the rest of the Jesuits finally left with the majority of the natives. On leaving the

---

[274] It apparently overlapped with the territory promised to other tribes and the Potawatomi feared the incursions of the hostile Pawnee. They also differed on the best location for farming and timber.

[275] Garraghan 2, pp. 600f, describes the process of leaving Sugar Creek and of the trial and error process of finding a spot to settle down.

[276] He obviously knew the superior would agree with his decision and did not want the waiting Potawatomi to be delayed further. There was a two-year limit to make the move from the time of the treaty signing; that may also have motivated him to move quickly once they had decided on a location.

Sugar Creek mission, they were deliberately set afire to the buildings to save them from misuse.[277] The Indians, despite their reluctance to leave, began the long trek.[278] The Jesuit party consisted of the superior of the mission, Felix Verreydt, Maurice Gailland, and Brother George Miles. The RSCJ were Lucille Mathevon, Mary Anne O'Connor, and Mary Layton with Joseph Bertrand as guide. They left Sugar Creek on August 16 and travelled in five large wagons, some of the party on horseback. The RSCJ were accompanied by a young boy named Charlot driving a small wagon and carrying the chickens.[279] Lucille mentions that they picnicked on the way on coffee, ham, and bread. Before eating, one of the Indians delivered a long blessing. They slept under the stars wrapped in buffalo robes, each group in its own place: the Jesuits, the Indians, and the RSCJ.

Maurice Gailland, SJ, (Jesuit Archives, Central South Province)

Maurice Gailland left a vivid description of the journey, how they camped out each evening, *à l'Indienne*, preparing their supper over a large fire. Before retiring they built up the fire to drive away the mosquitoes. "These plains present a strange and wild, but at the same time, a grand and beautiful appearance. Stretching out and away in the distance, they seem, like the ocean, to have naught but the blue sky for limit where the eye loses itself in their immensity."[280] While traveling they saw an innovative wagon that used two masts and sails to propel itself across this new type of ocean. Gailland learned that the inventor had only one problem: the high wind sometimes made this "ship" dangerous and difficult to control.

The group passed through the Ottawa territory, where they stopped to minister to a Catholic family and to have Mass. Proceeding through the territory of the Sauk (a people mentioned as quite hostile to Americans) they stopped with the Shawnee and slowly made their way to their new home.[281] They arrived at Christian Hoecken's place of residence on the Wakarusa on August 19. Despite its "temporary" location they saw twenty Indian lodges there. Hoecken's cabin also served as a makeshift chapel. He had been busy serving

---

[277] Garraghan 2, p. 600 says they were burned to "save them from desecration"—which would seem to point to only the religious buildings being burned. If all were burned, where did the remaining Potawatomi and the RSCJ live before leaving in August? Or was the burning done just before everyone left? Garraghan is not clear when they were burned.

[278] Accounts in Garraghan, *Jesuits of the Middle U.S.* 2, pp.193ff.

[279] Louise Callan says they were accompanied by a girl boarder named Charlotte; however, the Jesuit records say it was a boy named Charlot, and later in Father Gailland's diary, it is mentioned that he went hunting for the mission. See Garraghan 2, p. 613, for that reference. On p. 621, he is clearly identified as a boy. Fr. Hoecken also identified him as a boy, one of the Jesuit's first students.

[280] *Ibid*, pp. 2.602-3.

[281] *Ibid*. pp. 2.603.

the two settlements, baptizing and performing marriages.[282] Gailland was moved by the sight of the silver-haired priest wearing himself out in the service of the Potawatomi and immediately promised both to help him and to learn the native language. There they rested and waited for Louise Amiot who came in from Westport on September 1.[283]

No doubt this journey and the extended stops gave the RSCJ the opportunity to get to know Maurice Gailland, who had arrived at Sugar Creek eight days before they left. On his arrival he had been ill with a fever that caused him to hallucinate that he was back in his native Switzerland. Gailland would love and quickly master the Potawatomi language. He would be part of the mission until his death in 1877 and would be influential in shaping the RSCJ view of the natives and their mission with them.[284]

On September 7, the travelers parted from the Wakarusa to begin the last stage of their journey to the new Saint Mary's mission. When the party from Sugar Creek reached Saint Mary's mission on September 9, they had to cross the Kansas River at the ford. At first, high water prevented their crossing, but eventually they were able to cross on horseback or in wagons. The natives did not seem to be interested in crossing the Kansas River at the rocky ford or setting up camp. In one account, it was Lucille who took the lead across the river and started to clear away the head-high prairie grass in order to get tents set up for shelter.[285] There were two half-finished buildings on the site for the new mission, but they lacked "windows, doors, and floors, and any conveniences," according to Gailland, and they started to make them habitable. They were handicapped by the absence of Jesuit brother Andrew Mazzella, a skilled builder, who was ill and had stayed behind at Mission Creek.[286] There was

[282] Garraghan 2, p. 604.

[283] No reason for her being in Westport is given, but it was the place where they collected mail. Lucille's account is found in a letter in the Archives' special Collection: Potawatomi Mission box 10; also mentioned in Gailland's diary. Was she there to purchase supplies as well as collect mail? Westport was the supply stop for wagon trains heading to points west such as California, Oregon and down the Santa Fe Trail.

[284] Garraghan 2, p. 604. Father Gailland, who arrived for a few days before the move out of Sugar Creek, was welcomed by Christian Hoecken with joy, as he was the only priest who knew Potawatomi. Maurice Gailland immediately started to learn the language "During my short stay with Rev Father Hoecken, I applied myself to learn the first rudiments of the Indian language, and attended the daily instructions he gave to his little flock. At first the sounds of the words appeared to me very strange and difficult, but by degrees, and as I commenced understanding it a little, it became daily easier and smoother to my mind, and I found it to my great astonishment a rich and expressive though an uncultivated language. Its great defect is its paucity of words to express abstract ideas."

[285] Letter from Ellen Craney who lived at Saint Marys with Lucille at the end of her life. Louise Callan (RSCJ Archives, Callan Collection XII Ministry files Box 10) interprets the behavior of the natives as "lazy" but of course, this could also reflect their lack of interest in once again starting over in a new place and building everything again.

[286] Garraghan 2, p. 605 translated from Gailland's original diary written in Latin. Mazzella later joined them and spent many years at Saint Marys.

only an Indian trading post near the new site, but within two years there would be over fifty buildings, including fourteen stores. Here the Potawatomi would come to the office of the Indian agent to receive their annual annuity from the U.S. government as part of the treaty agreements. The soil was good, described as a rich black loam "so fat that if you tickled it, it would break into laughter."[287] Lucille enthusiastically described the area as an "earthly paradise for beauty of scenery, fertility of soil, abundance of fish and game. Of the latter there are wild ducks, turkeys, quail, and prairie chickens."[288]

Despite Lucille's good example and the start of building, many of the Indians stayed on the south side of the river at Mission Creek and Wakarusa Creek. Initially there were only three Indian families living around the mission. There had been other natives settled around the area, but they had been scared off by Pawnee raids in June and had not returned.[289] In mid-October, Christian Hoecken arrived after closing the settlement at Mission Creek. He brought with him natives who settled around the new mission; and there was hope that the others, seeing there was no longer danger, would return. As late as 1850, apparently about half of the Sugar Creek migrants were still camped on the south side of the river, and some were even still living at Sugar Creek.[290]

Building was finished on a two-story log house with five rooms near the creek in the west for the religious, and one hundred ten yards to the east was a similar residence for the Jesuits. On September 17, they put a cross on a hill overlooking the house to mark the mission; and in between the two dwellings, they built a chapel, which served the RSCJ, the Jesuits, and the mission population. The first recorded baptism there was performed in October. Eventually, the RSCJ's building was expanded on the arrival of Andrew Mazzella to include an assembly hall. The priests did not expand their building until 1865, but they erected a small log school house in 1849.[291]

---

[287] O'Connor, p. 59.

[288] Callan, *North America*, p. 294.

[289] Garraghan 2, pp. 610ff.

[290] *Ibid.* pp. 615f.

[291] *Ibid.* pp. 611ff.

Mission Church (KSHS)

Given the limited space, the two schools first accepted only five boarders each. When one of the students ran away, another quickly took his or her place. The girls participated in the domestic work of the house, and the boys helped with hunting.[292] The first students appear to have been Métis because the first full-blooded Indian was admitted in the spring. At Sugar Creek, the RSCJ had conducted a day school and also had boarders, but the Jesuits still had only a day school. At Saint Mary's they were able to open a boarding school. The Indians seemed much more willing to send their girls rather than their boys to the boarding school, and it was not until late in the mission's history that the boys' school enrollment equaled or surpassed that of the girls. In his visits to the different Indian settlements, Christopher Hoecken encouraged the parents to send their children to the school. There were soon forty-five to fifty girls in the Sacred Heart school. Despite the fact that half of the natives were not Catholic, Lucille says that "they are the very ones who often bring us their children."[293] The RSCJ also participated in adult religious instruction and in the next year prepared eighty-five Indian girls and women for Baptism and First Communion.[294]

At this same time, there appeared to be rivalry between the mission schools and that of the Baptists who had

---

[292] O'Connor, p. 262.

[293] Callan, North America, p. 294.

[294] Ibid. p. 295.

begun a school south of the river. Tribal divisions were reflected in the choice of schools, with families divided[295] between those who favored the mission school and those, some of them the more traditional Indians who had differences with the Catholic missionaries, who sent their children to the Baptist school. This division between the Mission Indians who were Catholic and those who became known as the Prairie Band of Potawatomi (traditionalists or, as the missionaries called them, "pagans") would continue throughout the history of the mission. The government would eventually support two schools—one Catholic and the other Baptist The rivalry between the schools was complicated, not only by the tribal differences but also by anti-Catholic, anti-foreigner and anti-Jesuit attitudes in both subsequent directors of the Baptist school and government agents. In a hostile report in 1849, a representative of the Baptist school referred to schools with "foreign influence," which no doubt meant the Jesuits and the RSCJ, who were mostly not U.S. born. This also may have reflected the "nativist," anti-immigrant sentiments of the time.[296]

The winter of 1848-1849 was especially severe. The river froze solid for eight weeks so that horses and wagons could cross well into February. Gailland found that the ink in his pen had frozen. On Sunday, December 24, the Jesuit records report that there was no sermon because of the cold, and they were unable to have midnight Mass. The mission priests each just celebrated a Mass on Christmas day.[297] The donations from other houses helped the RSCJ, who mention receiving linen, sugar, coffee, and rice from Saint Michael's and cash donations from other houses.[298] The priests missed the presence of Christian Hoecken[299] who had left in November with a party of Indians going to make maple sugar. One of the things lacking in the new mission was the sugar maple, of which they had had an abundance at Sugar Creek.

The *Annual Letters* of the Society that year reported that Lucille was at her wits end trying to obtain food for the community and pupils. In November 1848, Louise Amiot baked everyone a small hoe cake a day from

---

[295] Such as the Bourassa brothers; see Garraghan 2, pp. 623f. "The Baptist school drew chiefly from the Prairie Potawatomi, at least so Agent Murphy reported. Doctor Lykens's report of 1850 classifies the (Baptist school) pupils as six Chippewa, ten Ottawa and thirty-four Potawatomi. The school register for this or a closely subsequent year carries the names Bourassa, Beaubien and Darling (Ottawa), Petelle (Chippewa), Bertrand, Burnet, Laframboise and Wilmet (Potawatomi). Four Wilmets, Esther, Charlotte, Mary and Archange are entered. All of these are names also found in the mission student population." The Baptist school was never as numerous and closed and then reopened in mid-50's, closed later in 1858 and then during the Civil War. Some of the students were from the mission since the teacher asked for some French Bibles for her students in 1849. The differences may have begun earlier when part of the band that came to Sugar Creek settled at Saint Joseph's or Potawatomi Creek. Some people who had differences with the missionaries or grievances against them settled there. Although the Jesuits visited Potawatomi Creek, the majority of the population resisted conversion and remained traditional.

[296] O'Connor, pp. 106-7.

[297] Garraghan 2, p. 612.

[298] Callan, North America, p. 295.

[299] He appears to have been the most fluent preacher. Father Verreydt needed to use an interpreter.

the sack of corn meal she had brought, supplemented with venison killed by the Indians. An Indian told Lucille of a supply of pumpkins they could have if they could get the means to procure them. Mary Anne O'Connor, accompanied by several of the older Indian girls, went ten miles in a wagon to gather the windfall. The letter remarks that the "proffered luxury would serve as their only food." Lucille showed her creativity in making a sort of stocking for the chickens that prevented them from being frostbitten. She described how the snow covered the beds of the RSCJ and how the water in their drinking cups froze. She seems to have been a one woman campaign against the dirt of the frontier. She was the person who bathed and deloused the new pupils when they arrived. On weekends she was part of the effort to wash clothes and bedding. The records do not elaborate on how this task was accomplished in the dead of winter.[300] Although the natives also suffered from the cold that first Christmas, Maurice Gailland writes "that their faces were bright and cheerful despite the distressing conditions in which they had perforce to live; moreover, they brought the missionaries a timely New Year's gift in the shape of a quantity of venison."[301] Delighting him even further was the return of Christian Hoecken from the sugaring expedition.

Adding to the suffering from the cold was an outbreak of cholera in February. That disease was at its height by June, and classes had to be dismissed.[302] During the years of the mission, periodic outbreaks of disease and resulting class closures were reported. Some diseases were ones for which the natives had little immunity, measles and small pox. Others, such as cholera or typhoid, were spread by passing travelers bound for farther west. The discovery of gold in California the previous January had sparked traffic that spread disease along the Oregon Trail[303] from 1849 to 1855. Aided by some medical training Hoecken and Mazzella used the medicines at their disposal and consulted medical texts to care for the students.

At the end of September 1849 the vice provincial of the Jesuits, John Elet, and Pierre De Smet visited and were welcomed by the natives with drums and musket fire. This visit motivated some of the Indians who had settled on the south side of the river to cross over. Elet threw a barbecue for the Indians and the students on October 10. No mention is made of the RSCJ—were they in attendance, or did scruples about cloister prevent them? Elet instructed Christian Hoecken to build chapels for some of the outlying Indian settlements and to enlarge the Jesuit house so that they would have a refectory separate from that of the students, as well as to build more space for the school. When he left, he took Felix Verreydt with him, and shortly afterward Jean Baptiste Duerinck was sent as superior of the mission. Duerinck was forty and had great energy for his task, as well as skill as an administrator.

---

[300] *Lettres Annuelles*, 1849/50 and memoir at her death in 1876, typewritten English translation in RSCJ Provincial Archives, Potawatomi Mission, Box 2.

[301] Garraghan 2 (quoted p. 613) notes that the cold strained Gailland's Latin; he tried to find adjectives to describe it.

[302] Both Hoecken and Brother Mazzella had some medical training and served as mission doctors.

[303] It passed in front of the mission – identified today as the old Oregon Trail Route, an extension of West Missouri Road that parallels route 24 passing in front of the former mission before bending to the right on the way out of town.

He threw himself energetically into what he perceived as the task of "civilizing" the native students and teaching them to farm as well as evangelizing them.

Christian Hoecken like Pierre De Smet was a quintessential "Blackrobe" who filled the native culture's ideal of a "medicine man" since he was both a healer and a religious leader. A sense of his power can be seen in this tribute from one of the natives years later:

> Without interfering with the duties of his mission and [his duties] to God, he was among the Indians in their sports and hunts; and in the spring, when the Indians helped one another to plant corn, the most industrious figure in the crowd was the Jesuit Father, with a large plantation hoe, an apron sack full of seed corn and a big Dutch pipe in his mouth. He came, indeed, to teach the Indians civilization. He owned one yoke of oxen, poorly kept, going the rounds from one family to another to do the breaking up. It is said that he was charitable to an excessive degree. Being in the company of Indians so much, he spoke their language with the fluent ease of a native.[304]

Tragedy stuck in 1851 when this Jesuit pioneer, a strong friend of the Potawatomi, died of cholera, caught while traveling with Pierre De Smet to an Indian council in the far west. They were on a river boat and only 500 miles from Saint Louis, when the sickness struck and passengers starting dying. Christian Hoecken tried to use his medical skills to care for the sick and minister to the dying, when he himself fell victim to the illness.[305]

Maurice Gailland's diary is full of stories about both cholera and measles epidemics and their effect on the both the mission and surrounding settlers. Later in the decade during the building of Fort Riley, a plague struck again, and one hundred men died in ten days, including the Fort's commander. Before he died the commander sent a messenger to the mission asking for a priest to tend the dying. One hundred and fifty workmen deserted the fort, as well as the only doctor, who fled with his family to Saint Marys. (He was later court-martialed for his desertion.) The priest went to the fort, where his presence and sacramental ministrations encouraged those who remained and resulted in two conversions. When the priest went back to the mission, the grateful workers took up a collection and made a donation of $160.[306]

The Jesuit resources were stretched thin, and they were constantly being approached by other tribes with requests for similar services. Local Jesuit superiors were always shorthanded and begged for more personnel, lamenting that many promising missionaries were being used instead as teachers in other Jesuit schools.[307] When Christian Hoecken died, Maurice Gailland took his place in both ministry and in the hearts of the mission Indians. He had big shoes to fill, but until his death he was able to minister from the heart to his charges.

---

[304] Garraghan quoting *The Indian Advocate,* July 1890, cited in *Dial* (St. Marys, Kansas), March 1891.

[305] Garraghan 2, pp. 626-29 for a firsthand account of his death.

[306] O'Connor pp. 226-227.

[307] *Ibid.* chapter 29, p. 6.

In one of the villages Gailland had announced to the assembled Indians the news of their pastor's death, but as he was fatigued with travel he called upon an Indian catechist to address the congregation in his place. The catechist, having delivered a eulogy on Father Hoecken, added by way of exhortation, 'Our Father is dead—but another one has taken his place. Now you ought to look upon him as also your Father, we should have for him the same respect that we had for the other. He is deputed by the same Master, Jesus Christ, who has deputed both one and the other. The deputy has changed, not so the one who sent him or the prayers they taught us.'[308]

Gailland believed in visiting his people often, feeling that conversion results not from sermons "but solely by frequent visits and repeated proofs of friendship."[309]

The Jesuits and RSCJ sincerely felt that their educational project would help the Potawatomi survive in the world of farming and commerce that was engulfing them. They soon realized the model of a "reduction" in the style of Paraguay was not practical. In that model the natives, living in an isolated and protected settlement, far from the influence and corruption of the "white" world, would have been gradually introduced to western ways and allowed to adapt to them at their own pace. There was not enough time and the wave of settlers coming west was too great and would soon engulf them. In a letter to the Propagation of the Faith, Maurice Gailland celebrated the success of their efforts with the mission Indians. He had warned the natives that it is the Great Spirit who commands them to labor:

> The Great Spirit expects from them an absolute renunciation of their savage customs, that unless they show themselves obedient unto His voice, their lot will still remain deplorable, that the American government will refuse them the right of citizenship and continue to drive them back from their states, until at length their race will become entirely extinct.[310]

Despite his love for his people, he was unable to see that it was their culture that would enable them to survive and resist extinction. He was unable to realize that the goals of the government and those of the missionaries were not completely compatible. Until the 1880s, when government boarding schools became the norm, U.S. policy promoted and funded local religiously based schools. Civilization and Christianization seemed interchangeable. However, the values of acquisition and individualism promoted by the push to individual land ownership and abandonment of tribal membership worked against what the missionaries had been promoting—the values of sharing, caring for others and respect for personal dignity.[311]

---

[308] *Ibid.* 2, p. 631.

[309] O'Connor, p. 158.

[310] Garraghan 2, p. 632.

[311] *Encyclopedia of the North America Indian,* pp. 176-77, on Education and Goals of Euro-American culture.

The most successful members of the Potawatomi community engaged in commerce, not farming. In particular, the Métis members, perhaps because of their French trader traditions, set up businesses that were successful such as ferries, mills, inns and trading posts. The influx of people heading farther west provided customers. These same travelers traded household goods that they realized were superfluous: tables, pianos, bedsteads for more practical items for the journey ahead. Some native families' homes boasted items that would have fit into comfortable homes any place in the country. A lively trade in horses and cattle between the westward settlers and the mission Potawatomi also benefited local families.[312]

In 1849-50, the RSCJ community was composed of only five members: Lucille Mathevon, Mary Anne O'Connor, Julie Bazire,[313] serving as class mistresses, Mary Layton and Louise Amiot who were cooks. Julie Bazire[314] left after one year and was replaced by Julia Deegan, age twenty-five, a native of Callan, Kilkenny, Ireland, born in 1825.[315] Her death notice mentions that she immigrated to Saint Louis with her parents who were devout Catholics. In the 1840 U.S. census, there is a P. Deegan (Dugan) running a boarding house for canal workers in Saint Louis, but there is no indication he had a wife or children living with him. Local records indicate that a Patrick Deegan, who signed a petition in 1842, was from Kilkenny; perhaps he is this boarding house keeper from the census.[316]

Julia entered in 1849 in Saint Louis. That year Saint Louis was struck by a plague of cholera that was blamed on incoming famine immigrants. Did her family arrive during this difficult time? Were her parents deceased? In the 1850 U.S. census there are several Deegan families and the heads would be of the right age to be her siblings.

---

[312] R. David Edmunds "Indians as Pioneers: Potawatomis on the Frontier" *Chronicle of Oklahoma* #651, Winter 1987-88, pp. 340-353. He traces this aptitude for commerce to their French Creole roots as fur traders.

[313] Julia Bazire had a rather tumultuous life in the Society, serving while quite young as superior in American houses but eventually returning to England and later her native France where she appears to have died in an asylum in 1883. She was one of a number of RSCJ who were at the mission for only a year.

[314] Callan, *Philippine Duchesne*, p.702, quotes from a letter of Philippine to Amélie Jouve, writing about the work at the Potawatomi mission, "Mother Bazire found her work there distasteful, as has been the case in Saint Louis and Opelousas. They fear no place will satisfy her except France."

[315] A search of Kilkenny records was unsuccessful for her baptism although it may be too early, Around 1848-49 there were two Deegan families in Callan, Jeremiah, living on Mill and John on Flag Lane, although her family may have left before this record was taken (Griffins Valuation) these may be related to them.

[316] Census for Patrick has male inhabitants and one female slave. Two Missouri death records exist for a Patrick Deegan and the most likely for him is a man who died January 17, 1857, age forty-five, with a birth date of about 1812. Patrick Deegan might have been, like Julia, from Kilkenny. (Saint Louis Genealogical Society database lists a Patrick from Kilkenny who joined the Irish Repeal Association sometime in the 1840's).

Missouri death records and interment records have several older Deegans, but there is no indication when they arrived in the U.S.[317]

Julia arrived in 1850 at Saint Mary's when she was still a choir novice. Despite her youth, Julia was a class mistress and must have had some formal education either in the U.S. or in Ireland. She spent practically all of her religious life in Kansas, making her first vows there in 1851 and her final profession in 1860. She served as a teacher of English to the youngest students and helped in the parish or "poor" school.[318] Her motto was "*Ne rien demander, ne rien refuser*" (Ask nothing, refuse nothing). Toward the end of her life, she spent long hours in solitude in the infirmary. She died December 20, 1873, conscious to the end, after a three year lingering illness.[319] She was the first RSCJ to be buried in the new cemetery on the school grounds where the bodies of Louise and Mary Anne had been transferred from their original resting place near the mission chapel in 1869.

In 1849-50, Mary Layton was still the cook, but Louise Amiot is listed in the Society catalog as class mistress as well as working in the house. Another Irish immigrant, Sister Bridget Barnwell, age forty-two, from Urlingford, Kilkenny,[320] entered in 1843 at Saint Charles as a coadjutrix sister. She did not have as much education as Julia and could read but not write.[321] Bridget had lived with Philippine and been inspired by her. Her prized possession was a letter from Philippine that she wore in a pouch around her neck. She seems to have gotten the love of the natives from Philippine. She was loved by them and sometimes honored by receiving the gift of a scalp, which she accepted and then buried without question. She was known also to feed hungry Indians from the food she was cooking for the community.[322] Bridget made her final profession at Saint Mary's Mission and stayed until the closing of the mission in 1879. In her death notice, it was remarked that, besides her skill at cooking, she

---

[317] One problem is that Deegan can be spelled Deagan and sometimes Dugan, making identification of families difficult in the 1850 census.

[318] In the United States, the term "poor" school was not used, as it was in France. Philippine saw the title as alienating parents and keeping children away from the school in America. See Mooney, Catherine, *Philippine Duchesne*, who discusses this at length in section on cultural differences, pp. 126f.

[319] The illness is not identified but from the description, it might have been tuberculosis.

[320] Society register says Hurlingford, but this is incorrect as there is no town of this name in Kilkenny. Urlingford is in west Kilkenny on the border of Tipperary, not too far from Callan where Julia was born. For some reason in the 1855 Kansas census, she is listed as Margaret.

[321] According to some historians, this may indicate she was educated in a hedge school in Ireland where sometimes writing was not taught because of lack of materials, but students did learn to read. Other coadjutrix sisters from Ireland who arrived later could read and write, as did Mary Layton, but a few like Bridget could only read. (1870 census)

[322] Callan, *North America*, p. 302. This practice may have led to the later rebuke of visiting vicars about allowing strangers in the kitchen.

had a special gift for dealing with poultry and livestock. She was also said to have used the letter of Philippine in healing people.[323]

The three coadjutrix sisters had to milk the cows, care for the poultry, cook and bake for both community and students. It was logical that all of the religious needed to pitch in and help with the care of the house and students. Lucille was especially active "hoeing, weeding, gathering fruit or vegetables, carrying food to the cattle and swine…."[324] Since the school included both boarders and day students, those who taught were also trying to cover all of the classes, stretching their time and resources.[325] In 1855, Sister Amiot was still trying to supervise the work of the day students as well as work in the vestry and infirmary.

Painting of Mission (Jesuit Archives)

The sisters were used to receiving help from the students in these tasks. Indeed, it was probably part of the students' training. Some of that instruction would logically be done by the coadjutrix sisters who were skilled in these areas. There are mentions of the girls working in the laundry, caring for the livestock, milking the cows, and churning the butter. Occasionally the students still decided to wander away, and one sister writes:

> … (they) escaped our vigilance. It was not a rare occurrence after many hours of search to find twenty of them in the woods, sitting in a straight line in perfect order, and perfectly tranquil, so that it was impossible to even make them change their positions, until the fancy took them, when they all left as if by enchantment and suddenly returned to the house. Sometimes one of the Jesuit brothers was obliged to go out on horseback to look for them and to drive them back before him like a flock of sheep.[326]

Although Saint Marys, Kansas, even today, appears to be out in the middle of nowhere, U.S. Route 24, which passes in front, parallels the track of the Oregon Trail. Many wagon loads of settlers bound farther west passed in front of the simple two-story log buildings and wooden church. The travelers brought disease and crime to the town, but the sick cattle they abandoned augmented the small herd of cattle kept by the Jesuits when they were

---

[323] Notes of Marie Louise Martinez.

[324] *Ibid.*

[325] Schroeder mentions that they took double classes to cover them all.

[326] Monzert, p 1.

nursed back to health.[327] Some of the mission Indians built up a herd of cattle by trading ponies to the travelers for them. The mission augmented its income by selling provisions to the passing wagon trains. Ferries across the river were lucrative. Many settlers willingly paid the $5.00 toll, and one observer counted 700 wagons lined up at one ferry to cross.[328] The mission also lost population to the drive west after gold was discovered in California. Lucille mentions that a good number of the Métis were lured to the mines by reports that thousands of dollars could be earned in a short time. They went, leaving their families behind, on what was a two-month journey, hoping to return rich. She does not give the outcome, but it is likely that few returned and many disappeared, never to return.[329]

In 1851, the area, previously part of the diocese of Saint Louis, received its first bishop, John Baptist Miège, SJ. After he was appointed, his fellow Jesuits persuaded him to make his diocesan headquarters in Saint Marys. When he arrived hundreds of Indians greeted him in traditional fashion with displays of horsemanship and handshakes. The church was designated the pro-cathedral of Saint Mary (later the Immaculate Conception). Despite the impressive title, it was still the simple log church of the mission. His diocese was immense, stretching from the Missouri River to the Rockies and from the Red River in the south to the Canadian border in the north.[330] The new bishop was well suited to the frontier, traveling by horseback with his gun throughout his diocese, camping on the trail. Throughout his time as bishop, he traveled all over his immense diocese and was described by some fellow travelers, whose camp he stumbled upon, as tall and muscular, with an unshaven beard, a summer linen coat, and a gun over his shoulder.[331]

Despite their location on the frontier the community managed to celebrate Holy Week and Easter that year with all the pomp and circumstance of any parish in larger cities. About the same time that Bishop Miège arrived,

---

[327] Joseph Karol, SJ, "Church by the Trail," *Jesuit Bulletin* 1954, pp. 5-7. RSCJ Archives, Potawatomi Mission Box 2 folder 3 #11, "Something of Old Saint Marys."

[328] Edmunds, p. 349.

[329] Lucille Mathevon, Letter 1850. RSCJ Archives, Potawatomi Mission Box 2 folder 1 item I (also mentioned in O'Connor,)

[330] Perhaps both the size of his diocese and the immense task of financing it were reasons that Bishop Miège tried to resign four times, beginning in 1858 until he finally succeeded in 1874. Garraghan, *Jesuits of the Middle United States*, 3, pp. 4-5. See also 2, pp. 640f. As a Jesuit, he was allowed by his superiors to become a bishop because of the great need on the frontier. He did not want to accept the office; he was young, inexperienced and still had not made his final profession as a Jesuit. He tried to avoid the appointment, but church officials told him he was obliged to do so in holy obedience.

[331] Quoted in Garraghan 3, p. 16 note 23. The travelers were at first afraid of the stranger who came upon their campsite but were put at ease when he informed them he was their bishop.

two of the Indian girls went to Saint Louis with the intention of entering the Sacred Heart novitiate. No record remains of these women but it appears that they did not stay.[332]

Bishop Miège went to Rome, accompanied by the pioneer missionary Pierre De Smet in 1854, and he returned (despite a shipwreck on the way) bringing sacred vessels and items for the church as well as rosaries and medals for the Indians that had been blessed by the Pope. Saint Mary's Church acquired a bell, an organ, which delighted the natives, and a painting of the Immaculate Conception. "They were lost in wonder at the organ, for its mechanism was so simple that anyone who reads ordinary numbers, might, with little practice, produce a very pleasing harmony."[333] During this time at Saint Marys, many adults became Catholics; four hundred of them received Confirmation, and many children were baptized and received First Communion. However, in 1855 Miège moved the headquarters of his diocese to the town of Leavenworth on the Missouri River. Although it had few Catholics at the time, and no church, he felt it had more potential than Saint Marys, both for growth and for fast communication.

Lucille, Louise, and Bridget Barnwell still found bloody scalps at their doorsteps, which they accepted and buried. They took the practice, intended as a tribute, in stride, no matter what personal horror they might have felt. They must have felt the tensions as a result of the stories of war parties, raiding parties, and conflict between the tribes. The raids on the mission were usually not violent and resulted only in the theft of ponies. In 1852, the settlement was in turmoil because of rumor of an impending Pawnee raid. So many villagers decided to take refuge at the mission that "there was scarcely room to stand much less to move about. Even the Sacred Heart nuns caught the panic and, had the Fathers permitted it, would have made their general confessions in expectation of being tomahawked that very night."[334] Later that year the Potawatomi caught some Pawnee who were attempting to steal ponies. They were on the point of executing them when Maurice Gailland intervened and persuaded them to release the men. He told them that it was their duty as Christians and suggested that they invite the Pawnee chiefs to visit and to send their children to the mission school. He saw this act as the beginning of the conversion of the Pawnee. He also predicted that the alliance the Pawnee formed with the Potawatomi would aid the tribe as it hunted farther and farther west where they encountered more hostile tribes.[335]

---

[332] A check of novices for the period does not show any girls who fit, although there is one from Kansas and one from Illinois but both appear to be Irish. At least two girls from Saint Mary's Mission entered the Society in the 1870's and stayed (Johanna Hanrahan and Ann Caplice) but neither was Indian. Johanna entered in Kansas. In a letter of April 1852 Philippine tells Sophie that there are three Indian women who might make good candidates and suggests having a novitiate for such candidates in Kansas.

[333] O'Connor, p. 142. The picture of the Immaculate Conception was almost kidnapped by the rector of Saint Louis University who, when he saw it while it was on route to the mission, tried to keep it for the college in Saint Louis.

[334] *Ibid.* p. 88. One senses the good Jesuits had their hands full with the refugees without hearing nuns' confessions!

[335] *Ibid.* p. 92.

Boys in front of Saint Mary's Mission School, c. 1868 (Wiki Commons)

As a result of the ensuing peace, four Pawnee chiefs visited the school and were given a grand tour of the boys' school, where they were astonished that a study hall would contain eighty boys in order and quiet under the care of only one person. They were given a demonstration during a history and a catechism class of how learning worked, with the students reading and answering questions.

> The Pawnee chiefs marveled at how (the students) could read one another's thoughts by means of a book… they were informed that…a Pawnee chief could put his thoughts on a piece of paper in his own country and send it to the Pottawatomie [sic] chiefs at Saint Marys and the latter could read exactly the mind of the former.[336]

Eager to try this new technology, the chiefs picked up a book to see if it would talk to them but could not read it, and then they realized that the book really did not literally speak. They were equally entranced by the clock that the school used to tell when it was time to eat. It would be interesting to know if they thought the clock would be as useful as the book, since their own stomachs probably were as accurate as the clock in predicting the time to eat. They might have been surprised that the school children would eat at fixed times rather than when they were hungry as they did. The visit appears to have been a success since the Pawnee smoked the pipe of peace with the Potawatomi and shortly after sent thirty of their boys to the mission school.

The fears of the villagers and the RSCJ were well founded, for still there were clashes with other tribes. One reported by the Indian agent occurred in 1853 where Potawatomi warriors took scalps:

---

[336] *Ibid*. p. 94. Father Gailland told them that as a horse needed to be broken in order to be ridden their minds needed to be broken in order to read. Not the best analogy!

while out on their summer hunt (they) came in contact with the mountain Indians, and after a hard-fought battle, lasting more than half a day, succeeded in putting them to flight, leaving some twenty or thirty of their dead on the battle field. At least the Pottawatomies brought in about that number of scalps, over which they have been dancing for the last month. I learn from various sources that the mountain Indians came down expressly for the purpose of having a fight with the frontier Indians. They first came in contact with the Pawnees, and but for the timely aid of the Pottawatomies (who happened to be but a few miles off) would have killed to the last one, as they had them surrounded and had killed some ten or fifteen before the Pottawatomies reached the scene of action. All parties give the Pottawatomies great credit for their gallant conduct on that occasion. They lost in killed and wounded some four or five. From the best information I can get, the frontier Indians are not to blame, as they were fighting in self-defense. We anticipate a renewal of hostilities next summer if they should meet on the plains.[337]

From the same year as this raid there were two visitors who wrote their more peaceful impressions of Saint Mary's Mission. Visitor John C. Fremont[338] wrote:

In the fall of 1853 on an overland journey I spent a day at the Catholic station of St Mary's on the Kansas River among the Pottawattamie Indians. Under the impression of what I saw, I wrote then in my note-book as follows: October 25, Went to Uniontown…a street of log cabins. Nothing to be had here. Some corn for our animals and a piece of cheese for ourselves. Lots of John Barleycorn, which the men about were consuming…. October 26: High wind and sleet. Clouds scudding across the sky. About two o'clock we reached the pretty little Catholic Mission of St Mary's. The well-built, white-washed houses with the cross on the spire showing out above them was already a very grateful sight. On the broad bottoms immediately below are the fields and houses of the Pottawatamie [sic] Indians. Met with a hospitable reception from the head of the Mission [Jean Baptiste Duerinck]. A clear sky promises a bright day for tomorrow. Learned here some of the plants which are medicinal among the Indians. Among them *Asarum Canadense*—jewel weed—a narcotic, and *Oryngium Aquaticum,* the great remedy of the Pottawatamies [sic] for snakebites.[339] October 27: White frost covers the ground this morning. Sky clear and air still. With bowls of good coffee and excellent bread, made a good breakfast We already begin to appreciate food. Prepared our luggage, threw into the wagon the provisions obtained here and at ten o'clock took leave of the hospitable priests and set out. I was never more impressed by the efficiency of well-directed and permanent missionary effort than here at this far-off mission settlement, where the progress and good order strike forcibly as they stand in great contrast with the neighboring white settlement [Uniontown].[340]

---

[337] Connelley pp. 500f.

[338] He was a military officer, explorer, writer about the West, presidential candidate, military governor and state senator from the new state of California. He had passed at least 5 times through this area beginning in the early 1840's when he travelled with the scout Kit Carson on the way to California and Oregon.

[339] Duerinck had training as a botanist and probably was the person who informed Fremont.

[340] John Charles Fremont, *Memoirs of My Life* (Chicago, 1887), p 28 quoted in Garraghan 2, pp. 693-94.

Max Greene, another less famous traveler from the East, wrote how the very name, Saint Mary's, lent a poetic charm to the wilderness.

> Near the last named locality stands the Catholic Mission, a not ineffective institution. Its farms are in a flourishing condition. This is known as St Mary, the one golden word of poesy, sacred in art as in religion and beautiful wherever the beautiful is adored. It is meet that the chime of Sabbath bells should give the music of that holy name to the winds in those establishments, into which the whole of the Indian pension money finds its way. Gaudy patterns of flimsy calico, rating as high as the richest satin, saddles, bridles and spurs of the very commonest kind fetching a higher price than padded quilted articles of the same manufacture, and beads, rings, whistles, and little looking-glasses, all selling on the same rates. They give them out on credit till the quarter-day comes around, when the poor Indian punctually hands over his pension to those unconscionable harpies.[341]

Jean Baptiste Duerinck, superintendent of the Catholic Manual Labor School,[342] had this to say of the natives:

> The peace and harmony of this settlement is now seldom disturbed by war parties or alarming reports of invasion. The Pawnees have formerly been accused of stealing our horses, but no complaints have lately been heard on that score. Our Indians have this summer smoked peace with them whilst on a buffalo hunt in the upper country. The Pottawatomie [sic] Prairie Indians have not yet laid aside their wild and uncivilized mode of living; they are averse to work and live in wretched cabins and wigwams. They paint their faces and delight in all sorts of motley and fantastical dress and trappings. They are unfortunately addicted to liquor. Some unprincipled whites and half-breeds, too lazy to work, sell them whisky and cheat the intoxicated dupes out of their horses and ponies, and even out of their guns and blankets.[343]

In 1852 the U.S. government decided to establish a fort on the Oregon Trail about fifty miles west of the mission that came to be known as Fort Riley. This fort was designed to protect travelers on the way through Indian Territory from hostile natives and later became the headquarters of the U.S. Cavalry. While the principal task was to keep native people from attacking the wagon trains, it later became the local peace keeper between settlers. Mule trains, often more than fifty wagons long, would have passed by the mission bringing building supplies and workers as the population of the fort grew and its buildings expanded. Despite the distance from the mission, it appears that the priests there were called on to serve the fort population. In the summer of 1854, there

---

[341] Max Greene, *The Kanzas Region* (New York, 1856), pp. 45f.

[342] Jesuit superior quoted in O'Connor.

[343] Connelley, p. 498-499 available at http://www.kansasheritage.org/PBP/books/kshsroll/kshs_02.html. He is contrasting the mission Indians to their fellow Potawatomi who resisted conversion so perhaps should be taken with a grain of salt. His comments do point to the ongoing problem of alcohol abuse and the greed of the settlers.

is a record that Jean Baptiste Duerinck officiated at the marriage of a couple at Fort Riley, so the Jesuits appear to have extended their pastoral work to the fort.[344]

On June 28, 1854 the *New York Tribune* published an article about the mission in which the writer gives a view of the life there:

> Sermons are preached every Sunday, in Indian and English. The manual labor school is under their charge, assisted by eight lay brothers, and is in a flourishing condition. The number of boys admitted from October 1, 1852, till September, 1853, was seventy-seven, and the average number in attendance was fifty-two. The female department is under the charge of the "Ladies of the Sacred Heart"--a community of seven in number, three Ladies and four Sisters, who devote all their time to the school. The number of girls admitted from October 1, 1852, to September, 1853, was ninety-two, and the average attendance during the four quarters was sixty-seven. This missionary establishment enjoys great popularity among the Indians. Its site is said to be the loveliest spot in the Indian country. The mission buildings, with the adjacent trading houses, groups of Indian improvements and extensive corn-fields, all give it the appearance of a town. The mission farm is large, and more than one hundred acres are under very profitable cultivation. The stock of horned cattle consists of 250 head, and these afford a considerable part of the support of the mission.[345]

Despite the success of both schools,[346] there was a strain on the finances on account of the small government allowance. At one point the Jesuit superior was threatening to close the boys' school because they were unable to meet all their expenses from the subsidy plus sale of farm products. A crop failure due to persistent drought may have contributed to their problems. Part of the effort to bring "civilization" to the Indians included skills training. Both the Jesuits who ran a boys' school and the RSCJ who ran the girls' academy introduced the Indian students to farm labor, animal husbandry, and manual skills (cooking, baking, carpentry, masonry). The produce of the farm was sold and became part of the income of both schools. The government, which initially gave $500 per year, increased the amount from $50 per student to $75, but that did still not cover the expense. There were about seventy to eighty girls in the school.[347]

Jean Baptiste Duerinck writes to the Indian agent of his admiration for the work of the RSCJ observing:

---

[344] Barry, "Kansas before 1854," (Summer, 1967) p 179, continuation of previous article.

[345] William Cutler, *History of the State of Kansas*, first published 1883 by A. T. Andreas, Chicago, Illinois, Kansas Historical Society, "Indian History" part 8 quote from *New York Tribune* article, no page numbers given; available on their website http://www.kancoll.org/

[346] Tardieu, Account of Saint Mary's Mission, written about 1872 but using earlier sources. RSCJ Archives, Potawatomi Mission box 2. It appears that the Sacred Heart school had more students (85) than did the Jesuits at this time (50-68). But counts of students vary greatly as can be seen from the previous paragraph.

[347] Monzert p. 1 (1852).

If you enter the house during the work hours, you will find the inmates all at work with order and regularity, detailed in small parties under a mistress—some sew or knit, some spin, some cook and eat, others wash, clean up the rooms, milk the cows in the yard, or work in the garden. If you meet them all in one of the rooms, you wonder at their number, as frequently eighty of them will rise at once to greet you. If you happen amongst them during their playtime, you will see them all merry and happy, full of innocent sport and mischief, which on account of their sweet humor is never taken amiss. These girls are of a tame and modest turn while at school, but when they grow up and return to their people, the young men find them very sociable, talkative, fond of dress, and yet of a stern character when [the men] foolishly presume to take undue liberties with them.[348]

Evidently, the RSCJ were producing spirited Sacred Heart girls at the mission.[349] The "plain English education" involved sitting in a classroom, but the training in "housewifery" involved more activity, and Duerinck noticed that the "girls are…active and ruddy, nimble on their feet, and their waists, free of hoops and bands, they deem it a favor to work in the garden, to cook, to wash with their playmates, to sew and to spin. The place is a real beehive of industry."[350]

A visiting agent in 1857 remarked about the girls school that

The neatness and cleanliness of the school yard and buildings at St. Mary's give to it an air of comfort that is the admiration of all passers-by The female department of this school is under the management of nine Sisters of the Sacred Heart, with Madame Lucille as superior, and is frequently visited by distinguished strangers, who, after seeing the amiable manners, cleanly appearance, and cheerful looks of the Pottawatomie girls, and the fine order, system, and regularity with which the school is conducted, not only express their approbation, but wonder at seeing so fine an institution of learning within an Indian reservation.[351]

---

[348] Garraghan 2, p. 664, quoting his report for 1856 – he urges the Indian agent to visit and see for himself.
[349] O Connor p. 103 describes the influx of young white men seeking mission school brides who were able to see through the designs of their courtship. One young lady left her groom at the altar when she discovered he had a wife back home.
[350] O'Connor, p. 152.
[351] Garraghan 2, pp. 673-74.

Mission with its white fence (Wiki commons)

The relationship with the natives, especially those who were not Catholics, started to change in the 1850s. Previously the Jesuits had the practice of handing out food, clothing, and other aid to any who stopped by the mission. When Duerinck took over as superior, he decided that this practice was encouraging dependence and worked against the missionaries' goal of promoting self-sufficiency. He restricted aid to "the deserving poor." For this he was labeled "hard hearted." This lack of generosity must have puzzled the Potawatomi. It went against their strong cultural norms, especially the value of hospitality.

There is no record of what the RSCJ thought or did.[352] It seems that they may have continued the practice of giving food, since having strangers in the kitchen was one of the faults for which superiors vicar later chided them. Ironically, the very practice of the U.S. government providing an annual annuity and free education had accustomed the natives to receiving sustenance in return for their ceding their lands. This policy worked against the stated goal of developing self-sufficiency.[353]

In a report of 1855, the Jesuit school announced a new policy that the parents could no longer constantly visit

---

[352] Callan, *North America* p. 302. Bridget Barnwell is remembered as someone who was generous with the mission food supplies to the natives to the extent that she gave away food meant for the community.

[353] Duerinck was an energetic businessman with a hand in all sorts of business besides farming, he invested in a mill, bought and sold real estate as far away as Leavenworth, developed the farm with latest equipment and arranged for the mission to enter into business with the U.S. army to supply them during the building of Fort Riley and later for the troops stationed there.

and must leave their students undisturbed for the term.[354] There is no record that the RSCJ publicized a similar policy, and even after 1855 it appears that the parents continued to visit as they pleased up through the end of the decade.[355]

Even to their friend Maurice Gailland, the native unwillingness to learn "white" standards of economy and saving for the future looked like "shiftlessness." In 1855 he writes (and unwittingly gives a description of the native cultural value that worked against their becoming property owners):

> The Indian has no care for the morrow; he feasts as long as he has anything to eat. When he has plenty he shares it with everyone, and soon gets through his supplies. Economy is hateful to him; for he considers it miserly to hoard up meat and provisions for himself, while his poorer neighbors come round begging a meal. Since then, they had brought this poverty on themselves by their improvidence…it were out of question and beyond our means to support the whole nation, we often took occasion to teach the lesson that they must see in their present sufferings the necessity of working more industriously to provide against another famine.[356]

Gailland evidently felt this practice was successful and spurred the natives to more economical practices. It is also possible, given their traditions, that the natives took care of their own. While he sounded tough, Gailland also sought aid from settlers to collect provisions for those suffering want. Continued drought in the area would plague their farming efforts to such an extent that the Jesuits organized special prayers for rain.[357]

Pierre De Smet, in 1858, remarked on their progress in the faith and in education and farming skills.[358] But he also recognized that the natives' resistance to learning agriculture had not been eradicated. The missionaries still interpreted this attitude as laziness. "The old and the young, the father and the son are all equally averse to work. An Indian is frequently heard to utter this foolish complaint, that it is a pity he cannot plow his corn in winter when the weather is cold rather than in summer when it is hot!"[359]

Neither the RSCJ nor the Jesuits appeared to have comprehended the importance of the communal life for the Potawatomi. Sharing all in common, something Philippine sensed on arrival at the mission, which she attributed to the influence of Christianity, actually was a strong native cultural value. The explorer Perrot gave a long description of the Potawatomi value of harmonious relationships within the tribe. He describes the compassionate sharing,

---

[354] Garraghan 2, p. 665.

[355] Schroeder. This policy would change in the 1860's as more settler students entered the school.

[356] O'Connor, pp. 223-24.

[357] *Ibid.* pp. 224-25. Their prayers are successful at least in the area of the mission but Gailland takes a certain perverse delight that rain then fell and nourished their crops while those of the "pagans, twenty miles from the Mission, burnt up with the summer heats."

[358] Karol has a drawing of the original schools and church from this period.

[359] O'Connor, pp. 96-97, remarks of Duerinck to the commissioner of Indian affairs in 1854.

the care of the sick, and the sense of equality. "Chiefs (are) on an equal footing with the poorest, even with the boys with whom they converse as they do with persons of discretion…rebukes are given with great mildness." [360]

Potawatomi people St. Mary's Mission (Wiki Commons)

The Jesuit records still contain stories of conversions of natives during this time, some of whom are moved to do so by dreams and visions. Within the culture of this tribe, there was a tradition of boys at ten years old fasting for a day and seeking a vision and for teenagers fasting for several days in the wilderness alone in order to receive guidance from their guardian spirit. It is interesting that in the records available from the Jesuit school most of their Indian students were under twelve, which may indicate that teens moved on when this vision quest began. The use of fasting and seeking of a vision appears to have worked also in favor of conversion in the adult population. The Jesuits continued the practice of requiring converts to sacrifice their medicine bundles. But they now had enough knowledge of Indian medicinal herbs to allow "keeping those (medicines) good for sick and casting all else in the fire."[361] That Protestant missionaries were active around the mission is witnessed by stories of natives' reaction to proselytizing in their midst[362]. One Methodist missionary engaged in dialogue with

---

[360] *Ibid.* pp. 136-37, describes how they handle crimes with the penalty set by the elders to avoid wholesale revenge.

[361] *Ibid.* pp. 121-22. Medicines often were used also for divination and to give success on the hunt. This policy may reflect Duerinck's interest in botany.

[362] From the earliest days of the mission in Sugar Creek, there were many Protestant missionary efforts among the native people in the Indian Territory. Louise Barry, "Kansas before 1854," *Revised Annals of the Kansas Historical Society,* Vol. 29, #4 (Winter, 1963) pp. 429f., mentions visits by Methodists to their schools as well as Episcopalians, Baptists and Quakers.

one of the chiefs whom he found reading the Bible. In the exchange that followed, the native demonstrated his knowledge of the Bible by quoting it back to the minister, noting that Jesus warned of false prophets who would come in the form of lambs but in reality would be wolves. He invited the minister and his wife to go elsewhere to less-educated Indians.[363]

Throughout the 1850s the RSCJ community would be more or less stable and never be more than eight or nine sisters. In the catalog of 1855–56, the RSCJ community was only nine, five choir religious: Lucille Mathevon, Mary Anne O'Connor, Bridget O'Neill, Elisabeth Schroeder, and Julia Deegan. The coadjutrix sisters were Louise Amiot, Mary Layton, Bridget Barnwell, Marguerite Mahuny (Mahoney) and a novice, Ellen Cahill. The RSCJ ranged in age from twenty-seven to seventy-two. Louise was already very ill and would die within the year. Ellen is also listed as infirm that year but would make her first vows and final profession at Saint Mary's in 1864. She evidently regained her strength and was the community baker by the end of the decade and also responsible for caring for the boarders' refectory and the infirmary. She stayed at Saint Mary's until 1868 and died in 1899 in Chicago.

The RSCJ wrote less about their observations of the natives and their culture than did the Jesuits, but Lucille did record her observation of native medicines. One of the boarders had to be sent home when she developed severe paralysis that medicine was unable to alleviate. Imagine the surprise of the RSCJ when the girl returned to them after a period at home. She had been treated with poultices of native herbs and completely restored. Lucille seems to have gained an appreciation for the usefulness of the Indians' knowledge of healing herbs from this and other experiences.[364] However, she still had recourse to American medical knowledge, as is seen by an incident involving Louise Amiot. In the early summer 1852, right after Louise Amiot made her final vows, Lucille took her on the long and arduous journey back to Saint Louis to consult a doctor about her "lung trouble." This involved taking a wagon

> over land without roads, being obliged to traverse forests, immense prairies, over a country almost uninhabited. One day the driver having strayed from the way, and after wandering about during a whole day seeing night approach…declared that he did not know where he was. The travelers [sic] were very much frightened; but they had to resign themselves to spending the night under the beautiful stars…in the cart… and their driver slept beneath…Mother Lucille covered the sister the best she could and tried to make her rest, but for herself, she prayed…all that long night to preserve them from savage beasts which abounded in those parts.[365]

---

[363] *Ibid.* p. 114.

[364] RSCJ Archives, Series XII C. Ministry file, Callan collection, Personal Papers, Box 10.

[365] Monzert p. 1. She also notes that the driver was drunk, perhaps accounting for his getting lost!

The journey took three weeks and included a stop in Saint Joseph, Missouri, where they stayed with a former pupil from Saint Louis. Was her illness tuberculosis? Two other of the religious buried at Saint Mary's would die of similar illnesses, one of which would be diagnosed as tuberculosis.[366]

William A. Thornton, a military officer traveling to New Mexico via the Santa Fe Trail, left this brief description of the approach to the mission along the Kansas River, the mission itself, and the territory just beyond it as they left. He gives a picture of what visitors to the mission might have seen and experienced. Like many travelers, his party was suffering from cholera, which was an ever present danger to the health of the mission. He also noticed evidence of an early land speculator in the area. Thornton probably did not stop at the mission since he was travelling on the opposite side of the river. On July 2, 1855, the day before he reached the mission he writes:

> Marched at 6 a.m. Morning cloudy and prospect of rain. Route S.W. 10 miles and west 6 miles on the left side of the Kansas River. The prairie on valley of the Kansas River about three miles wide. Beautiful locations. The ridges rise about 50 feet. It is here that Governor Reeder is said to own 1200 acres, purchased at 90 cents the acre. Encamped at noon at Cross Creek and had many others sick in our wagons. Day very warm without rain. Suffered much from burned lips. General health good. Afternoon closed by the death and burial of two men. Thunderstorm during the night—distance 16 miles. July 3: Marched at 6 a.m. and reached a Potawatomi village known as the Mission at 8 a.m. The building of logs whitewashed externally, giving them an air of neatness. Schoolhouse and chapel. Many children well clad and at play. General appearance of the people very comfortable—distance 6 miles. Reached Lost Creek at 11 1/2 a.m., 15 1/2. Encamped at 1 p.m. on Vermillion Creek. Day oppressively warm—distance 19 miles. July 4: Marched at 5 1/2 a.m. Morning warm and cloudy. Rained during the day. Met many Delaware Indians returning from a buffalo hunt loaded with skins and meat. Reached the Big Blue River at 1 o'clock, crossed on a fine bridge and encamped. Sickness less and men in better spirits. Suffered much from burned lips and nose. Heavy thunderstorm which lasted five hours. One man died of Cholera—distance 22 miles.[367]

The RSCJ do not much mention the heat, wind, or storms of the area but this account gives an idea of what they experienced.

The RSCJ superiors back in Saint Louis were evidently concerned about the community out on the fringes. Bishop Miège seems to have received communication from Margaret Gallwey, RSCJ, around 1854 expressing her questions and concerns about the community's lifestyle, safety, access to and use of spiritual supports. From

---

[366] Julia Deegan is described as having a lingering illness, and Rosa Boyle is said to have had TB before arriving at the mission where she was sent for her health.

[367] Diary of William A. Thornton transcribed by Stephen Blair and posted on the website of the Kansas Historical Society. Blair is the holder of the diary of Thornton, who was his great-great grandfather. The journey was long, hot and plagued with illness. He, accompanied by officers, their families, and servants and over 130 soldiers reached the mission after a five-day journey from Leavenworth. They lost people each day from cholera.

the response, it seems that she was concerned about the motivation of religious who wished to join the mission and of "the danger of losing the spirit of the Sacred Heart." It would be interesting to know what specifically she considered the spirit they were losing since she had never personally visited the house. Did she have contact with Lucille and Louise on their brief visit in 1852?[368] The bishop is quite blunt with her saying,

> Permit me to remark that your imagination, which has already been more or less anti-Indian, greatly exaggerates the requisite qualities and the dangers to be feared; it carries you back too near the days of Christopher Columbus. There are no more dangers to be run here than in Saint Louis, Saint Charles, or Saint Joseph. Your nuns have both an ordinary confessor and an extraordinary one, three or four Masses daily, if they wish to assist at them, an instruction every fortnight, High Mass on Sunday. They are perfectly free to follow their Rule and customs; no one interferes with them or troubles them in the least in the enjoyment of all the privileges of their Society. They are fairly well housed and fed, they have eighty boarders, they work far more than they should which is your fault, dear Mother, more than mine…They are loved, respected and admired by all who know them, above all by their bishop.[369]

Possibly as a result of both these concerns and the need for an onsite visit, Amélie Jouve would be the first superior vicar to file a report on a visit to the mission when she came in 1856.[370]

In an 1855 letter from Sophie Barat to Amélie,[371] she urges her to "take care of your health…a visit to 'savages' is martyrdom. Mother Cutts lost her health that way: Of course, she fell into the water; which did not help. Fortunately they have a holy Bishop who takes a lively interest."[372] This may refer to a proposed visit of Maria Cutts in 1849[373] when she was prevented from arrival by bad weather. However, she appears to have made a brief

---

[368] Margaret was superior in Saint Louis and had made contributions to the Mission; she was mistress of novices at this time. Who was her source of information? Later she would visit the house as vicar.

[369] Callan, *North America* p. 297. He notes the advanced age of Lucille and Mary Anne O'Connor and urges her to send replacements to the Mission with the same spirit as they have.

[370] Mathevon, Letters, Callan collection. Mother Cutts had been scheduled to visit in the late 1840s but was prevented by widespread flooding and appears never to have made it to the mission. Elizabeth Galitzine did not leave any report of her visit in 1842. (See note below. Cutts may have made a visit in 1851 or 52 but left no record.)

[371] Amélie Jouve (1799-1880), a niece of Philippine Duchesne; she and two of her siblings entered the Society. She came to America in 1846 and comforted the aging Philippine with personal greetings from Madeleine Sophie Barat. She was appointed superior vicar in 1854 and would make a visitation to Saint Mary's in 1856. She returned to France in 1864.

[372] Letter #14, 1855, RSCJ Archives, Callan Collection, box 10 folder 2. In 1856, Sophie writes about Paris being torn up for urban projects and how she would rather "travel the Great Plains than Paris all torn up." Had she heard about visits to the mission from some other source?

[373] The House Journal of Grand Coteau has two mentions of visits to Sugar Creek from Mother Cutts, one in September 1844, when it notes she was prevented by the high mountains, and later in 1845 by floods and then low water, which did not allow the steamboat to navigate the river.

visit in 1852 or 1853, although there are no notes on her visit in the Sacred Heart archives.[374] On that visit she talked to Bishop Miège who was already planning to move his headquarters to Leavenworth and wanted RSCJ to establish a school there. She apparently was besieged by foundation requests from among others Saint Joseph, Missouri, and Dubuque, Iowa.[375] Miège would have moved to Leavenworth, Kansas, by the time the visitation to Saint Mary's would take place in 1856, and Amélie Jouve would visit him in Leavenworth on her way.

Mother Amélie
Jouve, RSCJ
(RSCJ Archives)

In a letter to Amélie Jouve written just before her visit, Lucille writes that "we wish to lighten your burden, Reverend Mother, by trying to be true Religious of the Sacred Heart; but when you come to visit us, you will find that your daughters of the prairie are not all saints."[376] She stresses that it is safe to visit. Is she addressing fears that developed because of news reports about Indian attacks on wagon trains headed to California?[377] Lucille mentions that they are on a military highway that extends to California and "no one need fear to join us in this frontier region."

Amélie Jouve was accompanied by two aspirants (religious in first vows) Bridget O'Neill, a native of Tipperary, Ireland, age thirty-eight, and Elisabeth Schroeder, born in Prussia, raised in Ohio, age twenty-seven.[378] Elisabeth left a vivid account of both the trip and her initial reactions to Saint Mary's. She described how they arrived via river boat at Leavenworth where they were received by Bishop Miège.[379] While there, Bridget O Neill professed her final vows. They then mounted a carriage, but the driver was unsure of the route to Saint Mary's, and they constantly had to backtrack. When they stopped at an

---

[374] There is no an annual letter for 1852-53 that probably would have mentioned even a brief visit. There are reports on visits of Vicars in the Potawatomi section of Archives but they start with that of Amélie Jouve in 1856. The Central Archives of the Society in Rome has correspondence from Maria Cutts but it does not mention a visit.

[375] Callan, *North America*, p. 505. It is strange that there is no vicar's report if she did visit the mission (the house journal contains no record) or was she too overwhelmed by the work at hand or too busy with a visitor from Rome, Anna du Rousiers.

[376] *Ibid*. Callan, *North America,* p.298. Is she perhaps remembering some of the concerns that Margaret Gallwey seems to have expressed and later communicated in her letter to Bishop Miège?

[377] Edmunds, *Indians as Pioneers*, pp. 341-42, points to the exaggeration of threat of Indian attacks in the press and notes that of the 316,000 emigrants traveling the Oregon Trail 1840-1860, Indians killed 362 travelers and emigrants killed 426 Indians.

[378] When they started they were both in first vows, but for some reason, perhaps because she was older, Bridget made her final vows. Elisabeth made her profession in Kansas at Saint Marys in 1862.

[379] E. Schroeder: transcript, RSCJ Archives, IV. K. Potawatomi Mission, box 2, tells how curious but compassionate passengers seeing these three women dressed in (definitely out of fashion) black secular clothing assumed they were widows and the two younger women, daughters of Amélie Jouve. They were asked how they would support themselves and replied they were starting a school. The passengers took up a collection for the cause (p. 1).

inn, it was full of oxcart teamsters taking provisions to the various military installations in the territory. The innkeeper, a Frenchwoman, let them stay in her room, vacating the bed while she and her baby slept on the floor. Amélie Jouve, however, did not use the bed since it was "occupied by a host of unpleasant insects" causing her to "retreat to a rocking chair where she passed the night in prayer."[380] They probably would have had a hard time sleeping anyway—it was very hot. For ventilation they opened the door to the porch, but on account of the overflow of drivers outside, "the night air was filled with sounds of cursing, swearing, talking, laughing, and snoring."[381] Elisabeth found it impossible to sleep and next day to eat breakfast. That inability to eat attracted the rough if kindly attention of one of the teamsters, who tried to convince her that she needed to eat. The French woman was much taken with Elisabeth, claiming she had known her in France, a place Elisabeth had never visited. The woman shared her life story with Amélie and admitted she had not received the sacraments in many years. Amélie asked her to promise to go to confession to the first passing priest. (She kept her promise, and the passing priest reported back to Saint Mary's that she was a "great fish.") After leaving the inn, they found the milk in their provisions had soured, and the driver, still clueless about the route, was able to replace it by milking a cow in a field they passed. Finally, they arrived in the evening to the waiting religious at Saint Mary's.

Elisabeth's first impression of Saint Mary's was not an especially happy one. "Seeing the poor little mission consisting of two log houses resting on the ground and containing only eight rooms my heart failed me as I thought of the beautiful convent of Grand Coteau, my first religious home where I had been so happy."[382] This impression was probably not ameliorated by her experience that evening when she and Amélie shared a room, and "no sooner had we extinguished our candle, when the crickets who live in the cracks of the floor became very friendly, even so far as to get on the beds, and chirped with all their might so that sleep or rest was impossible. I got up and lit the candle, remaining beside it to watch it as long as it burned so that Mother Jouve might get a little sleep."[383] Elisabeth has vivid descriptions of the poverty of the mission church with its whitewashed, canvas covered walls. The sparse chapel moved Amélie to tears, and before she left she appointed Elisabeth sacristan. The new arrivals received the traditional handshake from all the Indians the next day. Elisabeth would remain at Saint Mary's until the mission closed.

Elisabeth describes a sample Monday at Saint Mary's where she was not only sacrist, but a teacher and in charge of the children's clothing. The school had between seventy and eighty girls. Some were day students who lived nearby, and others were boarders. The day began before five when the RSCJ went to pray (half an hour for the coadjutrix and one hour for the choir sisters). At 6:15 there was Mass and breakfast Then the older girls milked the cows, and six to seven other girls helped bring the milk home and churn it. The younger girls helped

---

[380] *Ibid.* pp. 2-5.

[381] *Ibid.* p.6.

[382] *Ibid.* p.7.

[383] *Ibid.* p.7.

in the kitchen and with housework. She writes, "All had manual labor." At nine, classes began but with only three teachers, each took two divisions, and their day lasted until five, when once again the older girls milked and did housework, while the little girls went to Lucille to learn to knit. Elisabeth had a class of twenty to twenty-five big girls who liked sewing, fancy work and music. She initially found the group a bit of a handful[384] but seemed to grow into her job. She was impressed by the faith and devotion of her Indian charges. Her duties in the sacristy and vestry must have taken some time. She leaves a vivid description of Lucille's work at bathing and delousing the incoming students. Elisabeth played the piano[385] and recounts how an Indian man gave her $10 to teach his daughter to play but was disappointed that after a few days the child still had not mastered it.

The students who lived near Saint Mary's attended Mass each day, and families at a distance would come on Saturday and stay overnight. "On feast days the convent was full, they would sleep on the floor wrapped in their blankets and gave no trouble."[386] The Indians obviously felt right at home in both the convent and the church. "At Christmas and on the New Year the whole tribe would come to shake hands, wish us a happy feast and receive a piece of candy and cake. They are very fond of sweet things."[387] On another occasion she describes an Indian man who rested in the church during Elisabeth's adoration and proceeded to consume his entire package of candy, she adds, "I made a poor adoration that day."[388]

Life on the prairie was close to both weather and nature. Elisabeth writes that the log houses' cracks and air holes were "enough for wind, rain and rats. One night when it had been raining, I heard a queer noise, and I got up when I found myself standing in water which reached above my ankles. One day the door of my sleeping room was left open, and a large snake entered and coiled itself around the leg of my bed. Fortunately someone saw it and killed it before bed time. Such things often happened."[389] The prairie winters were especially severe: "our beds were often covered with snow and in the mornings we would sometimes find our bed clothes frozen around our mouths. Frequently while at our meals the water would freeze in our glasses… (Despite this) I never prayed with more devotion than in that old Church even when trembling with cold."[390] The first Christmas she was there Elisabeth arranged a Christmas crib in the church, which delighted the Indians. She describes how an

---

[384] *Ibid.* p.7. "Some were very smart, others lazy and troublesome" and later on (p. 11), "At first I had a hard time but soon I learned to manage them and I loved them."

[385] The mission received the piano early in the decade.

[386] Schroeder, p. 11.

[387] *Ibid.* p. 12. By this time the government had altered the natives' diet and sweets, previously wild honey and maple syrup or sugar, had been replaced by refined sugar and candy.

[388] *Ibid.* p. 13.

[389] *Ibid.* p. 13. She describes a sister finding that a swarm of bees had taken refuge in her room behind her bed. Not knowing where they came from, the sisters moved them to a beehive and soon had a dozen swarms.

[390] *Ibid.* p. 13-14.

Indian left twenty-five cents at the crib so the Blessed Virgin could get some clothes for the baby, who appeared cold. Enterprisingly, Elisabeth left the money there and by Epiphany had collected between $15 and $20 to use for linens and decoration of the altar of the church.[391]

As vicar making an official visit to the RSCJ community, Amélie Jouve was attempting to fulfill the mandate given her in the Constitutions to "watch continually over the faithful observance of the Constitutions and Rule…to maintain peace and union amongst the members of their community" (§297). The position of vicar was evolving in the Society, and after 1851 Sophie spent time training them in how to visit a house and evaluate the community and its works. She emphasized concern for the spiritual and physical wellbeing and health of the community, the physical maintenance of its buildings and grounds, as well as the financial stability and fiscal management of the school.[392]

Amélie seems to have expected the same level of "regularity" that was possible in the larger houses with which she was familiar.[393] She arrived in North America in 1846, bound for Montreal, but she made an out of the way detour to Saint Charles on a special mission from Sophie, bringing personal greetings to her aunt Philippine Duchesne. Once appointed vicar, she resided initially in Saint Louis, from where she quickly planned to visit the houses of the region, which included Louisiana, Missouri, and Kansas. Although briefly at Saint Charles for a few months in 1859, she moved her headquarters to Grand Coteau where she remained throughout the Civil War, until 1864 when she returned to France.[394]

During her visit, Amélie Jouve urged the nuns to maintain the separation between choir religious and coadjutrix sisters. It was the custom in other houses of the time for the choir and coadjutrix to lead rather separate lives. The first were mainly occupied with the ministry of teaching and administration, while the latter were engaged in domestic duties. At Saint Mary's that was often not the case. Teaching of manual skills to the students fell on choir and coadjutrix alike. The domestic labors had been shared between choir and coadjutrix from the beginning. Given the small number for most of the life of the community, any spiritual reading or conferences would probably have been done in common. The coadjutrix also had different prayer schedules and obligations and did not join the others for community recreation except on Sunday and special occasions. From

[391] *Ibid.* p. 16. Before Elisabeth made her profession, the question of her lack of a probation was raised. Father Diehl, Jesuit superior at the time, said, "This life at the mission was probation enough."

[392] Kilroy, *Society of the Sacred Heart*, p. 71.

[393] The Society *Constitutions* asked for a separation between the public and private areas of the house with an "entrance door… kept closely shut and shall open only from the inside" (#228). Visitors were received in an outer parlor and were accompanied by a companion (#228) and "Persons from outside the household are not to be brought into the interior of the house" (#229) although an exception was made for mothers wishing to see the students' living quarters. Silence within the house was a support to an atmosphere of contemplation.

[394] Callan, *North America*, p. 489. In 1864, she was recalled to Europe. She died in Orleans, France, in 1879.

the list of approved and heady topics for this gathering listed in rules for community recreation, one suspects they were probably largely silent. The assistant superior, in this case seventy-two year old Mary Anne O'Connor, was supposed to oversee the coadjutrix sisters. She was charged with their spiritual formation through reading the rule and Constitutions to them and giving them regular conferences. Until the 1860s the number of choir and coadjutrix would seem too small to separate for recreation, even if they had the physical space to do so. It is difficult to see how this would have been possible in their living situation of two log cabins with eight rooms for both RSCJ and boarders. The cabins had little privacy; students lived with the nuns, and the natives seemed to feel free to come and go much as they had in Sugar Creek. The RSCJ had no chapel of their own but went to the mission church for Mass, adoration and other prayers. In her favor, it should be noted that Amélie Jouve was trying to fulfill her mission as vicar to support the unity of the Society, no matter where it was situated. In her mind this was best done through regular observance of the rules of the Society.[395]

Maintaining silence and cloister were important, and Mother Jouve found Saint Mary's Mission wanting in this regard. The central authority of the Society (called the General Council) at its most recent meeting in France in 1851, made more concrete some of the rules around silence and cloister. Most of the RSCJ in Kansas would not have had the opportunity to study the 1851 decrees much less practice them. The coadjutrix were supposed to work in silence, but at Saint Mary's they were not working by themselves but directing and instructing the often lively native girls. There are references to Lucille's tendency to break into song while she was working.[396] The Potawatomi continued to feel at home in the school and came to visit and observe as they had always done. There was no way of isolating the visitors from the life of the students and the community.

Amélie was especially critical of some of the RSCJ and of the management of the house. Her confidential notes give a blunt report of her impressions of the community members and their gifts. She praises Lucille for her zeal but calls her "mentally limited" and asserts that she "holds little to regularity."[397] She feels that Lucille has too close a relationship with the younger Louise, which allows the coadjutrix sister to have undue influence on the superior and her running of the house. Mary Anne O'Connor is praised as zealous but with "little judgment or education, never formed to regularity." Bridget O'Neil, Elisabeth Schroeder,[398] and Julia Deegan are assessed as good but needing to develop or grow, although Bridget is deemed "limited." All three of these women had a more

---

[395] It would not be until after the reforms of Vatican II and a desire by RSCJ to have the Society become truly enculturated in the people they served that unity would be distinguished from maintaining uniformity.

[396] Craney Memoir, RSCJ Archives.

[397] Reports on Visits 1856, Amélie Jouve, translated by Marie Louise Martinez in her notebook on Saint Mary's Mission in the provincial archives in Saint Louis. Some general points are the same as in the report of Amélie Jouve's visit but not the individual assessments. Similar reports on individuals in other houses visited by the vicar are in the provincial archives.

[398] Jouve, visits to houses 1855-1859. Archives Martinez. In a visit to the house where Elisabeth lived in 1855, Mother Jouve had declared that "she should be a Sister."

recent formation in the Society than the others. Of the coadjutrix only Bridget Barnwell, "good, regular, devoted," and Marguerite Mahuny (Mahoney), "good," receive a positive evaluation. Both of these had been trained more recently also. As for the two pioneers, Mary Layton, now forty-eight, is called "poor in every way," and Louise Amiot, thirty-eight, receives the most negative review: "poor religious, spirit, [sic] crafty, runs everybody and everything." Ellen Cahill, still a novice, is ill and nothing more is said.[399] It appears from her visits to other houses that Amélie Jouve's English was limited. Given the number of Irish in this house and the small number of RSCJ, would their common language, especially of the coadjutrix, have been English? Of the twelve RSCJ, at least eight would have had English as their primary language.

It is possible to speculate on the community dynamics that the vicar saw and on which she based her evaluation. The lifestyle that blended the RSCJ, regardless of class, and the friendships that developed between women of the two classes of sisters probably contributed to what she saw as a lack of regularity, undue influence and lack of separation. She had no personal experience of living in the native culture or in this type of ministry.[400] The natives would have seen her strict interpretation of cloister as a violation of hospitality. Her brief visit may have given her some indication of what space limitations and the privations of the frontier meant, but she seemed much more concerned about the poverty of the chapel than the accommodations of the RSCJ. Louise, as the junior member of the community from its beginning, had probably been accustomed to taking a more active role in both house and ministry from the earliest days at Sugar Creek, where she was the only coadjutrix until the arrival of Mary Layton in 1844. Lucille and Mary Anne were both aging, and it would have been natural for her to take up the slack. Lucille seems to have had a special affection for the younger woman with whom she had shared so much. The tender concern of Lucille for Louise can be seen in the story of her journey to Saint Louis in 1852. Lucille also had a deep friendship with Mary Layton, which survived until their death in 1876.[401]

Most of Amélie Jouve's critique of religious discipline and the causes of the lacks were outside the scope of the local community to alter. She herself notes the tight quarters, small number of religious, and no personal visits by superiors for many years. Is it any wonder that different customs would evolve? Some of the women had spent their entire religious life at Saint Mary's without any time in other larger and more traditionally structured houses. While praising the work, Mother Jouve did not seem to take into account the effect of the ministry (which

---

[399] Despite her ill health, Ellen, a native of Ireland, would make her first vows at Saint Mary's in 1857 and her profession there in 1864. She died in 1899 in Chicago.

[400] Even in her assignment to the new foundation at Ile Jesus, Montreal she had much better conditions in which to live and more religious to serve in the ministry in proportion to the number of students. When she arrived back in the U.S., she lived at the Saint Louis house where she appears in the 1850 U.S. census as A. Jaques listed right after M. Gallwey.

[401] Reports on Visits 1856. To be fair to the vicar, she left similar notes for all the houses she visited with equally direct and caustic evaluations. She was not unsympathetic to the coadjutrix sisters, commenting that in one house they worked too hard and did not get enough rest and recreation.

she feels is done well) on the lives of these women who were struggling to do it. There are seventy to eighty girls receiving classes in religion, English, penmanship, arithmetic, dressmaking, homemaking, and gardening. She has the "consolation to see them turning into Christian women."[402] She continues that plans should be made to send more religious, build a separate community house for the "sake of regularity," not to let the Indians into the cloister, and to keep the distinction between the choir and coadjutrix sisters clear, especially in dress. There needed to be better order, silence, and regularity. She did not approve of the merger of the school's finances with those of the Jesuits and noted that they never give an account.[403] The Jesuits agreed to build another house.[404] According to the later visit of Margaret Gallwey, it seems that Lucille, wisely, did not put into practice some of the "regularity" that was counseled by Amélie Jouve.

The government appeared happy with the efforts of the sisters to "civilize" the Indians. Both the Jesuits and the RSCJ followed the main lines of the government curriculum, but the sisters seemed to add their own twist with teaching some additional academic subjects, and both continued to preserve the Potawatomi language. During the 1850s and early 1860s the school received visits from politicians from as far away as Washington. At one point the Vice President of the United States came with eight senators. "They were particularly pleased with the needlework. All wanted some article; the Vice President asked for a pair of moccasins. I took his measure and had finished the order by the time he came back, he was much pleased with them."[405]

In this period the Jesuits sought to woo other Indian tribes to settle down at the mission. They tried to convince them that maintaining their nomadic style of life was not viable. Feasts for visiting Indians included generous samples of the produce of the mission, its vegetables and fruits. Some of these tribes asked for the services of the blackrobes. Pierre De Smet wrote of their visits and the dialogue about the faith that was provoked by what the Indians observed. The school impressed them, and the

---

[402] *Ibid.*

[403] Not until 1869 would the finances be separated. The Jesuits received the subsidy paid by the government and administered it. The RSCJ would have only controlled cash donations made by benefactors or other houses to them.

[404] Reports on visits 1856. Given the economic woes of the Jesuit school, it is no wonder this did not happen. A new house was finally built only after more non-Indian paying students come into the school in 1870 and the RSCJ had control of their own finances.

[405] *Ibid.* p. 15. Unfortunately Elisabeth does not give the date that this happened (she was at the mission 1856-1879) or the name of the Vice President. It was probably after the railroad pushed its way west from Saint Louis. The Kansas and Pacific RR ran right in front of the mission, and travelers would stop and, in Elisabeth's words, they "destroyed everything" so not all visits were as pleasant as this one. The only U.S. Vice President with native ancestry, Charles Curtis, Vice President under Herbert Hoover, was baptized at Saint Mary's mission in 1860 by Father Dumortier. The most likely candidates would be John Breckinridge from Kentucky, who served 1857-1861 under President Buchanan, or Hannibal Hamlin, 1861-65 under Lincoln. If this incident happened later, it might have been Schuyler Colfax who served 1869-1873 under President Grant.

nuns of the Sacred Heart have conciliated the affection of the women and girls of the nation and are working with them with great success...the Indian chiefs quitted the establishment with hearts overflowing with delight and in the consoling expectation of having similar happiness in their own tribes at no very distant future.[406]

At the end of their visit the chiefs of the Crows, Cheyenne, and Arapahos put on a wild exhibition of their dancing, music and chant. They mimicked the process of stalking, scalping and killing their enemies. Were the RSCJ also in the audience during this violent exhibition? If not, it seems likely that they would have heard the music, war whoops and drumming.

Given the harsh conditions at the mission, the amount of labor, and her own ill health, it is hardly surprising that the youngest RSCJ pioneer, Louise Amiot, would die in 1857 at age thirty-nine. Despite her ill health, she "considered nothing too hard, nothing too servile in the labor of saving souls." During her sixteen years laboring at the mission "her command of the native dialect gave her great influence over the Indian girls and their parents, so that she could accomplish good that seemed impossible to others."[407] She was especially known for her needlework and the many students she trained in that skill. Despite her illness, she worked with the students, devoting herself to them to the end. The Indians went into deep mourning at her death. She was the first to die, and her body initially was placed in the common church cemetery. It was moved to a cemetery on the mission grounds in 1869 and in 1894 to its current location in the parish cemetery with her RSCJ sisters.

By the end of the decade something else was dying—the Indian school itself. Although the Indians would continue to send their children[408] through the 1860s, the changes in both the composition of the population, the funding of Indian education, and the honoring of Native American treaty promises was changing. In 1854, the Kansas-Nebraska act was passed, allowing the question of slavery in these territories to be settled by the vote of the settlers. This abrogated the Missouri Compromise, which provided that this portion of Indian Territory should be closed to slavery. A veritable tsunami of settlers flowed west and grabbed what land they could. But Kansas would not be a paradise for settlers because 1854 was a year of drought, grasshoppers, and crop failure. The drought and crop failure of 1854 was quite general throughout the United States; the best summary of its impact upon the West by a western paper is to be found in the Saint Joseph (Missouri) *Gazette*, issues of August and September, especially those of September 13 and 20. A report from Fort Scott, dated August 25, declared that

---

[406] O'Connor, pp. 135ff.

[407] O'Connor p. 250, also *Annual Letters* of the Society 1858, p. 379. Was it this success that Amélie Jouve saw as giving her a greater influence in house decisions than she thought was appropriate?

[408] Connelley, p. 511. The school at Saint Marys had a much larger attendance, (than the Baptist school) the boys numbering 103 and the girls 110. The average attendance was: boys, 75; girls 73 (1859). Father Schultz, Father Duerinck's successor, also strongly supported making the Indians into farmers and imposing white values upon them. See his reports p. 512.

As regards the emigration to Kansas Territory, I do not think many will be able to settle in this part for the next twelve months, there being almost an entire failure in the crops throughout this section of country. Prospects are really dismal here for all kinds of produce. There will not be 'hog and hominy' enough for the old inhabitants, much less for a large influx [of] emigration.[409]

Despite the grim prediction the settlers would flood into the Kansas territory.

Besides the availability of land the settlers coming to Kansas were also trying to make sure that their side, pro slavery or abolitionist, was represented when a vote was taken to determine whether Kansas would be admitted to the union as a slave or Free State.

In the years 1857 and 1858, the State had appeared so much in the papers that it was popular to come to Kansas. Emigrants from all over moved to Kansas to help. Many college students turned from a literary life to come to Lawrence, not for personal gain, but for a principle, to help make it free. Not only emigrants came, but many others to see the country. They nearly all had money and they had it to spend.[410]

Clashes between both parties resulted in enough destruction and deaths for Kansas to be referred to as "bleeding Kansas."[411] The abolitionist John Brown would stage a bloody assault on the pro-slavery town of Potawatomie Creek in 1856[412] in retaliation for an assault on the town of Lawrence, a Free State stronghold, established by New England abolitionists. Active recruitment of Free State settlers was carried on in New England, and settlers from Missouri, a slave state, tried to stack the deck by intimidating Free State immigrants.[413] Clergy were divided: the chaplain at Fort Leavenworth was the author of a pro-slavery pamphlet, "Slavery consistent with Christianity."[414] The New England immigrants were recruited by ministers, such as the Reverend Henry Ward Beecher, who were active in the abolitionist cause. Both North and South formed Emigrant Aid Societies in order to persuade their constituencies to move to the Kansas territory. No mention was made that this territory had been promised in perpetuity to the different tribes that had moved there from east of the Mississippi. The efforts of the abolitionist

---

[409] James C. Malin, "Dust Storms: Part One 1850-1860," *Kansas Historical Society Journal* (May 1946), Vol 14 #2 p. 133. Available also online at www.kshs.org.

[410] Elfriede Fisher Rowe, *Wonderful Old Lawrence*, pp. 101-103. Kenneth Spencer Research Library, University of Kansas, and Archives of the Kansas Historical Society.

[411] A term that originated with newspaper publisher Horace Greeley in the *New York Tribune*.

[412] Letter of Mahala Doyle, The Gilder Lehrman Institute of American History, primary source archive, New York Historical Society (also available on www.gilderlehrman.org). On November 20, 1859, she wrote a letter to John Brown before his execution after his failed Harpers Ferry assault that describes the murder of her husband and two sons by John Brown and his sons in 1856 at Pottawatomie Creek. Interestingly enough she owned no slaves nor had intention to own them.

[413] Rowe.

[414] Barry, "Kansas before 1854." The pamphlet was published in 1850 and he served until 1859 at the fort.

settlers were successful after much political strife. The "free soilers" dominated the incoming settlers so that by the time Kansas was admitted to the union in 1861, it would be as a Free State. The acrimony of the debate would contribute to tensions leading to an even bigger conflict to come, that of the Civil War of 1861-1864.

Within a year of the Kansas-Nebraska Act,[415] thirty to forty towns arose where previously there had been open prairie and forests. The town of Topeka, about twenty-six miles from Saint Marys, was founded in December 1854. The population of settlers in the area increased from fewer than 1500 to over 8600 by the following year.[416] In 1855, the first meeting of settlers to elect a representative legislature was held at Saint Marys. The spiritual needs of the settlers began to compete for the attention of the fathers. By 1859, there were so many settlers that the Jesuits assigned a priest, Louis Dumortier, just for their needs and to visit their remote homesteads.[417] That year the town was on the regular stagecoach route of the Butterfield Stage from Saint Louis to Denver. Plans were made to make the Kansas River a steam boat route with specially built vessels for its shallow depths and sandbars. The Jesuits looked forward to reducing the cost of getting supplies and of shipping the mission produce using their own river landing.[418] Between 1854 and 1866, thirty-five specially built steamboats worked the river.

One of the Jesuit brothers, John Murphy, left an account of his travels in 1858 from Milwaukee to the mission in the Kaw valley. He traveled through Chicago to Saint Louis and, since the railroad had not reached the mission, took a nine-day river boat to Fort Leavenworth. A government stage heading from there to Fort Riley, fifty miles west of Saint Marys, dropped him off at the mission. He described the landscape:

> The whole region was free and open. There were no gates, no fences, no proprietors, no sound or sight of human life. What a beautiful region was this broad expanse of uninhabited land...the landscape that spread out before us seemed as a vision and the long rows of neat log buildings of Saint Mary's mission entered into it. About these mission houses, the Indian wigwams could be seen extending out as from a center all over the valley...except for those...employed at the mission no white men (could be) seen. The Indians had undisputed claim to their hunting grounds, and game such as the deer, squirrel, and rabbit, was still abundant. The buffalo, although plentiful around Fort Riley, had forever left the prairies about Saint Marys.

---

[415] In 1854, the Kansas-Nebraska Act overturned the Missouri Compromise, which stated that slavery would not be allowed north of latitude 36°30'. Instead, settlers would use the principle of popular sovereignty and vote to determine whether slavery would be allowed in each state.

[416] O'Connor, p. 198.

[417] Garraghan 3, pp. 4-5. He covered a territory 200 miles by 50 miles. Cost of one shipment could be as much as $400.

[418] Political intriguing by the railroads forced the legislature to declare the river not navigable and allowed bridges to be built, which put an end to steamboats coming up the river. It allowed the railroads to build and dominate transportation of goods and people.

He describes the boys as a "happy crowd, always pleasant and joyful." They were fascinated by the mission clock, which could show the "progress of suns and moons with such precision."[419]

In 1858, Jean Baptiste Duerinck died in a tragic accident on the river on route to Florissant to make his tertianship.[420] His temporary replacement, John Schultz, was appointed his successor. He had some six years' experience working with the Potawatomi and with great struggle had learned their language. Schultz took over as administrator and immediately had to clean up the results of some of Duerinck's business deals gone sour. He also read the signs of the times about the situation of the natives. He saw clearly that the government policies plus the onslaught of settlers boded no good for the mission and its schools.

> It is not likely that the Mission will last many years. The Potawatomi are only three thousand and their number decreases yearly. The future has nothing promising for them. Hemmed in closely by the whites, they must perforce choose one of two evils, either retire to the Rocky Mountains or become farmers. In the one case they will fall in with the Sioux and Arapahoe, their enemies, and be exterminated, in the other, they will remain where they are and so be among scoundrels, who in exchange for trifles will buy their houses and farms and so reduce them to beggary.[421]

At the end of the decade there was wild weather alternating between heavy rain, snow (on Saint Patrick's Day) and heat. Blistering summer heat followed, causing the destruction of crops. Only with the help of outside donations did the schools survive. They were fortunate to bring in sufficient hay to feed their cattle while many other settlers were forced to sell livestock that they could not feed. Fortunately, 1861 would prove to be a year of plenty.[422]

---

[419] O'Connor, pp.258-59.

[420] This is a period of six to nine months of formal preparation for final vows in the Society of Jesus (Jesuits); it occurs ten to fifteen years after the man has completed his initial formation as a novice.

[421] Garraghan 2, p. 680. See note on this page about Duerinck's financial difficulties.

[422] *Ibid.* pp. 261-62.

THE WANING OF SAINT MARY'S MISSION, 1861-1869

In 1861, Jesuit John Schultz was replaced by John Diels.[423] At the end of the 1861 school year in September, both schools presented a public examination for state inspectors. Considering that the schools had passed through a small pox epidemic in which four students died and sixty were ill, the success of the schools was remarkable. The Topeka state report, after giving high praise to the boys' school, then commended the work in the girls' school adding:

> I need only say that the fine manner in which the girls sustained themselves during a lengthy examination in the several branches taught in the school, the perfect readiness with which they answered nearly every question proposed, is the best evidence of their thorough course of training and of the untiring zeal with which those ladies discharge their duties towards the children under their care. I have seldom seen children of the age of those examined today acquit themselves in a more handsome manner; and when we consider that many of them, who are pure Indians, have first of all to learn a language which they knew nothing of, we must readily admit that the efforts of the teachers…have been eminently successful.[424]

By 1861, the Jesuit school had accepted two non-Indian boys[425] one the son of the U.S. Indian agent and the other a young Irish American, who studied alongside the Indian pupils. That number steadily increased.[426] Diels was credited with the growth of the school and commended for his business skills. The Jesuits began to devote more time to the evangelization and sacramental care of Irish and German settlers. The priests envisioned the mission as a center of Catholic life, not only for the natives but for the many Catholic settlers. Realistically, the paying students would augment the meager amount paid by the government for each Indian student.[427] Ironically as the 1860s progressed, the number of Indian students also increased. So many of these students came that at times the Jesuits were unable to accept all the Indian students who wished to attend.[428]

In 1861, a new treaty was made with the Potawatomi, passed by Congress in 1862 and signed by President

[423] Garraghan 3, p. 51. He worked closely with Father Gailland and became fluent in Potawatomi.
[424] O'Connor, pp. 289-91.
[425] Craney tells how Lucille comforted one of the non-Indian boys who was having a rough time fitting in with the native pupils. He would come and cry on her shoulder. Later he attested that her support enabled him to stay in the school and finish his education.
[426] Garraghan p. 44.
[427] Garraghan p. 49. Jesuits tried to get government to increase the amount to $100 per student, without success.
[428] O'Connor.

Lincoln. It drastically changed the communal system of holding land that they had used. Each Indian family was to receive an individual land allotment; those who wanted to hold land in common could also receive some common allotments on the reservation; but all remaining land had to be divided, and what was left over would be sold by the government.[429] The Mission of Saint Mary's and the Baptist Mission on the other side of the river would each receive 320 acres. The tribe was as divided on this plan as were the missionaries.[430] Maurice Gailland, who evidently was present at the meeting when the agreement was signed, recorded the eloquent opposition of one of the dissenting chiefs, Shawnee, who pointed out that the natives had already surrendered several states worth of land to the settlers. He did not understand why the settlers needed to determine the fate of his people.

> A pretty thing this is, suppose a stranger comes into your home, and declares himself dissatisfied with the way your domestic affairs are managed, would you listen to his whims? What have we to do with the whites who are settling among us? If our manner of acting displeases them, why do they come in our way? Let them allow us to manage our own affairs. and we will let them manage their own.[431]

When a commissioner encouraged the chief to heal the divisions within the tribe, he turned the argument back on him, pointing out that the Americans were not a great example of peace since they were fighting a bloody war pitting the North against the South. In it brother was warring against brother, and he challenged them to first make peace among themselves before presuming to preach it to the natives.[432] After the treaty of 1861 was signed, there was a lot of back and forth in communication with the government over several years to clarify the terms of the mission's use of the land.[433] While the missionaries were opposed to some of the terms of the agreement, they appear to have accepted it as inevitable. They also realized that there would come a time when there would be no native people to serve from this site. They insisted that the land, if it be a gift or if they purchased it, would be theirs to use for the needs of the area population, whether Indian or settler. While the mission certainly profited from the allotment, they also felt that the allotment process would further educate the natives to the American method

---

[429] Charles J. Kappler, ed., *Indian Affairs: Laws and Treaties,* Vol. II. Washington DC: Government Printing Office, 1904. Also available at www.okstate.edu/kappler/vol2/treaties/pot0824.htm.

[430] Connelley (p. 504) remarks on the eloquent reports of the previous director Duerinck, who strongly supported allotment and must have influenced the thinking of the sisters. "The report of the superintendent, J. B. Duerinck, was somewhat harsh, and was evidently written to correspond with the demands of the political powers then in the ascendancy, and demanding the extinction, according to custom, of Indian titles through allotment of lands in severalty."

[431] Garraghan, p. 28.

[432] *Ibid*. p. 29. Despite his opposition, he was commanded by the commissioner that he must sign the treaty.

[433] It was not signed by the Potawatomi until 1867.

of owning property. It would allow the mission to develop and serve the local Catholic population.[434] From the native point of view, the division of land in this way was close to a sacrilege and did not motivate them to become land owners. Some were suspicious of the missionaries' motives. The settlers considered any uncultivated plains as wasted and unclaimed, while the natives did not feel the compulsion to plow the prairie grass. Complicating the tribal discussions was the presence of many Métis families who had a foot in both worlds.[435]

In 1861 the commissioner for Indian affairs visited the area. He wrote:

> St. Mary's Mission school seemed to be in a prosperous condition, popular with the Indians, and doing much good. The female department deserves particular mention for its efficiency in teaching the different branches of education. The exhibition of plain and fancy needlework and embroidery, executed by the pupils, creditably attests the care and attention bestowed by the sisters upon these children of the forest. It was plain to me that their hearts are in the work. I cannot speak so favorably of the school for boys, but assurances were given by the present conductor, who has recently taken charge of it, that its deficiencies should be remedied. Much of the improvement in the mode of life observable among the Pottawatomies is attributable to the schools.[436]

---

[434] For a view from the Prairie Band perspective, see Gary Mitchell, *Stories of the Potawatomi People* on line at www.kansasheritage. org, which has the opposite view especially since the mission wound up with over 2,000 acres of land by gift and purchase. He also carries the story of the band up to about 1995.

[435] Prairie Band website http://www.pbpindiantribe.com/tribal-history.aspx. Soon after, railroad interests, religious groups and politicians got involved in new treaty negotiations. But the tribe also experienced an internal divide: 1,400 members wanted the land divided into allotments coupled with the promise of eventual citizenship. However, a small group of 780 Potawatomi stood firm for communal holdings. They were neither interested in obtaining citizenship nor rejecting their heritage, and they held firm in their belief that no single person owned the land. This group became what is now the Prairie Band Potawatomi Nation. Two treaties, one in 1861 and another in 1867, carved the existing reservation with a land base of 568,223 acres into portions that accommodated individual interests. The railroad received over 338,000 acres, Jesuit interests 320 acres, Baptist interests 320 acres, and the rest was divided into separate plots. The Jesuits, although failing ultimately to make Kansas a center of Catholic interest, did eventually settle approximately 2,300 acres around Saint Mary's Mission.

[436] *Ibid.* Connelley, pp. 513-14.

Potawatomi family in front of cabin, about 1868 (KSHS)

In a report of 1862 the total tribal population was 2,259: 648 men, 588 women, and 1,023 children.[437] Three years later it was 1,992: 512 men, 501 women, 979 children.[438]

The violence in the Kansas territory both before and during the Civil War did not much affect the mission because of its location far from the capital of the state and from areas affected by the "bleeding Kansas" disputes and Civil War raids. Throughout the mid-1850s, there had been sporadic plundering and theft by bands of natives wandering the area; but apart from the raids mentioned in the last section, these problems did not touch the mission. During the Civil War, the mission was affected by the different political sympathies of Indian agents. One of the Jesuits had to flee the Osage mission when the tribe was split by sympathies for different sides of the conflict, and the Indian agent, who favored the South, felt the priest was on the northern side. The news of Quandrill's raid on Lawrence, Kansas, when one hundred and fifty people were killed and the town burned, would have alarmed the mission. Bishop Miège was in the town at the time, but the church and its clergy were not harmed. Two of the priests and three of the brothers were notified that they had been drafted. Pierre De Smet attempted to get a religious exemption for them without complete success. They could have paid a $300 bounty for exemption from the draft as did other Americans, but De Smet resisted that, since it would take funds from their mission of education. He also pointed out that under canon law they were forbidden to take up arms. It

[437] *Ibid.* p. 514.
[438] *Ibid.* p. 518.

appears that the priests and brothers did not have to report and were allowed to stay at the mission throughout the war, even though his petition was not accepted.[439]

During this time of change, pioneer RSCJ Mary Anne O'Connor died on December 8, 1863, at the age of eighty.[440] Maurice Gailland remarked on her death that she

> was distinguished by many virtues…graced with humility and constant application to her work no matter how lowly…with a burning zeal for souls. Because of her extraordinary gifts, lay women constantly sought her advice, and they never left her presence without experiencing a deep benefit for their own souls because of her good common sense…some converting to the Catholic faith.[441]

The harsh conditions in which the community lived would persist until the construction of a new building in 1870. Accounts of this time often focus on the cold as a particular hardship. Marie-Rose Monzert, stationed at Saint Marys from 1868 to 1876, wrote her remembrances, mentioning that

> house was built with logs interwoven with the cracks filled in with pieces of stone and mud; while…the interior was covered with cotton cloth, which swelled out and rose and fell like the sails of a ship when the wind blew. There was no other floor than a few planks laid on the ground. Almost all the rooms were separated one from the other, so to go to the refectory, to the vestry, to the infirmary, to the dormitory, one had to go through the yard exposed to the inclemency of the weather. Slipping in the ditch and getting snow filled shoes[442]

was inevitable, followed by the distraction of praying with wet feet in the cold church.

The children still managed to run off even in bad weather, and Rosa describes three children who left during the recreation for the mistress general's feast, despite a freezing rain with the ground so icy it was

> almost impossible to walk. Towards evening without any reason for discontent, these three small children from nine to ten years of age escaped. Two of them lived twenty and the third, thirty miles from Saint Marys. They reached home the third day; their clothes, soaked from the rain, were entirely frozen. At the end of three weeks, their parents brought them back to us, as if nothing had happened and asked above all that they should not be punished. I cite the example as only one among a hundred, because I was an eye-witness of this one.[443]

---

[439] O'Connor, pp. 265-74. Possibly because the Kansas quota for the draft was met and they had a surplus of over 3,000 draftees.

[440] One Society record gives 1795 as her birth date but based on this her birth date is probably around 1785. She was 40 at the time of entrance. In the Kansas state census of 1855, her age is 60; she is not found in either the 1850 or the 1860 U.S. census.

[441] Faherty, William Barnaby, SJ, *Saint Louis Irish,* Missouri Historical Society, 2001, p. 262 quotes Father Gailland's tribute to Mary Anne's "good common sense."

[442] Monzert, p. 2.

[443] Marie-Rose Monzert appears in the community catalog in 1868.

Rose had a surprise early in her career at the mission, when, as the person in charge of a dormitory who slept with the girls, she got up early to pray before the children were awake. She knelt with her back turned to the room. The children at some time during her meditation, dressed, folded their pallets and hung them to air and disappeared to go to the chapel—all without a sound. Turning she found an empty room.

The community in 1860-1861 was still small: only nine religious, five choir and four coadjutrix sisters. Lucille was still superior, assisted by Mary Anne O'Connor and one other professed, Bridget O'Neill. Julia Deegan and Elisabeth Schroeder were aspirants, who had not yet made their final profession. Mary Layton, Bridget Barnwell, Rosalie Arsenaux, and Ellen Cahill made up the rest. In all probability, the older students helped, as Elisabeth described in her memoir, with the domestic and farm duties. The teachers of English were evidently successful, as can be seen in the report given that year. In 1862, a small pox epidemic hit the schools; sixty students were infected, and four of them died. Some homes in the village had no one in the family who was not ill.[444] Despite this trouble, the school was able to present the usual showcase of student accomplishment at the end of the school year. John Diels described the visit of the examiners to both the boys' and girls' schools, which received a favorable review in the *Topeka State Record*. The paper particularly commends the "untiring zeal with which those ladies discharge their duties towards the children under their care."[445]

There is an extant Kansas state census of Saint Marys in 1865 giving the names and birthplaces of the sisters. No U.S. entries for this date appear in the Society catalog because of the Civil War. The RSCJ are enumerated as if they were part of the Jesuit household: Lucille Mathevon, superior of the female school; Julia Deegan, Elizabeth Schroeder, Bridget O'Neil, Ann Garrity, all teachers; Mary Layton and Rosalie Arsenaux, assistant teachers; Bridget Barnwell, female cook; Ellen Cahill and Catherine O'Meara as domestics. Unfortunately the census did not enumerate the boarders at either of the schools.

The census taken May 2, 1865, did mangle names, but it is unique in that it has exact birth places for some of the RSCJ. It appears that the county of Kilkenny was the birth place of Julia, Ellen, Bridget Barnwell and Catherine O'Meara; but Ann Garrity is from Mayo; Bridget O Neil is from Tipperary. Rosalie Arsenaux, born in Louisiana, and Mary Layton, born in Kentucky, are the only ones born in the United States. Lucille and Elisabeth were born in France and Prussia respectively. The census taker writes Lions, France, for Lucille's birth place; since she probably gave the information, the entry may reflect her French accent when she said "Lyon." A glance through the town census shows immigrant settlers from Ireland, Germany, Norway, Sweden, France, as

---

[444] O'Connor, p. 289.

[445] *Ibid.* p. 291. The writer seems quite surprised at the progress since many are "pure Indian" whose first language is not English.

well as from other parts of the U.S., only a few families are listed as HB—"half breed" or Métis.[446] There are no full-blooded natives listed in the town, although natives may not have been enumerated in this census.

In 1866, the vicar, Margaret Gallwey, made a visitation, and her recommendations indicate that she was not happy with the lifestyle of the RSCJ in Saint Marys.[447] She chided them since "the abuses specified by Mother Jouve have not been attended to (and) that "it is useless for Superiors Vicar to make their visits if the local superiors do not have their directions carried out."[448] Her admonitions range from insisting the coadjutrix sisters not leave the school gate to chase the cows, to denying Communion to those who have broken silence. It is difficult to get a true picture of the day to day relationships of the choir and coadjutrix sisters from other records, but hints can be gleaned from the reports of the vicars, Margaret Gallwey in 1866 and Rose Gauthreaux in 1869. Both were trying to make their relationship conform to the norm in other, more settled houses, indicating that it was not the same in Saint Mary's Mission. In 1872, when Aloysia Hardey (new assistant general on her way to Rome) and, 1873, when Elizabeth Tucker visited, they noted that the rules had been interpreted so strictly as to be destructive of the spirit of the *cor unum*[449] of the house.

The coming of the railroad that passed in front of the mission made the journey from Saint Louis only twenty-four hours instead of three weeks and allowed more supervision of the house by the superior vicar. Only by accepting paying boarding students would the mission school survive. Since the native families would no longer receive a subsidized education, the mission would need another source of income. This necessity put both the Jesuit school and the Sacred Heart school in competition with other schools run by their orders in Saint Louis and with the RSCJ in Saint Joseph, Missouri. That last school, founded in 1853 and less than 70 miles from Saint Marys, had experienced a successful boarding school during the last decade, and "students came from homes as

---

[446] The average family arrived in Saint Marys within the last five to seven years based on the birthplace of the youngest children, verifying the explosive growth in that period. Beginning in 1860, Indians living in town were counted in the federal census; whether Kansas followed this practice is not known, but only half-breeds are listed. The 1865 census took thirty-eight pages; the 1860 U.S. census was seventeen (oddly enough neither the Jesuits nor the RSCJ are listed in it), and the 1855 Kansas census was only eight pages. In it the RSCJ ("Nuns" written in margin) are part of the Jesuit household, which includes Bishop Miège.

[447] In the notes of Amélie Jouve about her visit as vicar to the house where Margaret Gallwey was superior, she writes that she was a bit of a "*grande dame*," more esteemed than loved in her household.

[448] Memoirs of the vicars' visits, handwritten reports Archives, Saint Louis, IV. K. Potawatomi Mission, Box 1, item c.

[449] *Cor Unum*: an expression used to describe the spirit of the community as being of "one heart."

far distant as the Rockies."[450] As the railroad system grew, it allowed students to travel from Kansas and other prairie locations to those more established schools.[451]

In the mid-1860s for the first time, the boys outnumbered the girls (110 boys to 78 girls). In 1866, John Diels reported that the schools were struggling because of a lack of space. He writes that despite positive reports from distinguished visitors, those reports also have noticed the "want of proper accommodations…but nothing has been done to remedy this great want."[452] He points out that similar institutions have received government appropriations, undoubtedly an oblique criticism of the policies of the current Indian agent who was hostile to the Catholic Mission and favored the Baptist school.

In 1866 and the summer of August 1867, the Asian cholera struck Kansas. At Fort Riley to the west of the mission, a detachment of soldiers was especially hard hit, and Louis Dumortier went to minister to them. Unfortunately he succumbed to the illness.[453] Since he had been working with the far scattered Catholic population, this death put more responsibility for their pastoral care on other priests in the personnel strapped mission. In a letter of 1867, Lucille writes that there are twenty-six white students and that the train now passes right in front of the house. These students were in the same classes with the Indian students, and she says that this has not made any difference.[454] However, in the annual letter to the Society for 1867-68, whoever wrote the letter indicates that there were some problems in the school because of the admission of the settlers' children.

> The country is being populated rapidly by white people, a great many of whom are Catholic. Since we opened our school to their children, our Indian girls have become very difficult to manage.[455] Still these dear Indian children are very numerous and give us great consolation…The number of our pupils is 142.[456]

There is no indication of what caused the problem. A picture taken near the end of the decade shows the girls who appear to be mostly Potawatomi.

---

[450] Callan, *North America*, p.507. When Amélie Jouve visited in July 1856, she authorized purchase of property to allow them to house the increased population at the academy and to open a poor school as well.

[451] O'Connor (p.340) notes that the Jesuits were concerned about this competition and were reluctant to allow the boys school to offer a more advanced curriculum on a par with their school in Saint Louis. This does not appear to be a Society concern but perhaps the proximity of the school at Saint Joseph's founded in 1853 may have contributed to the diminishing number of white students at Saint Marys in the 70's.

[452] O'Connor, p. 293.

[453] Garraghan 3, p. 41.

[454] RSCJ Archives, IV. K. Potawatomi Mission, Box 2. Letter Lucille Mathevon August 14, 1867.

[455] Were the Indian children experiencing hostility from the settler children? Did the school start using English only as a way of communication among the students and thereby abandoning the native language?

[456] Callan, *North America*, quoted p. 307.

During the late 1850s to well into the 1870s there appear almost every year in the community list younger religious (aspirants and even novices), perhaps as part of their training. Most stayed only a year or two, only a few more than five years. These include RSCJ such as Marie-Rose Monzert, a native of Switzerland, and Ellen Craney, who wrote their impressions of Lucille Mathevon and the mission.[457] Young RSCJ who came as novices or aspirants to Saint Mary's and stayed five years or more included Rosalie Arsenaux, Julia Deegan, Bridget O'Neil, biological sisters Catherine and Mary O'Meara, Madeleine Emmanuel, Ellen Cahill, Bridget Barnwell, Teresa Dowdall and Elisabeth Schroeder.

One of these young religious was Catherine (Kate) Regan, born March 25, 1831, or 1839[458] in Ireland. In the 1850 U.S. census, a girl C.A. Regan, age 11, is listed in the Saint Louis City House. This child appears in the student register as Catherine O'Regan. She made her First Communion in 1851 and is listed as a free student whose parents, unnamed, live in Saint Louis. In the 1850 Saint Louis census, there is a couple, Patrick, 50, and Margaret Regan, 47, who run a boarding house. They are of the right age to be her parents.[459]

Catherine entered in Saint Louis in 1860 but was sent soon after reception to Chicago and made her first vows there in 1863. Since she was accepted as a choir novice and is listed as a teacher in Chicago, she had received some education, at the Sacred Heart or elsewhere. Kate arrived at Saint Mary's probably around late 1865 or 1866 and appears in the community list for the year 1866-1867. She is in charge of works for the poor, probably the parish school. In the mission records the day school, parish school and poor school seem to be the same. She also may have been working with different sodalities for the students and in charge of classes for young women learning sewing or other marketable skills.[460] Catherine appears in the 1860 census in Chicago, one of twenty sisters as Kate M. a teacher with Anne Garrity, a fellow novice who also would serve with her at Saint Mary's. Her superior is Margaret Gallwey,[461] who will make a formal visitation as vicar of Saint Mary's in 1866. Did Catherine

---

[457] At Sugar Creek, one of the pioneers, Louise Amiot, came before her final profession. In 1843–1845, a young aspirant who did not persevere came with Catherine Thiéfry.

[458] In the U.S. census in 1860 her age is listed as twenty-nine; that would have made her twenty at the time of her First Communion. The Catherine listed in Saint Louis student register is eleven. The letters nine and one in some of the older records can be written in such a way as to be confused. Unfortunately, there is nothing in the *Annual Letters* at her death.

[459] With them are William, twenty-two; Louisa, two; Bridget, nineteen; James, seventeen; Elizabeth, fifteen, and Patrick, twelve. The last child Patrick is born in Missouri so it may indicate the family arrived in 1847. This census does not indicate relationship to head of house, but it is possible they are all members of the same family. The same census has a Patrick, twenty-six, and Catherine, twenty, in same household, who might be a married couple or brother and sister (and if so she might be our Catherine if her birthday is 1830 rather than 1839). There are also several other Regan families in Saint Louis in the 1860 census of the right age to be her parents.

[460] Her occupation is listed as *chargée des œuvres*.

[461] Margaret Gallwey was the founder of the Chicago house in 1858. She was also mistress of novices, which is probably the reason the novices went to Chicago with her in 1860.

travel with her to Saint Mary's? She is also listed in the catalogs of both Saint Charles and the City House in Saint Louis in 1862-1865, in Saint Charles in 1865-1866 and back again for a year in Saint Louis in 1866-1867. Margaret Gallwey was also the superior of the City House in 1850 so she might have known Catherine, if she is the Catherine O'Regan listed as a student there.

Catherine's health did not stand up to the rigors of the mission. This posting may have been seen by her superiors as beneficial to her because of the fresh air of the prairie as opposed to her previous urban assignments.[462] Bridget O'Neil, Elisabeth Schroeder and Ellen Milmoe were the only fellow teachers. Lucille was in poor health and would leave Saint Mary's the next year. All of the teachers had at least three different employments. Bridget was also in charge of the day school. The overwork combined with the severe weather conditions may have contributed to Catherine's death, perhaps the result of tuberculosis. Given these extreme conditions, it is not surprising that her career at Saint Mary's was a short one; she died at age thirty-seven on July 23, 1868.[463] Because she had not yet made her final profession when she died, she was listed as Madame Regan on the gravestone, the title used for aspirants and professed of fewer than ten years. She must have been buried briefly in the old cemetery with Louise and Mary Anne, since those bodies were moved to the school property only in 1869.

Rose Gauthreaux made a visitation in October 1869. Like the last two visiting vicars, her concern was with regularity and keeping the rule.[464] She writes that the relationship between the choir and coadjutrix sisters is "to[o] free" and she will insist on maintaining the distinction between the two classes of RSCJ. It must have been confusing to all of them, except those few who had lived in larger and more "regular" houses. All three of the professed coadjutrix sisters: Mary Layton, Bridget Barnwell, and Rosalie Arceneaux had experience with a more egalitarian style of relationship. Both Mary and Rosalie were American by birth. Was her concern that they were influencing the four younger coadjutrix sisters: Mary and Catherine O'Meara, Bridget Cununey, and Madeleine Emmanuel who were in first vows? By the time of the visitation, if the 1870 census data can be projected back to 1869, the school had two-thirds native students with one-third students from settler families.[465] She instructs the sisters not to "consider the pupils their waiters and call them to assist in any work without permission." This is very different from the practices of the first thirty years of the foundation. Manual work was part of the education of the Indian students, but it seems that the new students and their parents were looking for a different kind of education. Were there parent complaints about this practice? Mary Layton and Rosalie Arceneaux had

---

[462] Descriptions of the dust storms, droughts, frigid winter blasts and summer heat make the air seem less healthy on the prairie!

[463] No mention of Catherine is made in the *Annual Letter* of the next year.

[464] Callan, *North America*, pp. 634ff. Rose was an orphan of Creole heritage, raised at Saint Michael's where she entered in 1840. She served in Canada, Eden Hall near Philadelphia, and Saint Louis before being appointed superior in Chicago in 1867. She succeeded Margaret Gallwey as superior vicar in 1869.

[465] The 1870 census lists twenty-six of the students as "W" or white and twice as many as "M" Mulatto and "I" Indian.

had the experience of being assistant teachers.[466] The vicar reinforces the previous directive of Margaret Gallwey to maintain a "distinction between the choir religious and the sisters."[467] She sets up a number of sodalities and charges different sisters with their supervision, with separate ones for the "regular boarders" and "Indian students." By this year, there are seven coadjutrix sisters, and they appear to be doing all the milking and churning of butter done previously by the older students. In the past, cloister rules were relaxed so they could go outside the gate to get the cows, and that was now forbidden. After her visit, who will chase the errant bovines? She cautions that past pupils should not be allowed to freely roam about the house when they visit.[468] Given the primitive nature of their buildings, several unconnected cabins, it would seem almost impossible to accomplish a more regular convent life without a new building. The religious still had no chapel of their own and were using the main mission chapel.

> A small percentage of the Citizen Potawatomi succeeded as independent farmers and businessmen and thrived in the conditions established for them by the allotment and citizenship treaty of 1861. Far more, however, were quickly engulfed by adverse conditions and outside pressures from non-Indian settlers and corporate interests who desired their land and wanted them out of Kansas. When only a few Citizen Potawatomi managed to succeed, federal officials blamed the Potawatomi's inherent "Indianness" for those who failed to make the transition to agriculturalists. Such rationalization made it easy to ignore the mismanagement of the assimilation effort by the federal government and the onslaught of corporations and non-Indian settlers pushing for access to Citizen Potawatomi land. The forlorn Citizen Potawatomi who ended up in a general state of landlessness, despair, and poverty refused to succumb to their circumstances however.[469]

> Even though the assimilatory processes of allotment and U.S. citizenship ultimately led to mass dispossession of the Citizen Potawatomi…, it motivated them to create political structures and shape the tribe's legal status in ways that generated the opportunity to influence the outcome of the government's plan for their lives. The Citizen Potawatomi utilized their undefined status as both Native Americans and U.S. citizens to challenge the federal government and receive more advantageous allotment conditions in Indian Territory.[470]

Over the next decades the Citizen Band would use their sad experience with government policies to navigate the bureaucracy and acquire both land and a sense of tribal identity. Acceptance of citizenship was a survival strategy.

---

[466] Kansas State census 1865 lists this as their occupation.

[467] Memorial of Mother Gauthreaux, handwritten manuscript in RSCJ Archives IV. K. Potawatomi Mission Box 1, item c.

[468] *Ibid.*

[469] Information from Citizen Potawatomi Nation website www.potawatomi.org: article dated March 4, 2015; Dr. Kelli Mosteller, director of the Citizen Potawatomi Nation Cultural Center.

[470] Kelli Jean Mosteller, "Place, Politics, and Property: Negotiating Allotment for the Citizen Potawatomi, 1861–1891" Ph.D. dissertation, University of Texas at Austin, May 2013.

The Citizen Potawatomi eventually agreed to the assimilation effort, in part because they succumbed to these pressures, but they also made a conscious decision that it was a valid option for their community. Tribal members had experienced several forced removals in the preceding decades and they sought permanence and security. They wanted the social status, economic advantages, political agency, and assurance of protection from further encroachment by non-Indian settlers or another removal they believed private land ownership and U.S. citizenship would entail.[471]

In 1868, the divisions among the Potawatomi were tearing the tribe apart. William Connelley quotes the Indian agent's view of the process:

The Prairie band, which holds their diminished reserve in common, are, many of them, beginning to realize that they must soon change their mode of life or look out for another home. They are not generally prepared for a distribution of their lands in severalty[472] among the members of their band and to become citizens. Being fully conscious of that fact, they desire a separation of their funds from the funds of the sectionizing party, so that they may enjoy among themselves what is their own, and still live on as Indians, according to their ancient customs. It is only necessary to state that they are occupying eleven miles square of a good farming land, with a fair proportion of timber, surrounded by a country as well settled by farmers as any part of Kansas, and in the neighborhood of several small towns or villages, to make it apparent that they are not always at peace with all the world, nor is it probable they ever will be again until they find a home where there are no whites, or where whites are less aggressive than they are in Kansas. I have to suggest that an effort should be made at once to treat with the Prairie Pottawatomies, [sic] to buy out their lands in Kansas and induce them to seek a home elsewhere. It will be observed that the agent did not fail to embrace the opportunity to recommend that the reservation be sold and the Prairie band removed.[473]

Some of the un-allotted land was sold to the railroad (at a very cheap rate) and the further depletion of the Indian lands continued. The settlers even looked enviously on what little portion of the Indian reserve remained:

The idea seems to prevail among the white settlers that that particular reserve, with its valuable timber, pure water, and rich prairie soil, containing over seventy-five thousand acres within an hour's ride from the dome of our State capital, could never have been intended as a home for the Indian, the land to remain, to a great extent, uncultivated, and forever free from taxation. They enter upon these lands stealthily and take away timber, or make a contract with some worthless Indian for such timber as they want (the land being held in

---

[471] *Ibid*. Mosteller p. 9.

[472] This term refers to each Indian's owning his/her own land as his/her own property not as tribal member. In effect, it dissolved the relationship between the individual and the tribe.

[473] Connelley, pp. 518-519.

common they can buy of the same Indian in one part of the reserve as well as another), and under this contract they go on defiantly cutting and destroying.[474]

In a touching and heartfelt account, one of the Jesuit brothers, De Vriendt, writes how the natives were cheated out of their allotments or tempted to sell:

> I feel very sad, because I see now that my prophecy is going to be true. I have said to the Indians 'wo[e] to you when your lands shall be sectionized! You will be lost body and soul.' It is now only too true for I see the land-sharks cheating my Indians out of their land and property. They took some of them, all unsuspecting, to the saloon and there they treated them to a little whiskey and then to a little brandy till they saw the Indians commencing to talk. Then the rascally land-sharks would try to make a bargain with the Indians, telling them they would give them three hundred dollars and a buggy and a pair of horses for eighty acres of land, and saying it would be very nice for them to have a buggy and a pair of horses for 80 acres of land, and…to have a buggy to drive their families to church.[475]

He mentions other examples of Indians losing land, becoming homeless or being forced to move to Topeka, returning to the mission without anything. Some began drinking and were arrested for violent crimes or were killed by the train. He tells of visitors to Maurice Gailland being counseled to hang on to their land, mostly unsuccessfully. After telling several sad stories, the brother concludes:

> O my Indians, if you had never possessed land, how happy you would be! But alas, it was too late. Your destruction is the use of money. O my brethren, how my heart feels I cannot tell you. Almighty God is good. I hope He will not let my Indians perish. I hope He will make them poor again, without land, and make them live in a common reserve. I hope so. Then shall I feel happy.[476]

The missionaries had counseled the Mission Band to accept allotment but soon found out that was a very bad idea. It was the traditional portion of the tribe, the Prairie Band, who were able to hang on to their land during this time by accepting a collective and more communal way of administering land. Even they would be plagued by settler incursions and eventually would be forced to accept allotment.[477]

In 1868 there were thirteen religious, the choir religious outnumbered by the coadjutrix. It was Lucille's last

---

[474] *Ibid.* Connelley, p. 519.
[475] Garraghan, pp. 60f.
[476] *Ibid.* p. 60f; it is ironic since the missionaries had been the ones to persuade their people to accept the allotments.
[477] Allotment became official policy of the U.S. government in dealing with natives via the Dawes Act of 1887; previously it was the preferred method. The Prairie Potawatomi reservation of today still occupies a small portion of the land occupied by their ancestors in the mission period, near Mayetta, Kansas, north of Topeka. The Citizen Band reservation is in Oklahoma.

year as superior. The community included Ellen Milmoe, her assistant; Bridget O'Neil, Julia Deegan, Elisabeth Schroeder, Marie-Rose Monzert; and Mary Layton, Bridget Barnwell, and Rosalie Arsenaux, professed coadjutrix sisters; the O'Meara sisters: Mary and Catherine, Bridget Cununey, and Madeleine Emmanuel, a native of Bavaria, all in first vows.

Lucille was relieved of the charge of superior after the visit of Margaret Gallwey. She was asked to return to Saint Charles in 1868 because of her poor health. Her return was probably by train, a twenty-four hour trip that was a contrast to her original long journey to Sugar Creek and the 1852 three week journey to Saint. Louis. She must have left with a heavy heart, having seen the many changes taking place in the relationship between the Potawatomi and the government and her inability to be present to her beloved natives during this time of disruption. Ellen Milmoe, an Irish sister, who had come to Saint Mary's in 1866 was named in her place.

By 1869, the Mission of Saint Mary's now owned the property on which their buildings stood. The property was divided in an agreement between the Jesuits and the Society. For the first time the finances of the Society and those of the Jesuits were separated. Previously the Jesuits had negotiated and received the government subsidy and administered the sale of mission farm produce. They had supported the RSCJ and their school from what they received. Now the allotment process allowed the mission and its Baptist counterpart to own the land on which they were situated. Previously the land was part of the Indian land reserve. The Jesuits received 320 acres and purchased more for the two schools. The Sacred Heart school received "an ample piece of ground to erect buildings, with recreation grounds, a garden, orchard and pastures…of about 40-60 arpents (acres)…ten milk cows, (more if needed) some horses and other animals which belong to the farm…$10,000…and if needed… provisions for twelve or eighteen months."[478]

Part of the agreement involved supplying bricks so that the Sacred Heart school could have a new three-story building sixty feet by forty feet. Given the space issue, the Religious of the Sacred Heart began plans to build this sturdy brick building. Its four stories (rather than three) and many chimneys would stand out on the lowland, and it was dubbed the "Skyscraper of the Prairie." Started in April 1870, it would be completed for the school term beginning in 1871.

---

[478] O'Connor, pp. 336-37. Hardey and Gallwey travelled to Leavenworth to sign this agreement in presence of Bishop Miège and the Jesuit provincial. The Jesuits also promised to establish a brickyard that would supply sufficient materials for the new building.

Two students from Saint Mary's from the late 1860s to 1870s entered the Society: Johanna Hanrahan and Katherine Ann Caplice.[479] Johanna would be a postulant at Saint Mary's, receive the habit there as a coadjutrix sister in 1874 and make her first vows there. She would be one of the group of religious who would close the school in 1879. The admission of settlers' students in the late 60s, changes in the curriculum and in the community composition, the shrinking population of Indian students whose parents could afford tuition or who lived near enough to come as free day students would all mark the finish of the mission to the Potawatomi.

In 1869 the Jesuits had already accepted the future and the influx of non-Indian students. They could see that to operate a boarding school here in Kansas would be cheaper than in other more urban areas. The proximity to the train would allow students to come from a distance. In preparation for that day a charter was sought for each of the schools from the State of Kansas. Although Indian students continued in the school, the settler population steadily increased. A visitor to the mission wrote,

Skyscraper on the Prairie, four stories, side

    In December, 1869, I accompanied Father Diels to Kansas, being sent there to procure a charter for the proposed college at St Mary's Mission. We went from St. Louis to Leavenworth, where I preached on the Sunday before Christmas. Before leaving St. Louis I wrote down what I thought the charter should in substance be. On reaching Leavenworth we got a lawyer, a Mr. Carroll, to put the charter in due technical form. We then went over to St. Mary's. I found that the main portion of the Pottowatomy [sic] tribe still remained around the mission. On Christmas day and on the following Sunday I listened to a sermon in the Pottowatomy [sic] language, spoken by Father Gailland. I found that language peculiarly sweet to the ear, Father Gailland told me that it possesses peculiar power and richness.[480]

---

[479] Neither is in the 1870 census list, but both girls can be found in the school list, although Katherine is listed as Ann with other Caplice girls on the roster. Katherine, born 1859 in Leavenworth, Kansas, entered in 1884 at Saint Louis, made her first vows in Omaha, was professed in 1893 in Paris, and died in Canada in 1911. Johanna Hanrahan, born 1857 in Kentucky, entered 1874 at Saint Mary's and professed first vows there in 1877. She made her final profession after leaving Saint Mary's and died in 1944 in New Orleans.

[480] Garraghan, p. 50.

Gailland would publish his large volume of Potawatomi prayers, mediations, Christian doctrine, church history and hymns in 1869.[481] He recognized that the mission days were sadly over:

> We have arrived at the gloomiest page of the Pottawatomie [sic] mission; ...now, in accordance with the treaty stipulations, the Government begins in different installments to pay to them large sums of money. The whiskey comes along with the money and flows in torrents; nearly every house in Saint Marys is turned into a saloon. Sharks of all kinds follow the Indians wherever they go, and never lose sight of them night and day; they use all manner of frauds and artifices to get hold of the Indian's money and property...(who) in despair of ever redeeming his condition, plunges still deeper into drinking and all sorts of excesses...many of our neophytes have become quite negligent in the practice of their religious duties. Many have sold their lands and become homeless. Many...have met with a premature death. Some were drowned, some crushed by (railroad) cars, some fell by the hands of Assassins. What a sad spectacle it is for a missionary to see the work of so many years destroyed and his flock devoured by merciless wolves.[482]

The Potawatomi who remained around Saint Marys were faced with the prospect of staying or leaving. Many who had taken advantage of a provision in the 1861 treaty to accept allotment and citizenship had been cheated out of the land allotment and were living in poverty. Some of the leaders in the Citizen Band of Potawatomi, many of whom lived near the mission, took advantage of an 1867 treaty provision allowing them to move to a new reservation in Oklahoma Indian territory. In 1869 leaders had gone to the territory to select the site for the new reservation. In 1870-71, the RSCJ remarked that "Indians are few and scattered and most five miles away...[we] have abandoned the type of education we gave the Indian girls who are now received only as day students."[483] It would not be until 1872 that the first families would move. One obstacle was that, unlike other removals, this would be done at their expense.[484]

---

[481] A copy of this book can be seen on http://www.potawatomi.org/lang/culture and also an audio recording of prayers in Potawatomi today; this is the website of the Citizens Band in Oklahoma where many of the mission Indians from Saint Marys settled. The original is in the tribal archives.

[482] O'Connor, pp. 321-322 quoting Gailland. He consoles himself that there is a faithful remnant who have remained faithful to the Catholic faith.

[483] *Annual Letters* 1870-1871 reports that they have twenty-six white girls in the boarding school, although the U.S. census for that year lists both the white students and a greater number of Indian girls.

[484] Information from Citizen Potawatomi Nation website: article dated March 4, 2015: Dr. Kelli Mosteller, director of the Citizen Potawatomi Nation Cultural Center.

BUILDING AND CLOSING 1870-1879

Girls in front of Saint Mary's Mission School (Wiki Commons)

Although both the Jesuit and Society accounts say there were no Indian boarders after 1869, there are many listed in the 1870 U.S. census for Saint Mary's College. At the time of the census, the schools were still using their old buildings, although plans for new ones for each school had slowly begun. Between the two schools there were eighty-five white students: fifty-six boys and twenty-nine girls. Most of the students were born in Kansas, although some were born at a distance, coming from Ireland, Maryland, Ohio, Illinois, and New York. Both schools still had native students, because they are listed in the census and apparently were residents there in the summer of 1870.[485] There were one hundred and six native students, sixty-seven boys and forty-nine girls, all born in Kansas. It is interesting that the ethnic breakdown at the foot of the page correctly divides the students into white and Indian. But a later hand in a darker ink has eradicated the "I" next to each Indian student, blocking it out with a line or scribble. It does not seem they were mislabeled as many of the surnames are Potawatomi names found in other records.[486] Whatever the reason, it may be symbolic for what was the beginning of the end for the native school. The college for boys had four lay teachers besides the three Jesuit priests and eight lay brothers. One of the brothers was listed as Indian. These entries take up six pages in the U.S. census.[487] At the end of June, the

---

[485] Does the *Annual Letter* of 1870-71 reflect who was left at end of the next academic year, as it says no Indian girls were in the boarding school?

[486] For example the 1867 Potawatomi tribal census.

[487] Comparison of the surnames of the students with those of Potawatomi families who had signed the 1867 treaty or who otherwise appear in tribal records shows that many of the names are the same. The list includes an Elizabeth Slavin (perhaps related to Theresa Slevin/Slavin raised at the Sugar Creek mission. Theresa died in 1876).

temperature was recorded at 101 degrees, and it continued to be hot and dry. Despite this both schools held an exhibition in mid-July highlighting the accomplishments of the students.[488]

Beginning in 1870 the number of RSCJ increases each year. There are sixteen religious listed in the census (names in parenthesis are what the census taker wrote): Ellen Milmoe, a native of Sligo, Ireland who arrived in 1869, Bridget O'Neill, Mary T. Dowdall, Margaret Cornelius, Elisabeth Schroeder, Julia Deegan, Matilda Hamilton listed as teachers; and Mary Layton, Rosalie (Royella) Arceneaux, Sarah Ryan, Mary O Meara (Mara), Catherine O'Meara (Mara), Madeleine (Magchlin) Emanuel (Amanuel), Bridget Barnwell (Pammann) and Ann Lehane (Schane). All of the latter except Sara are listed as domestic servants; her occupation is seamstress. The youngest is Matilda Hamilton, age twenty-four, from Canada.[489] The coadjutrix sisters tended to be younger than the choir religious, with ages ranging from eighteen to fifty. Five of the eight coadjutrix sisters were born in Ireland, the three others in Kentucky, Louisiana, and Bavaria. Only three of the RSCJ are native-born Americans: Mary Layton, Rosalie Arceneaux and Margaret Cornelius. The two O'Meara RSCJ, who arrived one after the other in the mid-1860s, are blood sisters. Five of the coadjutrix sisters have enough education to both read and write except for Bridget, Ann and the O'Meara sisters, who can read but not write.

The sudden drop in Indian students[490] after this census was no doubt due to the upheavals in the tribe as well as the end of the annual fee paid to subsidize each student. With the advent of what would become predominately settler students, both schools needed to offer more advanced subjects and have better-prepared teachers. English was the common language of the school, and there are some indications that the native students were now forbidden to speak their own language.[491] It is likely that any use of Potawatomi in the Sacred Heart school ceased with the deaths of Louise in 1857 and Mary Anne in 1863. Lucille was the only RSCJ left who spoke the language. The RSCJ soon realized that it was difficult to mix the settler and Indian students, even if the Indian students' families could afford the tuition. They decided to accept the Indian students only as day pupils for free or for a small amount. Since many Indian families lived seven to twenty-five miles away, attendance even at the free school was difficult. The 1870 census of the local residents shows that there was a number of families in town with Indian ancestry. It is likely that these families formed the attendance at the day school.

Parents of settler students who formed the bulk of the boarders could teach their daughters how to manage a home but wanted them instructed in academics and the "accomplishments" or the fine arts: music, French, and deportment. Students would no longer help with the livestock, churn butter, or perform heavy domestic chores.

---

[488] O'Connor, p. 337, places this in July 1871 but it took place before the new building was in use (fall 1870).

[489] Not to be confused with another Matilda (Xavier) Hamilton, sister of Regis, one of Philippine's first novices, who died in 1823.

[490] O'Connor, pp. 337-38 shows that the Jesuits' Indian student boarders decreased over the next couple of years due to the lack of funding; funding from the government evidently ceased with the end of the 1870-1871 academic year.

[491] Murphy, p. 214. One native woman resident in Oklahoma testified that at this time they were forbidden to speak Potawatomi and punished if they did. (Also note in Trail of Death testimony of oral history collected in Oklahoma.)

These duties would require a greater number of coadjutrix sisters.[492] Students were required to bring their own bedding, clothing, towels, and wore uniforms only on special feasts. The uniforms cost extra, and one of the visiting vicars reminds the sisters not to allow the pupils to take home the uniform if they had not paid for it. Students stopped going home for breaks, as it was seen detrimental to their progress. Previously, the RSCJ had made their retreat during student breaks, so if the students remained, it probably meant some of the RSCJ needed to supervise the boarders, working in shifts, while others made their retreat.

In December 1869, a corporation was set up in the state of Kansas for the Society's school. The trustees who signed the articles of incorporation were Ellen Milmoe, Bridget O'Neil, Mary Dowdall, Elisabeth Schroeder, and Mary Layton. In early January they designated the superior as president and noted that all professed members of the institute were members of the corporation. They authorized the beginning of the building. By December of that year, with Rose Gauthreaux there, the structure of the corporation was rearranged to make her, as vicar of the West, president with Ellen Milmoe as vice-president and Margaret Cornelius as treasurer in charge of the construction. At this point, Mary Layton offered her resignation.[493]

One result, perhaps unexpected, of setting up the schools independent of government aid was that now they would be taxed.[494] The Jesuits attempted to get an exemption, but by 1872 they needed to raise the tuition for each student from $120 each to $150, with a discount for siblings. The RSCJ tuition was similar, but by 1878 was $170 per student.

The steady erosion of the Indian population is found in the reports of the Indian agents. In 1870 one reads,

> This much we have said in regard to that portion of the Pottawatomies [sic] who have or are gradually passing from under the supervision of an agent, leaving only those who have heretofore been known as the "Prairie band," comprising, according to the census recently taken, 419 souls, and now living in separate lodges as follows, to wit, one frame house, fourteen log cabins, and thirty-five bark lodges, as the only representatives in Kansas of the once powerful tribe of Pottawatomie Indians. They are located on a reservation in Jackson county, state of Kansas, fourteen miles north of Topeka, the capital of the state. Their reserve comprises an area of eleven miles square of beautiful rolling prairie, well-watered by two beautiful streams known as Big and Little Soldier creeks, along which the Indians' houses and lodges are located. The rich bottoms of these streams afford an abundance of the very best farming lands, with a reasonable portion of rail and saw timber, and quantities of small undergrowth, which afford comfortable retreats in winter for themselves and stock, while the rolling prairie lands abound with excellent building stone and a reasonable supply of stone coal. This portion of the

[492] It is a shame that we do not have any reflections of Mary Layton who witnessed these changes during her time at Saint Mary's Mission, 1845-1876.
[493] Minutes of the Corporation, Sacred Heart School, Saint Marys, Kansas, 1869-1878. RSCJ Archives IV. K. Potawatomi Mission, Box 1 item b.
[494] O'Connor, p. 348.

tribe adheres tenaciously to their ancient Indian customs, habits and superstitions, although much effort has been made to educate them to leave off their old habits of hunting, particularly now that the game has almost entirely disappeared, and idly passing away their time, to resort to the cultivating of their soil for a support. But they still continue to cling to their old flag and bark lodges, after the customs of their fathers.[495]

Throughout the conflicts over the treaty process, the tribe had divided into the Mission Band and the Prairie Band, the latter composed of the "traditional" natives who had preserved their culture and religious practices, either by not converting to Christianity or by keeping those practices alive secretly. Many of the Mission Band, who were more assimilated to American culture or from Métis families, chose to take the individual land allotment and accept citizenship. They were encouraged to do so by the priests of the Mission. Maurice Gailland writes of a group of two hundred who, in the late 1860s, had submitted their petitions for citizenship and waited to hear from Washington. In effect, they surrendered their tribal affiliation by accepting citizenship. It was only in 1924 that other Native Americans were considered U.S. citizens.[496]

Unscrupulous settlers took advantage of many of the natives, who had received allotments, to purchase their land. The Citizen Band of Potawatomi took advantage of the provision of the treaty of 1867 that allowed them to trade land in Kansas for new land in Oklahoma. They began the move to a new reservation and left the area in fourteen wagons in 1872 to trek to Oklahoma. The Jesuits wanted to follow their flock south but were prevented by their superiors who feared they would not have enough personnel. The Religious of the Sacred Heart focused on serving a new student population, and with personnel stretched thin by new foundations elsewhere, did not raise the question.[497] Some of the Mission Band did not go to Oklahoma. Some moved to the Prairie Potawatomi lands set aside in Mayetta or stayed in Kansas in settlements around Saint Marys.[498] Since the cost of the move to Oklahoma had to be paid by the natives, only the more affluent families could afford to fund the trip. In the 1870 U.S. census of the area of Saint Marys, Kansas, there are many families originally marked "I" for Indian that a later pen in darker ink has marked "M," probably for "mixed blood." They are families with significant real estate and personal property ($2000-$4000); and in cases where an Indian woman is married to a non-Indian husband the wife also has property of value. In some families the children are marked either "M" or "I."[499]

---

[495] Connelley notes that even becoming successful farmers did not spare the Prairie Band from eventual forced acceptance of the allotment in 1895.

[496] Allotments and citizenship were connected through the years in U.S. government policy. The 1924 Citizenship Act gave citizenship to those on and off the reservation. Voting rights for Native Americans were granted in 1948.

[497] The Benedictines, who later came to serve the Citizen Band, remarked that many were bilingual in French and English, a reflection of their time at Saint Marys and the mixture of Metis families.

[498] In 1867, one of the chiefs wished to forbid mission natives to come but it appears that they did since their presence is sufficient to provoke government opposition in the 1880's.

[499] By the 1880 census for those who stayed in Kansas these children often are marked "W" for "white."

In July of 1870, a cyclone came through and took off the half-finished roof of the new building as well as caused destruction of homes in the town. Classes continued for both settler and Indian students.[500] By September there were only twenty-one boarders at the school to inaugurate the new building. The school and the RSCJ began to enjoy some of the academic advantages of those in larger cities. One example can be found in the Jesuit records: Father Butler, evidently a scholar of Irish literature, passed through the mission and conducted a discussion about the modern Irish poets at the convent. Eight of the RSCJ were from Ireland and would have enjoyed the program, although given the growing separation of the two classes of RSCJ, the five Irish coadjutrix sisters might not have been included. By 1870-1871 the number of RSCJ had increased to twenty, almost evenly divided between choir and coadjutrix sisters, including seven in first vows and three novices.

When Lucille Mathevon was removed as superior in 1868, she left Saint Marys without comment and went obediently to Saint Charles. This decision was not popular with the local people, and there were protests from the inhabitants of Saint Marys to Society authorities, which evidently reached as far as the supeior general.[501] In November 1871, despite her continued poor health, Lucille was allowed to return to the mission. Her arrival was greeted with great rejoicing by the native people, who met her at the train with cries of joy. One of the men carried her from the train in triumph to the waiting carriage. During the following weeks many of the natives came to see her, and she provided a table covered with cakes, apples and candy to receive them.[502] In some respects, despite her longing to be back again, it was a sad homecoming. She certainly was aware of the diminishment of the tribal lands and the movement of the Indian students away from the mission and its school. Ellen Craney, RSCJ, who lived with Lucille, said that the news that she was to return restored her

> but when she reached her destination dismay followed; it was not her Saint Mary's and the fine new house had no charms for her. True, the old buildings were still there (in front of the college), but everything... (had) changed. With the old sisters[503] she lamented that muddy shoes were not allowed in the hall...that the furniture needed to be handled gently, etc....the Indians had moved and she saw little of them. What had happened to her beloved Potawatomi ate at her heart, and she would say with tears in her eyes: "Ah, it is not the same mission as before."[504]

---

[500] O'Connor, p. 337, dates this in 1871; however, the building would have been finished by then so it is likely it took place in the summer of 1870 unless he is referring to the Jesuit school building. Lucille returned in November 1870 and the building was finished by that time.

[501] Callan, *North America*, p.310, says the protests were strong for three years. Also mentioned in *Annual Letter* of 1877 in report of her death, p. 278.

[502] *Ibid.*

[503] Perhaps fellow pioneer Mary Layton, RSCJ, from the 1850's, Bridget O'Neil, Julia Deegan, Bridget Barnwell and Elizabeth Schroeder. Most of the other RSCJ had arrived from the mid to late 60's.

[504] *Annual Letters* 1877, p. 278.

She realized what the future would be and it came…"when not one child with a drop of Indian blood was in the school."[505] Was she able visit the new cemetery close to the house where her companions Mary Anne O'Connor and Louise Amiot had been re-buried along with newcomer Kate Regan? Did she wonder at the effect of the changes mandated by visiting vicars and what appears to be a different spirit in the house? Even the church serving the Indian families had changed. The local pastor announced in 1872 that it was no longer an Indian Mission. Joseph Moose, a writer and member of the Citizen Band, remembered that

> The Indians, like the early Christians of the Roman catacombs, (attended) the five o'clock Mass because at the other hours of Sundays, the church was crowded to its utmost capacity by the elite of the city and country… when an Indian encroached upon the pale face worshippers at High Mass, he was kindly given standing room near the door, with sufficient room to kneel…the Indians had two faithful friends who clung to them from first to last…a devout American Catholic lady…who rendered the piano accompaniment for their singing. The other was the now aged and feeble Maurice Gailland. Every Sunday morning, with bent form, palsied motion and tottering steps, he groped through the…darkness to say Mass and to give his catacomb Indian children the bountiful consolation of religion.[506]

While the school was undergoing both changes in pupils and teachers, the community had been experiencing changes that brought tension and stress. The number in the community rose to twenty-one in the 1871-1872 catalog. A new superior, Mary Ann Armstrong, arrived that year with Laure Freret and joined Margaret Cornelius, Julia Deegan, Elisabeth Schroeder, Mary Dowdall, Honora Bartley, and Matilde Hamilton, all choir religious, and two choir novices, Mary Stone and Bridget Donovan. There were ten coadjutrix, Mary Layton, Bridget Barnwell, Rosalie Arceneaux, Sarah Ryan, the O'Meara sisters Mary and Catherine, Madeleine Emmanuel, Anne Lehane, Eliza Whitty, and novice Margaret Swan. The school was labor intensive, and it seems that tensions arose as a result of the attempt to follow the directives of previous visiting vicars. Community morale was not good. One mark of the new, strict cloister was that for the first time the community had a sister appointed as portress: Sarah Ryan. In their former assembly of log cabins, it was difficult to have clearly delineated spaces for RSCJ and others. With a solid brick building, the entrance of which was barred by a sturdy door, the community was able to have clearly separate areas for the RSCJ and their students and visitors.

These tensions would be noticed by both Aloysia Hardey, who visited the community in 1872, and Elizabeth Tucker in 1873. The new superiors who had replaced Lucille had obviously enforced the admonitions of previous vicars to more "regularity" in keeping silence and cloister and insisting also on maintaining distinctions between choir religious and coadjutrix sisters. But these were being interpreted in a way that caused pain in the community, damaging the *cor unum*. It is also possible that the influx of new sisters used to living in a very different way in

[505] Craney.
[506] Murphy, p. 208-209.

larger "more regulated" convents and schools also led to misunderstandings. It must have been difficult for some of the pioneers, like Lucille[507] and Mary, as well as the RSCJ who had labored during the 1850s, to see the difference in community spirit. Aloysia Hardey, during her visit in 1872, admonished:

> the superior and those in charge should manifest great kindness in their intercourse with the sisters who have hitherto been treated rather harshly and in a manner so contrary to the spirit of the Society. No distinction should be made in the food served to the sisters in the refectory nor should the cast-off clothing of the choir religious be distributed to them.[508]

The community had incurred a debt as a result of the new building, which needed to be paid off with interest. Some of the tensions in community may have stemmed from too stringent efforts to economize. Hardey commented on the poor quality of the food, especially the meat served to all, and noted that it needed to be of "better quality, prepared carefully and supplied more abundantly three times a day. Bread and tea for *goûter*[509] to all without exception."[510]

The new building also had some limitations, and in her visit Hardey suggested heating improvements. Like the old cabins, it was not warm in the winter, and the many fireplaces did not give sufficient heat. In a subsequent visit in 1873, Tucker noticed that this recommendation of Hardey had not been followed. Therefore, the corporation authorized installing wood stoves. There was not enough water for the building in the tank they were using, and it was necessary to dig a well, install pumps, and connect it to the building via piping.[511]

Mother Mary Ann Aloysia Hardey, RSCJ (RSCJ Archives)

---

[507] Lucille was absent from 1868-1871 when superiors were trying to carry out the directives of the vicars and she remarked negatively on some of the changes she experienced when she returned. (See rest of this chapter where it discusses her return to Saint Marys). Is it possible she shared some of her observations with Hardey and Tucker?

[508] Memoir of Visits of Vicars 1856-1879, RSCJ Archives IV. K. Potawatomi Mission, Box 1.

[509] *Goûter*, the French word used in the Society for an afternoon snack or refreshment break.

[510] Memoir of Visits of Vicars 1856-1879. During this time, the mission was struggling to pay a large debt so perhaps this was one way they had chosen to economize.

[511] Sacred Heart Corporation minutes exist for the period 1869-1879: RSCJ Archives Potawatomi Mission Box 1. An ongoing issue was fixing the gate perhaps because of the new sense of enforcing cloister? Funds appear to have been short for many of the suggested repairs or improvements.

Adding to the workload of the community was the care of the parish or poor school. During her visit Elizabeth Tucker asked that Bridget O'Neil leave that occupation to spend more time supervising the coadjutrix sisters' duties. She was charged with giving instruction to the sister novices two times a week. She cautions the sisters about gossiping with one another about individual students. Tucker also supported Bridget O Neil's suggestion that students not kneel to ask pardon for their faults. In a communication of June 1875, she praises the community for its progress in putting her changes into effect but continues:

> I regret there exists a want of love and cordiality between some of…the [choir] Religious and the Sisters. Some of the latter are dissatisfied because they are under the impression that they are made to feel their dependence and subordinate position. *I am aware of the fact that the Sisters having been formerly on an equal footing with the choir Religious has in some measure contributed to the existing feelings,*[512] but charity demands that a remedy be applied. The choir Religious must evince more sympathy with the Sisters, never speaking to them with a tone of authority, never reprehending them especially before the pupils. At recreation treat them with cordiality and during vacation be pleased to aid them in their domestic employments for such is the expressed wish of our Mother General…bear in mind that *our Sisters are not servants but religious like ourselves and that they merit the esteem and affection mandated by our holy Rule…*[513]

Mary Layton must have welcomed the return of her friend Lucille and enjoyed the time they were able to spend together. They both must have welcomed the admonitions of Aloysia Hardey and Elizabeth Tucker about improving the atmosphere in the house and the relations between the choir religious and the coadjutrix sisters. Lucille had a close friendship all her life with Mary Layton and Louise Amiot. So close was she to Mary that at her death she promised to return for her.

Lucille's last years at Saint Mary's were marked by much sorrow. But she did have the joy in 1873 of celebrating with fellow pioneer Maurice Gailland the twenty-fifth anniversary of the founding of the mission at Saint Mary's. But the same year brought the sadness of witnessing the lingering illness of young Julia Deegan who was ill for three years before her death.[514] While she did not laugh as much as formerly, Lucille had not lost her smile. While her vigor was gone, she was described as bent but still having a firm step, with prominent eyes. This veteran missionary had worn herself out in service so much that one commentator notes that "the Indians used her kindness as one uses water without thinking of it, for they were sure to find it ever fresh, ever new"[515] One of the few changes she probably welcomed was the chapel where for the first time they had the Eucharist reserved

---

[512] *Ibid.* Tucker (my emphasis).

[513] *Ibid.* Tucker (my emphasis).

[514] The description of her illness suggests that it is possible that tuberculosis had claimed another victim at Saint Marys.

[515] Callan, *North America*, p. 302.

in their house. During the last few years of her life, Lucille was confined by illness, sometimes too sick to go to Mass or to be with the community.

Was she well enough to witness the students who participated in the annual Corpus Christi procession in 1875? The little girls, dressed in white, represented Irish, German, and Potawatomi people who lived in the town; they carried the flags of the different countries. Did she contrast it with the procession at Sugar Creek with the warriors on horseback? This one had two hundred and twenty-five carriages, and the Blessed Sacrament was carried in a flower-decorated carriage drawn by six white horses.[516]

Lucille spent a great deal of time in prayer and wrote on Christmas 1875 that she was trying to practice the virtues of the Infant: peace, patience and poverty.[517] That Christmas the RSCJ had midnight Mass in their little chapel. Although she prayed to die that Christmas, she had a sense that her suffering was not at an end. In February 1876, she remarked on how difficult it is to get old. She had a desire to go to heaven but had a fear of Purgatory that remained until the end. That month she contracted a respiratory infection and was moved to the infirmary; the community sent for the doctor. She did not improve, and the RSCJ took turns watching by her bedside. One of the last acts of her life was noticing the fatigue of the sister watching with her; she sent her away, urging her to rest since she (Lucille) had need of nothing. In the middle of that night she became worse, thus attracting the attention of the infirmarian, who sent for the priest to anoint her.

She was eighty-three years, two months and five days old, and much of her religious life had been spent in the service of the mission. Ellen Craney credits Lucille with being the "golden thread" that held the mission united. She had been a novice at Sainte-Marie when Philippine lived and worked there, thus creating a link with the founders of the Society of the Sacred Heart, Madeleine Sophie Barat herself. She was with Mary Anne O'Connor responsible for the re-founding at Saint Charles, and for "thirty-five years the heart and soul of the Indian Mission."[518] At Lucille's death the natives mourned deeply. Both Indians and settlers came to view her body, mourning her as friend and advocate, touching her body with their rosaries and medals with great reverence.[519] Many could not attend her funeral since the news did not reach them in time. But they are described as visiting her grave, chanting and lamenting, "The saddest looking people I ever saw."[520]

Mary Layton had joined Lucille in the infirmary in March 1876. The last month of her life she was paralyzed almost completely and could only use her right hand to say the rosary. She welcomed those who cared for her with a smile expressing her thanks for their help. The sister who had served others for over forty years was unable to

---

[516] *Annual Letters* 1877, p. 272.

[517] *Ibid.* p. 279.

[518] *Ibid.* p. 279 and Memoir of Ellen Craney who cared for Lucille at the end of her life.

[519] *Annual Letters* 1877, p. 280.

[520] Ellen Craney lived with Lucille and was present in house when she died and was buried.

help herself but waited in patience and peace. Lucille, who visited her each day, had promised her that she would return soon for her friend. Three weeks after Lucille died, Mary followed her, on March 30, 1876.[521]

In 1876 the United States celebrated its centennial, and the celebrations included a look back at the events of the previous one hundred years. In the local newspaper that year, a journalist enumerated the many achievements of the area starting with the settlers' election of a representative assembly at Saint Marys in 1855. "…we had an Indian school at Saint Marys for the education of the boys and girls of the tribe. Now we have Saint Mary's College, occupying one building worth over $100,000, and the Academy for young ladies, occupying a fine brick structure, costing nearly $100,000. These two institutions for the education of youth of both sexes are not surpassed by any in the state."[522]

The corporation minutes of the mission show the struggle to economize while paying back their debt of $22,500, to upgrade the building's heat and water, and repair fences and gates. An additional expense was the need to hire a lawyer to settle difficulties about insurance papers. They needed more land, a chicken shed, replacement bricks for those damaged by frost, shade trees, and inside plumbing. An economic crisis in 1875 hit the area on account of a plague of locusts and subsequent crop failures. It is not until 1876 that they succeed in installing indoor plumbing with water conveyed to the house. By 1877 they will have repaid some of the debt but are still struggling to fix the fences, which, despite the rules of cloister, appear to have been a low priority.

The years 1874 and 1875 might have been known as those of the locusts and the earthquake. Of the two, the locusts were more dangerous, since they destroyed crops needed for cattle fodder, and the earthquake did no damage. Less fodder for cattle meant selling off much

Skyscraper on the Prairie, front view

of their herd. The RSCJ reported that the locusts were so many that they blocked the sun.[523] During early June, the Jesuits instituted a novena to ward them away from the mission fields. On June 11 the plague began migrating

[521] Unlike that of other pioneers, there is never any mention of what Mary's relationship with the natives was. There is no mention that she knew the native language, but she must have spoken French so could have communicated with the families that blended those two cultures.
[522] NEWS ARTICLE: A HISTORICAL SKETCH OF the Early Days of Pottawatomie County. Prepared for the Occasion of the Centennial Celebration, July 4th, 1876, by Hon. L. R. Palmer. Microfilm at the Kansas Historical Society Archives: reel S-60.
[523] *Annual Letters* 1875/76.

north and was completely gone by the 18th.[524] That was the year that the splendid Corpus Christi procession that had begun long ago with two hundred mounted horseback riders was now reduced to being led by only six boys on Indian ponies.[525]

There is no indication in Society records that the RSCJ at Saint Marys were aware of events taking place in the West, where armed conflict was occurring between native people, especially the Lakota and the Cheyenne, and the U.S. Army. Fort Riley, near the Mission, was the headquarters of the U.S. Seventh Cavalry, formed there in 1866. George Custer, an army officer[526] known for his heroism at the Battle of Bull Run, came to Fort Riley in 1868 to join the Seventh Cavalry. He would serve with the Seventh Cavalry from Fort Riley until 1871, when the unit was sent to support in the South during Reconstruction. In 1873, it would move to Fort Abraham Lincoln in the Dakota Territory. The following year Custer would lead an expedition into the Black Hills. Lakota people from the Dakota Territory resisted the U.S. army, and under Chief Sitting Bull met the Seventh Cavalry at the battle of Little Big Horn in 1876, in which Custer and his five hundred men suffered complete defeat and all died.

As the number of students diminished, the community grew in size. By 1875-76 there were twenty-three RSCJ: ten choir religious: Mary Ann Armstrong, who had been appointed superior in 1871; Bridget O'Neil, Matilde Hamilton, Lucille Mathevon, Elisabeth Schroeder, Margaret Knapp, Mary Dowdall, Octavie Robidoux, Theresa Carroll, and Ellen Craney. The thirteen coadjutrix sisters outnumbered the choir sisters: Mary Layton, Bridget Barnwell, Rosalie Arceneaux, Sarah Ryan, Mary and Catherine O'Meara, Madeleine Emmanuel, all professed; Anne Lehane, Margaret Swan, and Mary Anne Summers in first vows; and two novices, Johanna Collins, Ann Reynolds, and Postulant Johanna Bresnahan. Lucille Mathevon and Mary Layton would die before the year was out.

The last of the seven RSCJ buried in the grave at Saint Marys was Rosa Boyle, born May 21, 1825, in Philadelphia.[527] She entered the Society in 1853[528] in Saint Louis at the age of twenty-seven and made her vows in 1855. Her parents were James Boyle and Ellen Campbell, both born in the United States.[529] All we know about

---

[524] O'Connor, p. 372.

[525] *Ibid.* p. 378. Other aspects seem as grand with 200 wagons and a parade through town.

[526] Custer had a less than stellar record before the Civil War, graduating last in his class at West Point. He achieved a celebrity status after his performance in the Civil War. It seems unlikely that local newspapers would not have covered him and his exploits.

[527] A Sacred Heart school near Philadelphia was founded in 1842, too late for Rosa to have been a student there. She may have encountered the Society through retreats given for laywomen in Saint Louis or through one of the Jesuits.

[528] The 1850 U.S. census for Saint Louis has no Rosa Boyle and few families with that name. A search of the American Catholic Historical Society published marriage registers 1799-1826 does not yield a wedding for this couple, but there is a number of Boyle families: Hugh, Neil, and two James but none with wife that matches. Her family is not listed in other sources such as *All Trails West: The Founding Catholic Families of Pennsylvania*, although other Boyles are.

[529] Rosa is listed at Kenwood in the 1870 census, and it indicates both her parents as American born.

her family is that it was one "where faith and devotion were hereditary.[530] There is a number of entries for Boyle marriages in Old Saint Joseph's (and Saint Mary's), Philadelphia, but none for this couple. Rosa probably was baptized in this parish, which was divided into two in 1833.[531] It is one of the oldest Catholic churches in the United States.[532] In the 1790 census there were two James Boyles in Philadelphia, living near this church, both weavers. Other census years continue to list one or more James Boyle families, but up to 1840 there is only one with a child of an age to be Rosa.[533]

By the time Rosa was considering entering the Society, she was living in Saint Louis,[534] where there was a good-sized Irish community, which had swelled with numbers of immigrants after the Irish famine of 1847-1848. In 1849 a cholera epidemic hit the city along with the destruction of the waterfront by fire. Orphans abounded both from disease and disaster and from being abandoned by parents or guardians. Some were left by prospectors heading west to the gold mines of California. As a result, the number of orphanages in Saint Louis doubled in the next twenty years. Rosa was active in her church, working with the poor, and president of the Children of Mary Sodality at the Jesuit parish. It would be interesting to know why Rosa decided to enter the Society of the Sacred Heart rather than other American congregations that were working directly with the poor. Rosa evidently struggled with the decision to enter because "the good she was doing in the world caused her to find difficulty in renouncing it. Faithful to grace, she at length triumphed over every obstacle and was received in Saint Louis, April 7, 1854, by Margaret Gallwey."

Rosa had leadership skills, and even before her final profession, when assigned to Saint Louis, she was in charge of the coadjutrix sisters[535] in addition to being the sacristan.[536] One month after her final profession in 1861, she was made superior at Saint Joseph, Missouri, leaving there in 1867.[537] Later she continued working with the coadjutrix sisters after

---

[530] *Annual Letters* 1876-77 on occasion of her death, p. 281.

[531] Records available for baptisms published from the American Catholic Historical Society only cover to 1810.

[532] Founded by the Jesuits in 1733, it was a refuge for Catholics fleeing religious discrimination laws in Maryland. Only in William Penn's colony were they free to worship. Thomas Fitzwilliam, a signer of the Declaration of Independence, and Commodore John Barry were members. Members of the Continental Congress, such as George Washington and John Adams, attended services here. The first Catholic commemoration of the Declaration of Independence was held in this church.

[533] In the burial records for the Old Cathedral cemetery, there are three James Boyles the right age to be Rosa's father; one died age fifty in 1851; if he was Rosa's father, might his death be the reason the family moved to Saint Louis? However, there is an equal number of James Boyles buried in Saint Louis around the time Rosa lived there, one of whom might also have been her father.

[534] The Saint Louis Irish community was large at this time and there are many Boyle families in Saint Louis, but for some reason they do not show up in the 1850 census.

[535] She is in the 1860 census: twenty-one choir religious, twenty coadjutrix sisters.

[536] A sacristan was responsible for setting up for Mass and other services. She cared for the linens, altar clothes, vestments and the vessels used such as the chalices, plates, candlesticks etc.

[537] Callan, *North America*, pp. 672-73. Saint Joseph, founded in 1853, was a "poor" or day school founded to care for the many Catholic settlers' children. By 1868, it had 150 students.

she became assistant superior in Saint Louis in 1868.[538] In 1870 she is listed in the U.S. Census for Albany, New York, as a resident of Kenwood. She had a similar position in Chicago in 1874 and 1875. Both those houses were large and had nearly fifty RSCJ. Saint Mary's community, although the largest in its history, would be half that size. The move to Kansas with a smaller number of coadjutrix sisters was a lighter employment. Since Rosa was ill, her superiors may have hoped that the better country air of Kansas would improve her health.

By the time Rosa arrived it is unlikely that there were any native students as boarders and few as day students. In 1877 there were only nineteen boarders at the school, although the number of day students is not recorded. When Rosa died in 1877 at age fifty, the writer of the report was eloquent on her virtues, praising her as a "perfect" novice, who in her religious life was as "wax in the hands of her superiors." The report gives a hint of her spirit; she evidently spoke her mind and "gave her opinion candidly without being deterred by human consideration."[539] Rosa was the last RSCJ buried in the small cemetery on the grounds of the Sacred Heart school.

The same year that Rosa Boyle died, the veteran missionary to the Potawatomi, Maurice Gailland, also died. His biographer gives a vivid account of how he wore himself out ministering to those of his charges who remained, since he was the only priest who spoke their language. He also cared for the many Catholic families that had moved into the prairies of Kansas travelling great distances in all kinds of weather.

> A call in the winter season from a sick Indian residing twenty-three miles from Saint Marys was promptly answered by Gailland, but on crossing a river only a short distance from the mission, he fell through the ice and had to continue on his way with clothes frozen to his body. He had perforce under the same circumstances to spend the night in the Indian's hut and return home the following day. Twenty four hours of this physical hardship and exposure had their result, the missionary thereby contracting a paralysis from which he never fully recovered. For some time subsequently he was still able, with the aid of horse and buggy, to go some distance on his ministerial rounds but to ride horseback was now beyond him,[540]

An article written for *The Pottawatomie Chief* in January 1878 gives descriptions of the area around the mission as well as the mission itself.

> The traveler is particularly struck with the beautiful country around Saint Marys. In the Kansas Valley, on the Kansas Pacific Railway, twenty five miles west from Topeka, surrounded by some of the best bottom and uplands to be found west of the Mississippi. The city and country around is settled by a thriving and

[538] The *Society Catalogue* for Saint Louis 1868-1869 lists her as assistant superior, class mistress and responsible for the direction of the coadjutrix sisters.
[539] *Annual Letters* 1876/1877.
[540] Garraghan 3, p.64: after a final sick call he was brought home ill in 1877, reviving sufficiently to say his last Mass on the feast of Saint Ignatius and dying in August of that year.

industrious class, who are rapidly redeeming the time and the land. The location of Saint Marys in the center of the celebrated Pottawatomie reservation, renders the trade of a goodly portion of four counties tributary to it. The magnificent valley of Mill Creek stretches away to the southwest, which, with a great bend in the Kansas river, gives a large proportion of bottom and timber lands, and with plenty of good water makes this a most desirable locality for the settler. The scenery, with its variety of timber, prairie and upland slopes, the fruit orchards and the rivers is unsurpassed in Kansas.[541]

It is obvious why the settlers had coveted the area and by this time had completely taken it over. The college is one of the attractions of the new Kansas and the journalist continues to brag.

The College is a most elegant structure, built of brick— by our esteemed citizen Mr. M. Ward—and is four stories high; standing in the East part of the city, and surrounded with all the buildings, shops, studies etc., forms quite a village; while the grounds are beautifully laid out and adorned with shrubbery, evergreens and various rare and costly plants. The building was erected at a cost of $100,000, and is…furnished in the most approved modern style. [It is not clear if he is referring to the new building erected by the Jesuits or that of the Sacred Heart but it appears to be that of the Jesuits.] Rev. F. H. Stuntebeck, is conceded by all to stand pre-eminently at the head of his class as an educator, and is a man of great executive ability, as the workings of the institution from day to day and from year to year, plainly prove; for never is there anything else than the utmost harmony, system, regularity and precision…The faculty consists of ten or twelve professors, and teachers of music, languages etc., of course including every branch to be taught to educate from the primary to the classics. The attendance, from all parts of the country is annually large and includes students from every State in the Union. While the home attendance by day students is almost universal. The terms of tuition are—for the session of ten months, from September 1st, to June 30th, of each year—$150, for boarders, and $3 per month for day scholars. In the case of the boarder, the above tuition fees cover all—board, rooms, washing, medical attendance, etc. There is no institution of learning in all the West, in which the tuition charges are not at least double, compared to those of ours, where the same attention and instruction are received by the students. The Academy or Convent for the education of young ladies, stands near, and is the counterpart of the college, in buildings, surrounding and educational advantages. The institution is presided over exclusively by ladies, under the direction of the "Mother Superioress." The health, comfort, and advancement is [*sic*] watched over with the most zealous care. The tuition is $85 for a five months session, or $170, for a full term of ten months. This includes, board, books, washing and rooms. Day pupils are admitted for $15 per session.[542]

The same newspaper article outlines the many changes that occurred in this small town during the 1870s. It now has a Catholic church separate from the mission, along with a Swedish Lutheran and a Congregational church. Methodists also meet but have no church building. There are three hotels and two restaurants. The commercial

---

[541] Microfilm at the Kansas Historical Society Archives: reel S-60.

[542] *Ibid*. Not clear in text what a "session" was, i.e., a month or five months.

establishments are all founded within the last ten years and include thirteen stores with general merchandise, drugs, clothing, shoes and boots, groceries, jewelry, and furniture and hardware. There are harness shops, lumberyards, two blacksmith shops, a livery stable, two barbers, two land offices, and two grain merchants. The town boasts three doctors, four lawyers, and three saloons. Public buildings include a city hall and a post office. There is a railroad depot, a steam mill, and two newspapers.[543]

Despite the evident growing prosperity of the area, the Sacred Heart school did not grow, and the number of girls diminished each year. Although the Jesuit school was filled with boys, prairie farm families evidently did not feel like making a similar investment in their sisters' education. Two other Sacred Heart schools, in Saint Joseph, Missouri, and Saint Louis, may have siphoned off prospective students, given the ease of rail travel. But the actual catalyst for the closing was a catastrophic fire in February 1879 in the new Jesuit building that left over ninety boys and their teachers homeless. The sisters housed the Jesuits and their students in the "Skyscraper on the Prairie" and moved their sixteen students into the cloister with the religious. Three days later they found housing in town for their students so they could finish out the year. It was ironic that the number of RSCJ in the last two years of the school's existence was the largest in its history—between twenty-three and twenty-six.

Of the RSCJ who closed the school in 1879, there remained none of the original pioneers. Only seven of the twenty-six, Bridget O'Neil, Theresa Dowdall, Rosalie Arceneaux, Bridget Barnwell, Elizabeth Schroeder, and the O'Meara sisters, who had arrived in the 1850s and 1860s, would have had memories of the days when it served native students. The superior, Mary Bourke, had arrived in 1877, replacing Mary Ann Armstrong. By this time the community probably resembled more closely, in its schedule and customs, those of large convents in other parts of the Society. It had space for the choir religious and the coadjutrix sisters to follow the customs practiced in other houses and to receive formation designed for their needs.

It is interesting to speculate what might have been the future of the mission if in the crucial years of the 1860s the religious had not been bound by cloister and been able to follow their students[544] to their new home. Both single-sex education and strapped community finances probably would have prevented them from opening a day school on the Kansas reservation.[545] On the other hand, it is possible that it was a blessing in disguise that the RSCJ did not become involved in running a government boarding school or day school of the 1880s. Well into

---

543 *Ibid.* microfilm reel S-60.

544 The Citizen Band was later served by the Benedictines.

545 O'Connor, p. 317. The tribe did succeed in having schools on the reserve one of which was staffed by the Quakers.

the twentieth century, these institutions [546] included practices designed to rob the native children of any vestiges of their culture and language. The bitter memories of those natives who were forcibly removed from their parents, forbidden to speak their language or practice their religion and culture still persist among the elders of many tribes today. Not until after the second Vatican Council in the 1960s would RSCJ truly realize what it meant to work with indigenous cultures with true respect.

---

[546] Government boarding schools had the explicit goal of exterminating native culture by removing native children from parents, often by force. They were known for their coercive methods and harsh punishment. It is estimated that there was a total of 500 such schools both on and off reservations. Both boarding and day schools were sometimes run by missionaries. In the 1960s and '70s Indian tribes gained control of schools through various acts of Congress. Sherman Indian School in Riverside, California, is the only surviving government boarding school, but it is run by Native Americans and promotes native culture. Over thirty tribal colleges exist run by tribal authority.

Epilogue: The Future of the Potawatomi and the Society of the Sacred Heart

The government system of Indian off-reservation boarding schools began in 1879 with the foundation of Carlisle Indian School in Pennsylvania and grew by the end of the century to over one hundred such schools. Their goal was to totally eradicate the native culture. "Christianizing" the native led the government, despite the American principle of separation of church and state, to promote the Christian (preferably Protestant) religion as a tool of this process.[547] Another freedom guaranteed by the Bill of Rights, that of freedom of religion, was ignored, as native religious practices, even on the reservation, were criminalized. Natives were forbidden to engage in ceremonies such as the Sun Dance or to possess ritual articles used in their religions.

These regulations seem to have been a response to fears generated by a number of native prophetic movements in the late nineteenth century. In the 1870s religious movements began, which gave participants a sense of hope in the midst of oppression and loss of territory. Circle dances, always a part of native rituals, were performed at night to facilitate the coming of a new age. The Ghost Dance originated among the Paiutes and spread to other tribes. The Drum Religion, similar to the Ghost Dance, became popular with the Potawatomi. Many of these movements blended native rituals and practices with elements of Christianity.[548] Some of the movements prophesied that the natives would regain their lands; settlers would disappear, and their dead would rise, provided the dances were performed regularly. The movement urged a return to native spiritual practices and balanced living. The Ghost Dance increased resistance to the Dawes Act of 1887 among the Lakota. In 1890, the U.S. government broke up the large Lakota reservation into five smaller pieces, leading to further unrest and the presence of U.S. troops.

[547] Although the enforcement of some these laws ceased sooner, they were officially revoked only by the American Indian Religious Freedom Act of 1978. Vine Deloria in his work "God is Red" (1972) wrote on both native spirituality and native views of other religious beliefs.

[548] Christopher Vecsey, *The Paths of Kateri's Kin,* (University of Notre Dame, 1991) Vol. I, p. 250, discusses the modern day practice of the Drum among the Potawatomi. Other movements were the Indian Shaker Church and the Earth Lodge Religion.

The killing of Sitting Bull,[549] a native political and spiritual leader, later that year on December 14, 1890, and the massacre at Wounded Knee two weeks later, December 29, 1890, are attributed by native historians to the fear generated by the Ghost Dance. Those killed at Wounded Knee had just performed a Ghost dance and were on their way to take refuge at Pine Ridge Agency with another band of Lakota. They were massacred by the Seventh Cavalry Unit of the U.S. Army, George Custer's' unit. Fort Riley, near Saint Mary's Mission, was where the U.S. Cavalry was trained. Witnesses reported that soldiers cried out "Remember Little Big Horn" as they killed over two hundred natives, mostly women and children.

Among the Prairie Potawatomi, the Big Drum Dance, or Dream Dance, was introduced by contact with bands in Wisconsin in the late 1870s. Initially it was promoted as a way to rid the natives of whites and Christian Indians as well as to restore their traditions. As it developed, it reinforced native solidarity and resistance to the dominant American culture. Some of the Prairie Potawatomi members migrated to Skunk Hill in Wisconsin to join other traditional Potawatomi who practiced the Drum Dance about the turn of the twentieth century.

The practice of land grabbing was not over when the Society closed its mission in Saint Marys. The disastrous Dawes[550] Act in 1887 gave the government the authority to force Indian nations to accept individual allotment whatever previous treaties had given them. It led to further erosion of Indian rights and property, since it dealt with individual Indians and not with the tribe as a nation. The goal was eradication of Indian identity as well as the opening up of vast western lands to accommodate the growing U.S. population. The railroad began actively promoting the migration of settlers through ads, such as those in the Kansas Historical Society collection (1878-1889) touting the area as one for "A new home in an old settlement," one in which "you will buy a farm as cheap as on the border of settlement and yet with all the advantages of and surrounded by a high civilization."[551] One of the advertisements has a profile of Saint Marys as a place where the farmer will find a market for his goods and be able to purchase all he needs in its stores. The College of Saint Mary is mentioned as one of its attractions.

Gary Mitchell, tribal historian, outlines the process: "The reservation must go!" became the cry of eastern reformers determined to fashion Indians in their own image and therefore to proclaim them self-reliant citizens. As a result, in 1887, Congress passed the Dawes Act or the General Allotment Act of 1887. The government deemed this law a "virtual necessity." Congress said it could no longer protect Indian lands from further settlement and

---

[549] He was the leader who directed the Lakota force that defeated Custer's 7th Cavalry at Little Big Horn 1876. He resisted treaties that broke up the Lakota land, led a band of natives to Canada, and returned in 1881 when they found it too difficult to survive there. He had achieved a certain celebrity not only for the defeat of Custer but also as a member of Buffalo Bill Cody's show in 1885. He refused to become a farmer and made a living of his celebrity, selling photos and autographs much to the chagrin of the local Indian agent who had insisted he return to the reservation from the show after just a year. He was killed while being arrested on suspicion of supporting the Ghost Dance movement.

[550] The author of the act, Henry Dawes, felt that owning property was the mark of a "civilized" person.

[551] Kansas State Historical Society advertisements for RR lands.

the demands of the railroads and other enterprises. The basic provision of the General Allotment Act was to give each Indian a private plot of land on which to become an industrious farmer. To hasten assimilation, the law provided for the end of tribal relationships, such as land held in common. It stipulated that reservations were to be surrendered and divided into family-sized farms, which would be allotted to each Indian. The supreme aim was to substitute mainstream American civilization for tribal culture. Since the railroad had purchased the land left over from the allotment for about $1.00 an acre, there was immense profit to be made from taking Indian land.[552]

The Prairie Band Potawatomi still persistently refused to accept individual allotments of land or the right of the government to make such a disposition. In the 1880s, they were beginning to make a success of developing agriculture and stock herding. Unfortunately, settlers began to look with envy on their success. The natives had planted orchards and built a school. Ironically, they were starting to do what the government and the missionaries had told them to do—settle in one place and take up farming. In Indian agents' reports from the period, it is clear that they would like to buy up the land that the tribe had made successful. Persuasion to accept allotments consisted of withholding federal payments due the Prairie Band and giving double allotments of their land to settlers, Indians from other tribes, and the residing agent's relatives. By the 1880s and 1890s, government policy clearly tended toward forcing the Indians to accept allotment. Mission Potawatomi who had moved onto the reservation opposed the allotment based on their own sad experience. The government was suspicious of their influence and in 1884, 1886, and 1891, these former Saint Mary's Mission Indians were ordered to move off the reservation. When they refused, the US Seventh Cavalry moved in. Finally in 1894, they removed the Mission natives, and in 1895 the whole tribe was forced to accept allotments. Much of the land finally allotted to them was too poor to farm, and they received no financial credit and little help of any kind.[553]

William Connelley observes that in the 1870s the agents were prejudiced against the tribe, feeling that there was a class of the Prairie Band opposed to progress.

> It was composed of the priest and medicine men—the men who held to the old traditions and customs of the Pottawatomies. This inclination to preserve the ancient rites was always condemned by the agents and missionaries. They always saw, as they supposed, in this attitude, a sort of defiance of Christian influence. In reality there was no intention to stand in opposition to the missionary efforts. It was the love of the old order and the faith and reverence held in and for the ways of ancient days, so strong in the human heart. If the agent and missionaries had but rightly read Indian character in this respect, they would have permitted and encouraged the free exercise of the old ceremonies. The Indian would have added the Christian religion to his own—which those individuals did who adopted it. It requires time to divest a people of religious customs and

---

[552] Gary E. Mitchell, *Stories of the Potawatomi People*, self-published, 16095 N. Road, Mayetta, Kansas 66509-9087. Also on http://www.kansasheritage.org/PBP/books/mitch/mitchbuk.html.

[553] Prairie Band website and additional information from Connelley; See also Mitchell's *Stories of the Potawatomi People*. Both books are available on www.kansasheritage.org.

feelings. As the generations passed the old pagan practices would have passed, for the vital elements must and will survive and subvert the superfluous in human life. The old rites would have survived as folk customs, folk lore. Much of beauty and much of ethnological value would have been saved—much that would have benefited both the white and Indian races.[554]

In the early part of the twentieth century, the movement to extinguish native culture continued as government policy resulted in the forcible removal of native children from their families. However, there was a growing understanding on the part of some American social reformers that the policy was unjust and flawed. Helen Hunt Jackson, an early activist for native rights, wrote in 1881 *A Century of Dishonor,* criticizing the U.S. government treatment of native peoples. She authored a report on the condition of the Mission Indians of California in 1883 that was inspiration for legislation that failed to aid them. When those reports were ignored and the legislation failed, she wrote *Ramona* in 1884, incorporating her research in fictional form to raise public awareness.[555] In the 1930s, tribal governments were recognized, although this step sometimes led to tribal division and conflict.

The legend of the "vanishing Indian" and the stereotypes perpetuated by the popular "cowboys and Indians" movies were pervasive in mainstream American culture. Many Americans assumed that the Indian had indeed "vanished" and so were surprised by the Indian protest movements of the 1960s. Native civil rights, education and advocacy movements such as the National Congress of American Indians (NCAI), the National Indian Youth Council (NIYC), and especially the American Indian Movement (AIM) brought native issues to national attention. In 1969 in *Custer Died for Your Sins,* native author Vine Deloria wrote of the damage done to native culture by the evangelization methods of Christian missionaries. In 1970, *Bury My Heart at Wounded Knee,* by Dee Brown, introduced Americans to the history of native people. In the 1972 classic work, *God is Red,* the same author introduced many Americans to the roots of the Indian movement and the many protests over Indian rights that occurred during the 1970s. Media attention and participation by younger activists gave the movement energy and prominence.

William Connelley's book quoted in this account continues the story of the Kansas Potawatomi reservation and the Prairie Band through the beginning of the nineteenth century. Gary Mitchell's *Stories of the Potawatomi People* gives the history through 1995 and disagrees with Connelley on major points, especially the role of the missionaries. Information on the Citizens' Band can be found in *Potawatomi of the West* by Joseph Murphy, OSB.

The Prairie Band Potawatomi website brings up to date the history of those who settled north of Topeka on the reservation. Two other Potawatomi tribal websites may be of interest for insight into modern day Potawatomi

---

[554] Connelley, p. 523. Whether the Prairie Band would agree that this would happen seems unlikely. Native accounts of this period such as Mitchell's give a different perspective.

[555] She hoped to achieve for Native Americans an awareness of injustices that would parallel what the popular success of *Uncle Tom's Cabin* had done for the abolitionist movement.

life: Citizens' Band in Oklahoma and Pokagon Band in Michigan.[556] The Catholics living on the Prairie Tribe reserve built a chapel, Our Lady of the Snows. A picture of Saint Philippine Duchesne is in the chapel. Served by the Jesuits in the 1940s, it later came under diocesan priests' care. Today the parish of Saint Dominic in nearby Holton, Kansas, serves the mission.[557]

Nearly one hundred years after the close of the Saint Mary's Mission, the deliberations of the Second Vatican Council allowed native people to accept Catholicism without abandoning their own culture and those native spiritual practices consistent with Catholic teachings. Before this development, missionaries had assumed that adoption of western (European) culture was a prerequisite everywhere to becoming Catholic.[558] The Council urged missionaries to look for the signs of the Spirit working within other cultures and religions and to enter into dialogue with them. The "Declaration on the Relation of the Church to Non-Christian religions" or *Nostra Aetate*, proclaimed by Pope Paul VI on October 28, 1965, states: "Likewise, other religions found everywhere try to counter the restlessness of the human heart, each in its own manner, by proposing ways, comprising teachings, rules of life, and sacred rites. *The Catholic Church rejects nothing that is true and holy in these religions…* [The church] regards with sincere reverence those ways of conduct and of life, those precepts and teachings which, though differing in many aspects from the ones she holds and sets forth, nonetheless often reflect a ray of that Truth which enlightens all" (paragraph #2). Another document from the Council, the decree *Ad Gentes* on the mission activity of the church (paragraph #26), affirms that "the approach of the missionary is one of reverence for their culture." This way of thinking revolutionized the encounter with other religions and affected the way missionaries approach people in their work of evangelization. The document urges anyone who is going to encounter another people to have a *great esteem for their patrimony and their language and their customs.*"[559]

In the United States, the Tekakwitha conference and local Tekakwitha circles were formed to promote the canonization of Kateri Tekakwitha as the first Native American saint. They also enabled native Catholics to explore aspects of their own spirituality and to recognize the compatibility of many of those practices and rituals with the

---

[556] Prairie Band website http://www.pbpindiantribe.com. Archbishop Charles Chaput is a member of this Potawatomi band; The Citizen Potawatomi band website http://www.potawatomi.org/ and the Pokagon Potawatomi Band website http://www.pokagonband-nsn.gov/.

[557] Vecsey, pp. 250 ff. on drum religion and its persistence into the twentieth century. Also has interviews with Potawatomi in Mayetta, Kansas, on views of church and religion.

[558] Short-lived experiments in genuine dialogue did occur, such as the one of Jesuit Matteo Ricci, a successful missionary to China in the sixteenth century, who sought to dialogue with Chinese scholars and adapt Christian practices to include Chinese culture. His innovations were condemned in the early eighteenth century. Pope Benedict XVI recognized him as a model of respect for other cultures. A contemporary of Ricci, Jesuit Roberto DeNobili, in India, adapted his preaching and practice of Christianity, incorporating local cultural customs. He pioneered Hindu-Christian dialogue.

[559] Emphasis mine.

Catholic faith. The church sought to become less Euro- or Western-centered, although it would not elect a Pope from outside Europe until 2013. Through the Tekakwitha conferences and in local workshops, native priests, religious, deacons, and laity, as well as nonnatives, learned about the spirituality of the people they serve and ways to integrate practices and symbols into liturgy and catechesis. The Council encouraged the formation, not only of a Catholic laity indigenous to the culture, but also clergy, religious, and catechists from the same culture who could express the faith out of their own lived experience.

When the Society of the Sacred Heart withdrew from Saint Mary's School in 1879, it was no longer serving the Potawatomi people for whom the school had been founded. The remainder of the tribe who stayed in Kansas were living in Mayetta, Kansas, north of Topeka while others had moved to a new reservation in Oklahoma. The Jesuits purchased the building and its grounds. The "Skyscraper of the Prairie" building was enlarged and incorporated into the Jesuit College after 1879 and still stands today, although without chimneys and with a different roof. None of the original cabins stand, having burned during the course of the years. The old log chapel of Bishop Miège was torn down, and a new one replaced it.

The College of Saint Marys for young men continued and experienced success, graduating its first students in 1882. In 1890, a teacher at Saint Marys, plagued by insomnia, wrote what was to become the most popular Catholic boys' novel: *Tom Playfair*. He based the character on a typical student of his day and set it at Saint Marys. Over the next twenty-five years it would be translated into many languages, becoming a sort of Catholic *Tom Sawyer*.

The Jesuit school had continued success as a college until the Great Depression, when it was forced to close. The buildings were used as a Jesuit seminary from 1931 to 1967. The seminary closed in 1967, moving to Saint Louis University. In 1972, the Jesuits attempted to give the land and buildings back to the tribe and held a ceremony formalizing the transfer.[560] The transfer needed government approval, and government bureaucracy led to the plans falling through. The property passed through various realtors' and developers' hands, one of whom acquired an option to purchase it in 1977 and made plans to sell it as a Job Corps training center. This plan was

---

[560] In the original transfer of lands to the missionaries in 1867, the land was supposed to be used for the education of the Potawatomi students. (Mitchell.) Coming from a native perspective, this writer felt that the Jesuits abandoned the natives and participated in the same sort of land grab as the other settlers. This attempt seems to be aimed at redressing this issue.

opposed by the town and fell through. It eventually was acquired by the schismatic Society of Saint Pius X in 1978, which now uses it as their United States center and a school.[561]

The system of two classes of RSCJ continued in the Society, and a look at Society records shows that many of the coadjutrix sisters in the United States, just as in the days of Saint Mary's, were immigrant Irish women. But the number of these vocations diminished as immigrant women were able to profit from the better education available in the United States. Given the cultural distaste for this system in the United States, native-born American women took advantage of opportunities for religious life in[562] American-founded religious congregations, which had not adopted this system. Although coadjutrix sisters continued to be present in the communities in the United States, many were immigrants from other countries, especially Poland, Malta and Latin America.

In 1964, the system of the two classes of choir and coadjutrix was abolished in the Society, although actual changes in attitude would take much longer. The rule of cloister was changed when, following the decisions of Vatican II, the Society had to identify itself as either monastic or apostolic.[563] The community at Sugar Creek, and in the first twenty years at Saint Mary's, was probably more like communities of RSCJ after Vatican II in its adaptation to the ministry and to the circumstances in which they lived than those existing at the same time in other parts of the Society. They had unwittingly, perhaps, because of necessity, incorporated American attitudes of equality into their relationships with one another and formed friendships across class lines.

In documents of the Society composed after Vatican II, the Constitutions of 1982, approved in 1987, and the Chapter of 1988, there is a renewed sense of how the Society's vocation as an apostolic religious community is lived out and how God is to be found in everything that touches the lives of the members. Each person's gifts are important: "Whatever the service entrusted to us, we stand together; united in our common mission" (Constitutions §30) The Society in over forty different countries is able to explore being truly incarnate in each

---

[561] The Society of Saint Pius X was formed in France, in 1976, by clergy who opposed to the liturgical reforms of Vatican II. They first focused on maintaining with Vatican approval the form of the liturgy in Latin that existed before the council. They became a schismatic group when their leader, Archbishop Lefebvre, ordained priests without the permission of the Vatican. Although there has been some attempt to reconcile the group with Rome, at this writing that has not happened. They also express opposition to other Vatican II decrees, especially the one on religious liberty. As recent as spring 2015, a bishop of this group was excommunicated a second time for illicitly consecrating a bishop for the Society. News from 2016 indicated a desire on the part of Pope Francis to reconcile this group with the mainstream church.

[562] Both Dubourg and Philippine Duchesne had sensed this from the beginning but they were not able to implement their insight into the Society's structure at the time.

[563] In order to take "solemn vows" women who entered religious life were bound to cloister, a monastic structure. During the nineteenth and twentieth centuries, the institutional church was adapting to the new forms of religious life that were evolving outside of the monastic structures and engaged in apostolic works that took them outside of a stable monastery setting. The process of developing a new form of religious life, the apostolic, found inspiration in Vatican II, and the process of experimentation and return to the original charism or inspiration that it encouraged.

culture and surroundings.[564] When it described an international apostolic community, the General Chapter of 1988 recognized that: "Little by little the process of enculturation is changing the face of the Society, giving us new energy and life…moving us…towards a deeper sense of our internationality. It is the unifying strength of our charism that commits us to deepen this dialogue among cultures." Throughout, the document speaks of the ways that being open to other cultures deepens personal understanding and is a transformative experience. The document encourages "learning the language and symbolic expressions of the people among whom we live." Although the pioneers at Sugar Creek and Saint Mary's did not have this explicit insight, they were able intuitively to know that they must meet the people they served with respect and love. It is not reasonable to judge the work of the early missionaries among the Potawatomi by the standards of today. In so far as the culture of the time and their formation allowed, and sometimes in spite of it, they were able to serve from the heart. In the process of attempting to welcome the native people and make them partners in the educational project, they were faulted for adaptation of their own culture and lifestyle to that of the people they served. They modeled hospitality, respect for native language, and fidelity to relationships forged with the people they served.

Since the freedom from cloister and the reforms of Vatican II, individual members of the Society in the United States and Canada[565] have served with Native Americans: Irene Packer, who served as librarian at Rose Bud Reservation in South Dakota, Esperanza Jasso in the native reservations of southern California near Mecca, Carol Putnam in Indiantown in Florida with indigenous immigrant people from Central America and later in Mecca with California Native Americans, Carlota Duarte among the indigenous people of Chiapas, Mexico, and Sheila Smith with First Nation peoples in Canada. A group of RSCJ serve and have served as teachers, catechists, and fund raisers at Saint Joseph's Mission in Soboba, California: Marianna Torrano, Mary Gen Smyth, Judy Roach, Adele Schroeder, and Deanna Rose Von Bargen. In 2002 they began St. Jude's, a primary school for native children, to incorporate native culture in the process of education, coming full circle back to the initiative begun at Sugar Creek in 1841. Once again the RSCJ were beginning a small educational enterprise with Native Americans.

---

[564] Prior to this, the Society with all its French customs was inserted into each country where a foundation was made. The exodus of all the French members in the early twentieth century to other houses in Europe, Africa, Asia, and the Americas added to the preservation of the French character of the Society.

[565] RSCJ in many other countries serve indigenous tribal peoples, examples that come to mind are Mexico, Latin America, Africa, Indonesia and India.

Sources and Bibliography

Primary sources

RSCJ Archives: Provincial Archives, Society of the Sacred Heart, United-States-Canada Province, Saint Louis, Missouri.

Annual Letters, Society of the Sacred Heart. RSCJ Archives

Community House Registers: Saint Charles, Saint Louis, and Saint Marys. RSCJ Archives.

Craney, Ellen, RSCJ. *Memoir of Lucille Mathevon.* Handwritten manuscript.

De Charry, Jeanne, RSCJ, ed., *Saint Madeleine-Sophie Barat, Saint Philippine Duchesne, Correspondence.* 4 vols. Translated by Barbara Hogg, RSCJ, Joan Sweetman, RSCJ, April O'Leary, RSCJ, and Mary Coke, RSCJ. Rome: Society of the Sacred Heart, 1988-1999.

Philippine Duchesne, RSCJ, Frontier Pioneer, Complete Writings, privately printed, 2018.

Gailland, Maurice, SJ. *Letters* and *Diary.* Latin and French, partial English translation. Midwest Jesuit Archives.

Kansas State Census 1855, 1865, and 1875.

Kersaint, Henriette de, RSCJ. Memoir of Mother de Kersaint. RSCJ Archives, Martinez Collection.

Mathevon, Lucille, RSCJ. Letters, unpublished copies in both French and English translation, RSCJ Archives.

Minutes of Sacred Heart Corporation Saint Marys Kansas 1869-1879. Handwritten notebook. RSCJ Archives.

Monzert, Marie-Rose, RSCJ. *Memoir of Lucile Mathevon.* Typed manuscript.

Reports of visits of Superiors Vicar to Saint Marys, Kansas. Handwritten reports to 1870 in French and later English. RSCJ Archives:

> Amélie Jouve, July 1856;
> Margaret Gallwey, May 1866;
> Rose Gauthreaux, October 1869 and April 1870;
> Aloysia Hardey, April 1872; Elizabeth Tucker, October 1873;
> Susanna Boudreau, May 1878.

Schroeder, Elizabeth, RSCJ. *Memoir of Saint Marys,* handwritten manuscript. RSCJ Archives. Potawatomi Mission Box 2.

Tardieu, Catherine de, RSCJ. *Account of Saint Marys Mission.* Unpublished French and English translation. RSCJ Archives: IV K Potawatomi Mission Box 2 Folder 1.

U.S. Census. Missouri, 1830-1870.

U.S. Census, Pennsylvania, 1790-1850.

U.S. Census, Kansas 1870 (1860 has no record of the mission)

Secondary sources

Callan, Louise, RSCJ. *Philippine Duchesne: Frontier Missionary of the Sacred Heart.* Westminster, Maryland: Newman Press, 1957.

Callan, Louise, RSCJ. *The Society of the Sacred Heart in North America.* New York/London/Toronto: Longmans, Green and Co., Toronto 1937.

Faherty, William Barnaby, S.J. *Saint Louis Irish: An Unmatched Celtic Community.* Saint Louis: Missouri Historical Society Press, 2001.

Garraghan, Gilbert, S.J. *The Jesuits of the Middle United States.* 3 vols. Chicago, Illinois: Loyola University Press, 1984. Online: http://jesuitarchives.org/virtuallygarraghan/

Houck, Louis. *A History of Missouri from the Earliest Explorations and Settlement until the Admission of the State into the Union.* 3 vols. Chicago: R.R. Donnelley and Sons, 1908. Reprint: Forgotten Books, 2017. http://www.ohiomemory.org/cdm/ref/collection/p16007coll27/id/6771

Kappler, Charles J., *Indian Affairs: Laws and Treaties. 2 vols.* Washington, D.C.: Government Printing Office, 1904. Online at: www.okstate.edu/kappler/vol2/treaties/pot0824.htm

Karol, Joseph, SJ, "The Church by the Trail." *Jesuit Bulletin* 1954, pp. 5-7.

Kilroy, Phil, RSCJ. *The Society of the Sacred Heart in 19th Century France.* Ireland: Cork University Press, 2012.

Kinsella, Thomas, *The History of Our Cradleland,* 1921. http://skyways.lib.ks.us/genweb/miami/kinsella/kinsel04.html

Martinez, Marie Louise, RSCJ. Notes: 17 boxes of materials collected about the history of the Society (cited by box); include testimony given for Philippine's process of beatification from RSCJ who had known her; notes on the Potawatomi for a proposed but unfinished history, letters of Lucille Mathevon and Philippine Duchesne, correspondence about Saint Mary's Mission, magazine articles, etc.

O'Connor, John, S.J. *Jesuit Missions in the Kaw Valley.* Unpublished manuscript. Midwest Jesuit Archives (translates and uses house journal, letters of priests and especially diary of Father Gailland.), 1925.

O'Laughlin, Michael, *Missouri Irish: The Original History of the Irish in Missouri, Including Saint Louis, Kansas City, and Trails WeSaint* Missouri Historical Society, 1984; revised edition 2004.

Rollings, Willard H. *Unaffected by the Gospel: Osage Resistance to the Christian Invasion, 1673-1906: A Cultural Victory.* Albuquerque: University of New Mexico Press, 2004.

Rowe, Elfriede Fisher. *Wonderful Old Lawrence*. Elfriede Fischer Rowe papers, Kansas Collection, RH MS 958, Kenneth Spencer Research Library, University of Kansas, and Archives of the Kansas State Historical Society.

Van Ravenswaay, Charles. *Saint Louis: An Informal History of the City and Its People, 1764-1865*. Champaign, Illinois: University of Illinois Press, 1991.

Other Manuscripts and Books about Native Americans in general and Potawatomi in particular

Connelley, William Elsey. *The Prairie Band of Pottawatomie Indians*. Reservation, Jackson County, Kansas. Secretary of the Kansas State Historical Society. www.kansasheritage.org. Typed manuscript also available at Kansas Historical Society: www.kshs.org.

Cook, Sarah E. and Ramadhyani, Rachel B. compilers. *Indians and a Changing Frontier: the Art of George Winter*, Catalogue of the George Winter Collection of the Tippecanoe County Historical Association, Lafayette, Indiana.

Curtis, Sarah A., *Civilizing Habits: Women Missionaries and the Revival of French Empire.* Oxford: Oxford University Press, 2010.

Edmunds, Russell David. "George Winter: Mirror of Acculturation," in *Indians and a Changing Frontier: the Art of George Winter* (see above Cook) pp. 23-37.

------*Indians as Pioneers: Potawatomis on the Frontier*. Chronicles of Oklahoma #651. Winter 1987-88 pp. 340-353.

------*The Potawatomis: Keepers of the Fire*. Norman, Oklahoma: University of Oklahoma Press, 1978.

Hickman, Laura, "Native Daughters: Saint Mary's Mission School among the Potowatomi." Unpublished paper, University of Nebraska. RSCJ Archives

Hoxie, Frederick E. ed. *Encyclopedia of North American Indians*, Boston/New York: Houghton Mifflin, 2001.

Killoren, John J., S.J. *Come Blackrobe: De Smet and the Indian Tragedy*. Norman, Oklahoma/London: University of Oklahoma Press, 1994.

Mitchell, Gary E. *Stories of the Potawatomi People: From Early Days to Modern Times*. www.kansasheritage.org, published in several issues of the *Topeka Capitol Journal* February- November, 1995 and available from author at 16095 N Road, Mayetta, Kansas 66509- 9087.

Mosteller, Kelli Jean. "Place, Politics, and Property: Negotiating Allotment for the Citizen Potawatomi, 1861 – 1891." Ph.D. Thesis, University of Texas at Austin. May 2013.

147

Murphy, Joseph, O.S.B. *Potawatomi of the West: Origins of the Citizen Band*. Shawnee, Oklahoma: Potawatomi Citizen Band, 1988.

Palmer L.R. *A Historical Sketch of the Early Days of Pottawatomie County*. Prepared for the Occasion of the Centennial Celebration, July 4th, 1876. http://skyways.lib.ks.us/genweb/pottawat/newspap5.html

Perrot, Nicholas, Bacqueville de La Potherie (Claude – Charles Le Roy M. de), Morrell Marston, Thomas Forsyth, *The Indian Tribes of the Upper Mississippi Valley and Region of the Great Lakes as Described by Nicolas Perrot, French Commandant in the Northwest; Bacquevile de la Potherie, French Royal Commissioner to Canada; Morrell Marston, American Army Officer; and Thomas Forsyth, United States Agent at Fort Armstrong,* Volume 2 (Google eBook), Paul Radin, Gertrude M. Robertson Vol 2 (Google eBook) Translation of French published ca 1864 The Arthur H. Clark Company, 1912. https://archive.org/details/indiantribesofup02blairich

Sleeper-Smith, Susan, *Indian Women and French Men: Rethinking Cultural Encounter in the Western Great Lakes.* Andover, Massachusetts: University of Massachusetts Press, 2001.

Vecsey, Christopher. *The Paths of Kateri's Kin*. Notre Dame: University of Notre Dame Press, 1991.

Willard, Shirley and Susan Campbell. *The Trail of Death 1838*. Rochester, Indiana: Fulton County Historical Society, 2003.

Printed in the United States
By Bookmasters